teach yourself...

WORD 5

LEO J. SCANLON

ADVANCED COMPUTER BOOKS

MANAGEMENT INFORMATION SOURCE, INC.

COPYRIGHT

TABLE OF CONTENTS

This book is a practical guide to version 5 of the popular Microsoft Word word processing program. It is "practical" in that it shows you how to use Word to perform everyday tasks. It describes Word from the user's point of view, emphasizing the composition and revision of informal and formal correspondence, reports, and form letters.

This book's discussion of Word is illustrated with simple yet realistic examples, and each chapter concludes with practical hints and warnings and a summary of the key points. Most chapters also include a series of questions and answers that address common problems.

INTENDED AUDIENCE

This book assumes no prior word processing or computer experience beyond the simple ability to start up your computer. With this in mind, everything is explained in plain English, and technical terms are used only when absolutely necessary.

Furthermore, the pace is relaxed, and new topics are introduced only as they are required to do useful work. The assumption is that you are primarily concerned with using Word to simplify your writing tasks, not with learning every possible command or nuance.

WHAT KIND OF COMPUTER SHOULD YOU HAVE?

Word requires an IBM Personal Computer (PC, XT, AT, or PS/2) or compatible with at least 384K bytes of available memory and either two floppy disk drives or one floppy disk drive and a hard (fixed) disk. Owners of other computers should consult their dealer or Microsoft Corporation to determine whether Word will run on their machines as well.

WHAT THIS BOOK CONTAINS

This book contains twelve chapters and three appendices, which are summarized as follows:

Chapter 1 begins with a general overview of word processing and then describes the features, applications, and requirements of Word. It also describes how using Word differs from ordinary typing.

Chapter 2 teaches you to actually begin using Word. It describes the methods required for casual jobs such as personal correspondence and household lists. Here you learn how to correct typing errors, divide text into paragraphs, print documents, and save your work on disk.

Chapter 3 discusses the preparation of formal correspondence with stricter and more precise formats. This involves setting margins and tabs, right-justifying, handling multipage letters, numbering pages, underlining, and centering. This chapter also shows you how to set up tables and how to use abbreviations for material you refer to often.

Chapter 4 describes how to use Word's built-in Speller to locate and correct spelling errors. It also discusses the use of Word's Thesaurus to obtain a list of synonyms for a word and replace the word with a synonym if you want.

Chapter 5 describes the composition of reports and other longer documents, which involves learning about double-spacing, running heads (headers and footers), bold print, subscripts and superscripts, footnotes, and endnotes. You will also learn how to use the **mouse** to edit text, how to produce backup copies of your work, and how to manage disk space and disk files. Finally, you will learn how to use Word 5's graphics capabilities to insert graphic images (pictures and drawings) into your documents.

Chapter 6 is concerned with revising text. It explains how to move and copy material and how to use search and replace operations to correct and update documents.

Chapter 7 explains how to work on different parts of a document or parts of different documents simultaneously, which involves dividing the screen into "windows."

Chapter 8 describes how to tailor Word to your specific needs by making it apply a "style sheet."

Chapter 9 shows you how to prepare form letters.

Chapter 10 describes how to save text and commands you use often in **macros**. Once you have defined a macro, you can make Word "replay" it at any time by mentioning its name.

Chapter 11 tells you how to make Word number outline entries automatically.

Chapter 12 describes a variety of features that are handy for preparing reports. It tells how to make Word number items in a series (chapters, sections, and tables) and how to make it generate a table of contents, index, or list from words or phrases in a document. It also describes Word's useful **cross-reference** feature, which keeps track of in-text references to figures, tables, and pages. This chapter also explains how to perform mathematical operations and how to draw lines and boxes. Finally, you will learn how to put comments, or **annotations**, in a document.

Appendix A describes commands in the computer's Disk Operating System (DOS) that you can use to perform "housekeeping" operations on your disks.

Appendix B summarizes Word's key commands.

Appendix C summarizes Word's menu commands.

WHAT YOU WILL LEARN

This book will give you a firm grasp on using Word to prepare letters, reports, term papers, contracts, legal documents, forms, lists, and memoranda. You will learn how to correct typing errors quickly and easily, set up different page formats, work with the mouse, produce print formats such as underlining and bold, generate a table of contents and index, and handle tables, equations, quotations, references, and footnotes.

In short, this book will teach you how to use Word to simplify a wide range of everyday writing jobs.

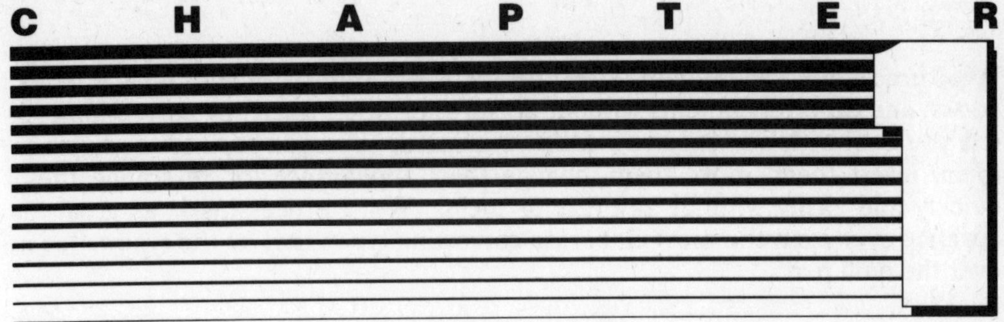

ABOUT WORD PROCESSING AND MICROSOFT WORD

This chapter helps you get started by outlining the major features and typical applications of Word, the new features of Word 5.0, and the equipment required to run Word. It also discusses the differences between typing and word processing and gives keyboarding hints to help you make the transition from typewriter to computer keyboard. It also discusses the names used for hard and floppy disk drives and provides special instructions for hard disk users.

Word processing is the electronic creation of letters, reports, memoranda, articles, books, and other documents without erasures or other unsightly corrections. It lets you deal with words as you do in your mind: You can replace them, erase them, insert them, move them, change their appearance, or rearrange them quickly and easily without any fuss or mess. Word processing is as great an advance over even the most elaborate correcting typewriter as the typewriter is over the quill pen.

Thus, even at its simplest level, word processing is a tremendous convenience. You can turn out professional-quality letters, reports, articles, term papers, and manuscripts even if you can't type very well. No more using special correction tape or fluid, cutting and pasting, or trying to insert typing into copies. Instead, you can simply enter your material, make your corrections and changes on a display screen, and print the final copy.

Not only is word processing faster and more convenient than regular typing, but it also gives you much more freedom to change and improve your work. Even in a near-final draft, you can easily correct mistakes that you would never change by hand. You can reorder your ideas, improve your explanations, remove or change repetitive words or phrases, or insert material at the last minute. In short, word processing lets you concentrate on what to say rather than on just making what you say look right. It's even better than having someone type for you because it's faster, more accurate, and more convenient.

You can perform more tasks with word processing than you could even consider doing manually. For example, you can do the following:

1. Build a library of standard letters, paragraphs, clauses, or other material that you can have ready for immediate use.

2. Insert material from other sources (e.g., contracts, invoices, or financial statements) without retyping.

3. Merge materials to create longer documents.

4. Produce special formats such as underlining, bold print, subscripts, and superscripts.

5. Check an entire document for misspellings, incorrect or obsolete material, repetitions, misuse or overuse of words and phrases, and improper formats. You can also make all the required changes or corrections with simple commands.

6. Automatically add features such as headings, wider or narrower margins, and page numbers.

7. Copy and change documents without destroying the originals or producing work that looks sloppy or unprofessional.

8. Produce customized or personalized form letters, notices, and memoranda that look like original typing.

All these features can dramatically increase both the quantity and quality of your work. Once you have worked with a word processor for a while, going back to an ordinary typewriter is comparable to living without your automobile, television set, or refrigerator. Word processing is a tremendous advance in convenience, speed, and ease of use.

"But," you may ask, "isn't it difficult to learn? Don't I have to be a computer expert?" The answer to both questions is no. You can become a competent word processor in a relatively short time. You need not understand computers or computer programming any more than you would to operate an automatic teller machine, an electronic cash register, or a calculator.

One of the best features of word processing is that you can learn gradually. You need not master every aspect of it to do useful work. You can start by simply using the word processor as a correcting typewriter. Then, as you gain experience and confidence, you can try its more advanced functions. The more you learn, the more you can do, but each step is worthwhile by itself. This step-by-step approach is the one taken in this book.

WHAT IS MICROSOFT WORD?

Microsoft Word, or Word for short, is a word processing program designed by Microsoft Corporation for use on an IBM Personal Computer — PC, XT, or AT — an IBM Personal System/2 (PS/2), or a compatible computer.

Major Features of Word

Word can perform the following tasks:

- Insert or delete characters, words, lines, sentences, paragraphs, or pages of text. (A **character** is any letter, number, punctuation mark, or other symbol on the keyboard.)

- Automatically rearrange text after insertions or deletions to produce lines of the proper length.

- Control the format and appearance of a printed document.

- Justify text to create an even right margin.

- Move or copy text to anywhere in a document or even to a different document.

- Save documents on disk for later use and read them back when needed.

- Search an entire document for certain characters, words, or phrases.

- Produce centering, underlining, double-underlining, bold print, subscripts, superscripts, and other special formats.

- Arrange text in winding, newspaper-style columns or side-by-side paragraphs.

- Abbreviate lengthy phrases, names, addresses, titles, or even entire paragraphs. Word will expand the abbreviations at your request.

- Number the pages in a document.

- Number titles in an outline automatically.

- Generate an index and table of contents for a document.

- Keep track of footnotes so that they always remain on the same page as their references.

- Add rows or columns of numbers in tables.

- Draw lines or boxes within a document. This lets you create bar charts and enclose text within boxes.

- Check a document for spelling errors, and correct those errors.

- Provide synonyms for a selected word from a built-in thesaurus, and replace the word with a synonym if you request it.

- Display parts of several different documents or several different parts of the same document simultaneously. Thus, you can look at old correspondence, financial reports, invoices, or contracts. You can also copy significant sections of them into your current work.

- Produce "personalized" form letters from a mailing list.

- Establish standard forms, called **style sheets**, for letters, reports, contracts, articles, or newsletters. You can then switch formats by simply activating a style sheet.

New Features of Word 5.0

Version 5.0 of Microsoft Word can perform several additional tasks, including the following:

- Insert graphics produced by a drawing program in a document, and let you resize, modify, and rotate them to fit your requirements.

- Give you a preview of how your pages will look before you print them.

- Match in-text references to a **target**, such as a page number or a numbered outline entry, paragraph, figure, or table. If you change the number of a target, Word changes every mention of that number automatically.

- Combine several disk files to produce a single document.

- Print text in color on a color printer.

- Establish **bookmarks** that you can reach easily from anywhere in a document.

- Include reviewers' comments as footnote-like **annotations**.

Typical Applications for Word

Word has many applications. Typical users include the following people:

- Managers, business people, and government or other white-collar workers who want to produce memoranda, reports, notices, price lists, schedules, mailings, and formal correspondence.

- Students who want to write assignments, term papers, theses, and disser-tations.

- Researchers who want to prepare proposals, articles, studies, forecasts, talks or presentations, and status reports.

- Writers who want to produce articles, essays, scripts, stories, poems, and books.

- Lawyers, bankers, accountants, and other professionals who want to generate contracts, notices, briefs, wills, transcripts, financial statements, and reports.

- Teachers who want to prepare lectures, class rosters, assignments, notes, and tests.

Of course, you can also use Word at home for letters, invitations, club or organizational mailings, rosters, and other lists, schedules, bulletins, newsletters, notices, and creative or nonfiction writing.

Equipment Required

To use Word 5.0, you need an IBM Personal Computer, or equivalent, with two floppy disk drives and at least 384K bytes of available memory, and a printer. You can also use a computer that has one floppy disk drive and one hard disk drive, such as an IBM PC XT, AT, or PS/2.

Floppy disk drives "read" information from thin, flexible magnetic media called **diskettes** or **floppy disks**. Diskettes are readily available in computer stores and most office supply stores. A hard disk is a recording mechanism capable of holding much more information than a floppy disk. Disks serve the same purpose as tapes used to record and play back music, language lessons, or dictation.

THE KEYBOARD

If you're used to working on a standard typewriter, you may be intimidated by all the oddly marked keys on the computer's keyboard. A brief explanation should help you understand what they do.

There are three groups of keys, as shown in Figure 1.1. The white keys in the center are like those on a typewriter. However, on the keyboard for the IBM PC and XT, there is a key marked \ and | between Z and the left Shift key. (Shift is marked with a wide upward-pointing arrow or the word "Shift.") If you are a touch typist, be careful to avoid pressing this extra key instead of Shift. On the IBM PC AT keyboard, the \ key is located at the upper right corner of the central key group, so you will not have this problem. Note that the keyboard also includes some extra symbols such as the following: [ ], { }, ', and ~.

Figure 1.1   IBM Personal Computer keyboard.

Control Keys

The darker keys on either side of the central, lighter colored keys are **control keys**. They affect other keys or make the computer do something other than just entering a character. Figure 1.2 shows the control keys you will use most often with Word.

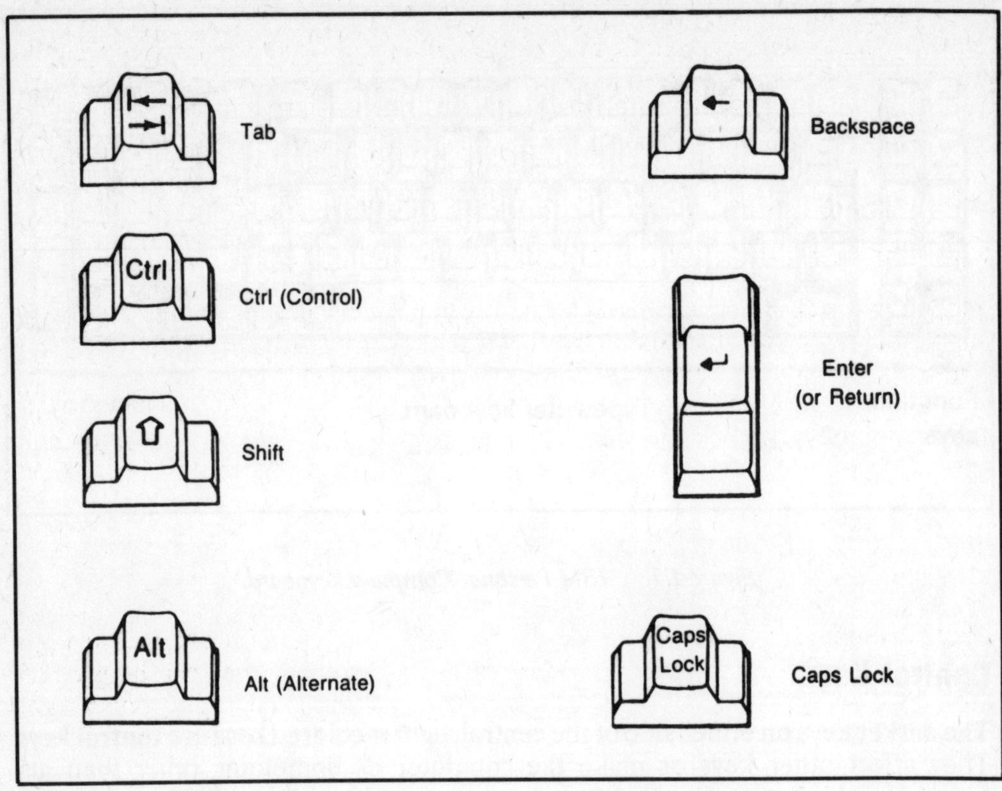

Figure 1.2   Frequently used control keys.

The Shift key has already been mentioned. The key with the arrow pointing down and to the left is the Enter key, the equivalent of Return on a typewriter. On a typewriter, you press Return at the end of each line. When using Word, you press Enter only at the end of a paragraph or to skip a line. The computer divides normal text into lines automatically. The dark key (to the left of "Q") marked with both left and right arrows is the Tab key; it is used to move to the right, just as on a typewriter.

The key with the left arrow, above the Enter key, is the Backspace key. On a typewriter, pressing Backspace moves the carriage or typing element one character to the left. When you use Word, pressing Backspace not only moves to the preceding character, but erases that character as well.

Caps Lock is a handy variation of a Shift Lock key; it locks in capital letters but leaves the nonletter keys (such as punctuation) in lowercase. Be careful with Caps Lock. Pressing it once locks in capital letters, but pressing it again returns the keyboard to lowercase. The IBM PC AT keyboard has a green indicator that lights when Caps Lock is on, but most PC and XT keyboards do not. Fortunately, Word provides its own indicator: it shows the abbreviation **CL** on the bottom line of the screen.

Of course, you can always press a letter key and see what appears on the screen. One added feature is that when Caps Lock is on, you can also press Shift to enter lowercase letters. Nonletter keys always work normally.

Among the other control keys, you will only use Esc (Escape), Ctrl (Control), and Alt (Alternate) with Word. Their functions will be described later.

Numeric Keypad

The keys on the right side of your keyboard, shown in Figure 1.3, are like the keys on a calculator. They're called a **numeric keypad** because they can be used to enter long sequences of numbers, such as item prices, grades, and population figures. The regular number keys in the typewriter section are also available, but they are sometimes harder to reach.

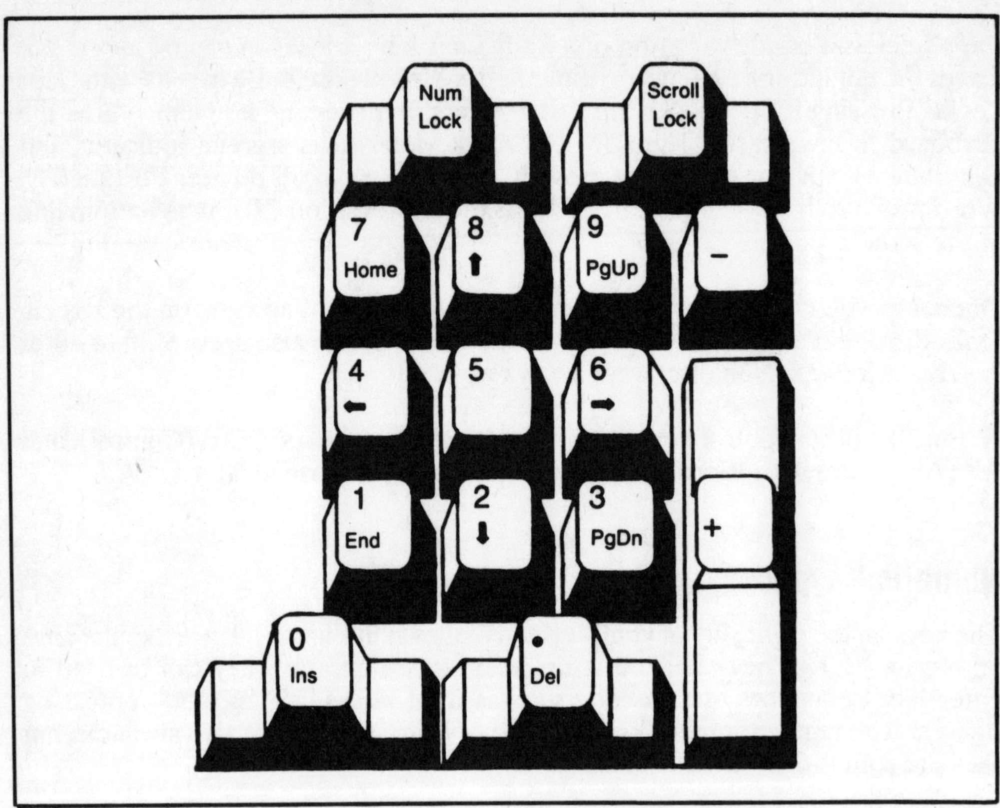

Figure 1.3   Numeric keypad.

Note that four of the light keys on the numeric keypad are marked with arrows. They provide you with a way to move from one place to another on the screen. The Home, End, PgUp (Page Up), and PgDn (Page Down) keys in the keypad are also movement keys, but they let you move greater distances than the arrow keys do.

The Ins (Insert) and Del (Delete) keys at the bottom of the keypad are used to replace existing text or remove material from it.

Note that the keys in the numeric keypad have markings for two functions. Pressing the Num Lock key changes these keys from one function to the other (i.e., if Num Lock is on, pressing these keys produces numbers on the screen; otherwise, the keys perform the actions just discussed). As with Caps Lock, the IBM PC AT has a special green light that indicates which case is active, but most PC and XT keyboards do not. Here again, Word provides an indicator; it shows NL on the bottom line of the screen.

Function Keys

The keys labeled F1, F2, F3, etc., at the far left or along the top of your keyboard are **function keys**. With Word, you use these keys to give the computer special commands such as to print, indent, or save a document on the disk.

Keyboard Hints

The following hints will help you use the PC keyboard effectively. Be particularly careful if you are an experienced typist; some keys are not where you would expect, and blind reaching will result in a lot of errors. Watch the screen closely until you become accustomed to the keyboard.

1. Note the difference between the space bar on the PC and on a typewriter. Pressing the space bar on the PC actually enters a space; that is, it blanks the current position on the screen. This is different from a typewriter, where the space bar moves the carriage or typing element to the right without affecting the text. The right arrow key on the PC's numeric keypad is equivalent to the space bar on a typewriter.

2. Be aware of whether Caps Lock and Num Lock are on or off. Most of the time you will want them off. Fortunately, as previously noted, Word indicates when they are on by showing either **CL** or **NL** on the bottom line. If you are getting all capital letters or are getting numbers when you meant to move somewhere on the screen, check the screen and turn the lock off. The usual problem is pressing a lock key by accident, particularly pressing Caps Lock when you meant to press Shift.

3. Note that on most keyboards Caps Lock is below the right Shift key, not above the left Shift key, as Shift Lock is on most typewriters.

4. Don't reach too far when you intend to press Enter. It's a large key, but there are keys to its right, which is unlike the situation on most typewriter keyboards.

5. Type symbols carefully. Particularly watch the locations of common ones such as quotation marks (") , hyphens (-) , and apostrophes (').

6. Watch what you're doing when you press control keys (Alt, Ctrl, or Shift) and function keys. It's easy to press the wrong key, and the effects are often very different from what you expect.

DIFFERENCES BETWEEN WORD PROCESSING AND TYPING

Although word processing is similar to typing, there are some differences that affect everyday work:

1. Word processing involves a long list of commands. More capabilities usually mean more commands (and more potential errors). Don't try to memorize commands; the commonly used ones will become habits, while you can always look up the less frequently used ones in the appendices at the end of this book, in the Word manual, or on the keyboard template or Pocket Guide that comes with Word. Word also has a **Help** command that you can use to get a description of the commands at any time.

2. What you see on the screen is not necessarily what comes out on the printer. Your printer may not be able to produce subscripts, superscripts, or bold print, even though Word can show them. Your printer may, on the other hand, have special typefaces and features such as compressed print that you cannot see on the screen. Furthermore, the printer's letters and spacing may look different from the computer's, and your printer may not even be able to produce certain characters. You will become familiar with the differences after a while, but this distinction can create problems initially.

3. Floppy disks require special treatment. You should save them in their paper jackets when not using them, label them carefully (using only a felt-tip pen), and store them upright in a box or special container. You can turn off the PC with disks in the drives, but *never remove a disk when the computer is using it* (i.e., when the red drive light is on). Disks need not be handled like precious jewels, but you should handle them as carefully as your best records or tapes.

CREATING A HARD DISK STARTUP FILE

When you turn on a computer that has a hard disk, it always starts in the primary or **root** directory (i.e., C>\). To switch it to the subdirectory that contains Word, you must type **cd \word5** at the C>\ prompt and press Enter. Then, to start Word, you must type **word** and press Enter. This requires only a few simple commands, but remembering commands is annoying.

To make your job easier, you can create a short program, or **batch file**, that both switches directories and starts Word when you type **word** and press Enter. To create this startup file, proceed as follows:

1. At the C> prompt, type **cd ** and press Enter to put the computer in the root directory, in case it isn't there already.

2. Type **copy con: word.bat** and press Enter.

3. Type **cd \word5** and press Enter.

4. Type **word %1** and press the **F6** function key; then press Enter.

DISK DRIVE NAMES

Your computer recognizes its disk drives by specific one-letter names, and you must know these names for some Word operations. For a computer with two floppy disk drives, the left drive is called **A** and the right drive is called **B**. On an IBM PC AT, the drives are stacked vertically; the top drive is A and the bottom drive is B. If your computer has a hard disk, it is called drive **C**, or some higher letter.

Note to Hard Disk Users

Sometimes in this book, you will be instructed to insert a certain disk in drive A or B. If your computer has a hard disk, disregard these instructions. If you've copied the Word program to your hard disk, all the programs you need are on the hard disk, and Word will automatically store the documents you create on it, too. Therefore, *hard disk users only need to insert a floppy disk into the computer when they are explicitly copying information to it to create a backup.*

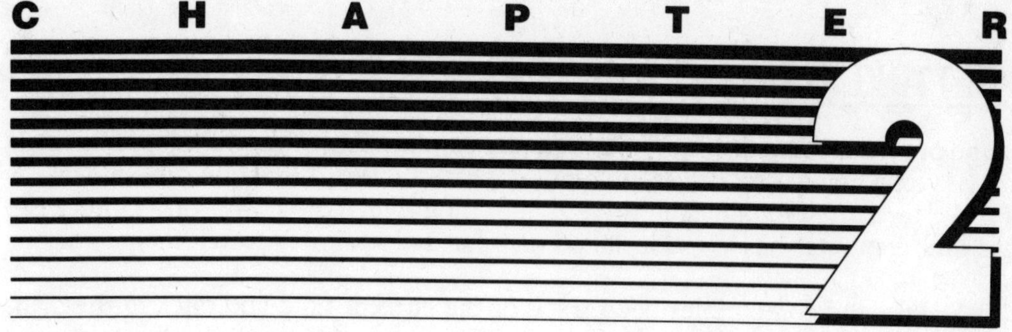

INFORMAL WRITING

Word lets you quickly write informal documents such as notes, personal letters, or shopping lists. In this kind of writing, you use the PC much like an ordinary typewriter.

Notes, personal letters, and shopping lists come and go. Most people don't keep copies of these types of documents or use the same ones twice. Other informal documents are worth keeping, such as lists of names and telephone numbers, Christmas card lists, class rosters, or an inventory of your household effects or insured valuables. This chapter shows you how to use Word for both temporary and permanent documents. You will start with a letter to a friend.

GETTING STARTED

The procedure for starting Word depends on what kind of computer you have. If it has only floppy disk drives, put your copy of the Word *Program* disk in drive A and a formatted data disk in drive B, and then switch the power on. Otherwise, if your computer has Word installed on a hard disk, simply switch the power on.

IBM PCs and compatibles keep track of the current time and date so they can "stamp" that information on the files on disk for your reference. If your computer is one that has a battery-powered clock and calendar, it already knows the time and date. Otherwise, you will be asked to enter those values. Thus, if your computer asks for the date, type it in the form *month-day-year*, and then press Enter. For example, on May 29, 1989, you would type **5-29-89** and press Enter.

Similarly, if the computer asks for the time, type it in the form *hours:minutes* and press Enter again. The computer uses the international (military) time standard in which midnight is 0:00 and 11:00 p.m. is 23:00. For example, to specify 2:25 p.m., type **14:25** and press Enter.

If your computer has floppy disks, the screen will show A>. Type **word** (**WORD** or **Word** will also do; the computer is not particular in this case) and press Enter again. If your computer has a hard disk, at the C> prompt, type **word** and press Enter.

Text Area

In either case, entering **word** makes Word display its starting screen (see Figure 2.1). The bordered area will display the text you enter from the keyboard. There is a small rectangle with a diamond inside at the upper left corner of this area. The Word manual refers to the rectangle as the "selection"; in this book, it is referred to as the "cursor." Either way, the rectangle indicates where you are working.

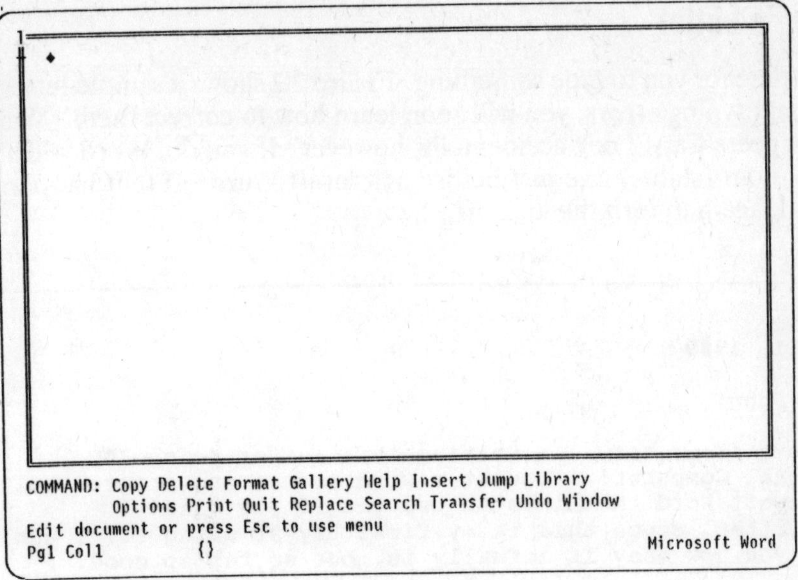

Figure 2.1   Word's starting screen.

The diamond is Word's **end mark**. It indicates the end of the document. Because you haven't entered anything yet, the cursor and end mark coincide.

The Edit Menu, Message Line, and Status Line

Below the text area is a list of commands, called the **Edit menu**, that let you tell Word what to do with your text — copy it, print it, etc. Finally, the bottom of the screen contains a **message line** and a **status line**. The information on these lines will be discussed later, when it is pertinent.

Mouse Pointer

If your computer station includes a mouse, somewhere on the screen you should also see a small blinking square (if you have a green or amber "monochrome" display) or an arrow (if you have a color display or a Hercules graphics card). This is the **mouse pointer**. As you move the mouse forward, backward, or sideways on your desk, the mouse pointer will move up, down, or across the screen. How to use the mouse in Word will be further discussed in Chapter 3.

Entering a Letter

It is now time for you to type something. Figure 2.2 shows a sample letter. Don't
worry about typing errors; you will soon learn how to correct them. Watch that
you don't press Caps Lock accidentally, however. If you do, Word will show **CL**
on the bottom (status) line just before **Microsoft Word**. If that happens, press
Caps Lock again to turn the lock off.

```
May 11, 1989

Dear John:

Believe it or not, I'm writing this letter on my IBM
Personal Computer! I bought a word processing program called
Microsoft Word that lets me use the PC just like a
typewriter. Since this is my first try at using it, I can't
tell you how easy it actually is, but so far so good.

Pat and I want to invite you, Sandra, and Robby to our new
summer cabin by Bender Lake. To paraphrase an old joke, when
can you drop in? Write soon.

All the best,



(Type your name here)
```

Figure 2.2   Sample letter to a friend.

To begin, type the date. The first letter will appear at the cursor's location in the
upper left corner of the text area. The cursor moves to the right automatically as
you type. Now press **Enter**, the large gray key that has an arrow pointing down
and to the left, at the right of the main keyboard. (On some keyboards, Enter is
marked with the word "Return.") The computer's Enter key is similar to the
Return key on a typewriter; that is, it moves the typing location indicator (cursor)
to the beginning of the next line.

Because the salutation starts two lines below the date, press Enter again, and then
type **Dear John:**. Now press Enter two more times to reach the line where the
body of the letter begins.

Type the body of the letter, but *don't press Enter at the end of each line*. This is a major advantage of word processing over ordinary typing. Word keeps track of how long each line is and brings the cursor down to the next line automatically. Press Enter only when you reach the end of a paragraph or want to skip a line.

After you type the closing (**All the best,**), press Enter four times to reach the line for your name; then type it and press Enter once more. This final Enter makes the letter disappear, leaving only your name on the screen. Don't worry, the letter is still in the computer; you don't *see* it now because Word displays only 19 lines at a time, and the final Enter moves the cursor to line 20.

Windows

The Word manual refers to the text area on the screen as a **window**. You can think of a window as a page in a tablet. When you finish writing a page, you turn it over and continue on the next one. The old page is still there, but you must make a conscious effort (that is, turn the page back) to see it. Word keeps track of how far down the screen you have worked and "turns the page" (changes the window, in its terminology) automatically.

CORRECTING ERRORS

You may have made some mistakes when you typed the letter. Fortunately, correcting errors is easy with word processing. After all, the errors are only on the screen, not printed on paper.

To correct an error, you must first move the cursor to it. Do this with the arrow keys and the other directional keys on the numeric keypad. Remember that you can't use the space bar to move over material as you can in typing because it will actually enter spaces.

Moving the Cursor

As you could probably guess, the arrow keys on the numeric keypad move the cursor in the direction they point to — that is, right (6), left (4), up (8), and down (2). However, the arrow keys only move the cursor one character at a time horizontally or one line at a time vertically. To move greater distances, you can use some other keypad keys, as follows:

- Pressing Home moves the cursor to the beginning of the current line.

- Pressing End moves it to the end of the current line.

- Pressing PgUp or PgDn — short for Page Up and Page Down — moves it up or down one full screen (window), that is, 19 lines at a time.

Note the positions of the arrow keys on the numeric keypad. Be sure Num Lock is off when you press them. If it is on, Word will show **NL** on the status line just before **Microsoft Word**, and if you press the keypad keys while Num Lock is on, you will be entering numbers instead of moving the cursor. If Num Lock is on, press the Num Lock key to turn it off.

Not only do the arrow keys have directions marked on them, but they are also placed according to the way they point: the up arrow key is above the others, the left-arrow key is to the left, and so on. These keys **repeat**; that is, they keep the cursor moving as long as you hold them down.

If you have followed directions so far, the letter is on the screen and the cursor is on the line below your name. Press the up arrow key. It will move the cursor up one line each time you press it. Move up a line or two, and then keep your finger on the up arrow key until the cursor reaches the top (date) line. The cursor will not move higher.

Now press the down arrow key until the cursor is on the first line of the second paragraph, the line that starts with "Pat and I." (If the cursor moves too far, use the up arrow key to backtrack.)

Suppose you really meant to type "Pam" instead of "Pat." In the next section, you will see how to correct this mistake.

CHANGING CHARACTERS

Changing a character with Word is like changing one with a correcting typewriter: move the cursor to it, delete it, and then type the new character. To change "Pat" to "Pam," use the arrow keys to move the cursor to the "t" in "Pat." Now press the Del (Delete) key below the numeric keypad, and then type **m**. The "t" has vanished, and "m" is in its place. If you made any other one-character mistakes, correct them now.

It's just as easy to change several characters. Simply move the cursor to where the changes begin, press Del once for each character you want to delete, and type the new characters. Remember that a space is also a character — it's the "Invisible Man" of the character world.

Inserting Characters

To insert characters, simply move the cursor just to the right of (that is, just beyond) where you want the insertion, and then type the new characters. Word will insert them just to the left of the cursor. If the extra characters make the line too long, Word automatically moves the excess characters to the next line and rearranges the paragraph to make every line the proper length.

To see how insertion and deletion work, try them on your example letter. Specifically, assume someone notes that "Sandra" should be "Saundra."

To change "Sandra" to "Saundra," move the cursor to the first line of the second paragraph, and then to the "n" in "Sandra." (Note that you should place the cursor just beyond — to the right of — where you want the insertion.) Now press **u**. The extra letter makes the line too long, so when you move the cursor to any other line, Word automatically moves the word "summer" to the next line and rearranges the rest of the paragraph as follows:

Pam and I want to invite you, Saundra, and Robby to our new summer cabin by Bender Lake. To paraphrase an old joke, when can you drop in? Write soon.

If you see other corrections that need to be made, make the appropriate insertions or deletions now.

Deleting to the Left

You can delete a character you just typed by pressing **Backspace**, the left arrow key above the Enter key. Pressing Backspace deletes the character just to the left of the cursor. Note how this differs from Del, which deletes the character *at* the cursor position. Del is more natural, but Backspace is handy because the cursor moves when you delete.

Suppose, for example, you meant to type **r**, but when you look at the screen, you see **t** instead. You can't just press Del because the cursor has moved to the right, but you *can* press Backspace and then **r**.

Overtyping

To change more than two or three consecutive characters, you can press the F5 function key to put Word in the Overtype mode. In this mode, Word replaces old characters with ones you type. It also reminds you that Overtype is on by showing **OT** (for "overtype") on the status line. Word stays in Overtype mode until you press F5 again.

Overtype is handy for corrections that are about the same length as, but quite different from, the originals. For example, suppose you type "He can precede" when you mean "He may proceed." To correct this error, move the cursor to the "c" in "can," press F5 to put Word in Overtype mode, type **may proceed**, and then press F5 again to put Word back in the Insert mode. Sometimes this is quicker and more natural than inserting and deleting.

Home and End Keys

Pressing the **Home** key (7 on the numeric keypad) moves the cursor to the beginning of the current line, while pressing the End key (1 on the numeric keypad) moves it to the end of the line. This is easier than holding down the left or right arrow key.

Home and End also provide a quick way of moving the cursor to the top or bottom of the screen. If you hold the **Ctrl** (Control) key down and then press Home or End, Word will move the cursor to the top left corner or bottom left corner of the screen, respectively.

CHANGING WORDS

You can handle words as sequences of characters — that is, insert or delete them one character at a time as you have done previously in this chapter. However, Word does provide ways to handle an entire word, rather than just one character, at a time. Pressing F8 tells Word to operate on the current word (word to the right), while pressing F7 tells it to operate on the preceding word (word to the left).

Deleting Words

To delete a word, position the cursor just ahead (to the left) of it or on any character in it; then press the F8 key followed by the Del key. F8 makes the cursor cover the entire word and any spaces between it and the word after it. If the deletion makes the line too short, Word automatically rearranges the rest of the paragraph. It also shrinks the cursor to its original, single-character length.

To see how this works, delete the word "Microsoft" from the first paragraph of the example letter. To do this, move the cursor to the "M," and then press the F8 key followed by the Del key. The entire word disappears. Note also how Word rearranges the rest of the paragraph. Now it has the following form:

**Believe it or not, I'm writing this letter on my IBM
Personal Computer! I bought a word processing program called
Word that lets me use the PC just like a typewriter. Since
this is my first try at using it, I can't tell you how easy
it actually is, but so far so good.**

If the cursor is on the space that follows an unwanted word, you can delete the word by pressing F7 (instead of F8) followed by the Del key. This option is handy for erasing a word you just typed. F7 and Del together remove whole words in the same way the Backspace key removes individual characters.

Moving the Cursor One Word at a Time

You can also use F7 or F8 to move the cursor quickly. Pressing F7 moves it one word to the left, while pressing F8 moves it one word to the right. Like the arrow keys, F7 and F8 repeat; that is, the cursor keeps moving as long as you hold an arrow key down. Note that when you press F7 or F8, Word widens the cursor to cover each word it comes to as it moves along.

Deleting a Group of Words

Suppose you want to delete several consecutive words. You could delete them one at a time with F7 or F8 and Del, but there is a way to remove all of them in one operation.

To select a group of consecutive words, press F6 to put Word in the "Extend" mode (EX appears on the status line), and then press F8 to move the cursor to the right, or press F7 to move it to the left, pressing the appropriate key once for each word. As the cursor moves, Word highlights each word it passes. When the cursor covers all the words you want to delete, simply press Del, and they will all disappear.

To see how this works, remove the clause "Believe it or not" from your example letter. To begin, move the cursor to the "B" in "Believe," and then press F6 to put Word in the Extend mode. Now press F8 five times to select **Believe** , **it** , **or** , **not**, and the comma after "not." (Note that Word thinks of a comma as a word by itself. This and other similar peculiarities will be discussed later in the chapter.) The cursor now covers the entire clause, so press Del to delete it.

As usual, Word rearranges the rest of the paragraph. The paragraph in its final form looks like the following:

**I'm writing this letter on my IBM Personal Computer! I
bought a word processing program called Word that lets me
use the PC just like a typewriter. Since this is my first
try at using it, I can't tell you how easy it actually is,
but so far so good.**

SELECTING FROM MENUS

In the next section, you will print the letter you have just prepared. This involves selecting the Print command from Word's Edit menu at the bottom of the screen.

Word provides three ways to select a command from a menu:

1. Position the mouse pointer on the command name and press the left mouse button.

2. Move the cursor to the command name, using the arrow keys or Tab, and then press Enter.

3. Type the capitalized letter in the command's name.

Regarding option 3, note that the first letter is capitalized in most command names; however, if a menu has more than one option that starts with the same letter, a letter *within* one of the conflicting names is capitalized. For example, Word's Format menu contains two options that begin with an "s":

```
FORMAT: Character Paragraph Tab Footnote Division Running-head Stylesheet
        sEarch repLace revision-Marks pOsition Annotation bookmarK
```

Typing **s** or **S** selects **Stylesheet** (because **S** is capitalized), whereas typing **e** or **E** selects **sEarch** (because **E** is capitalized). Similarly, this menu has three options that start with R and two that begin with P. Word has also set them apart with different capital letters.

PRINTING THE LETTER

Now that you are done editing the letter, you will want to see how it looks in print. **Print** is an option in the Edit menu, which is located below the text area.

To begin, turn your printer on and, if necessary, switch it to the "on-line" or "selected" mode. Now press the Esc (Escape) key to tell Word that you want to select a command. Note that the first command in the main Edit menu is highlighted, but you don't want this command.

To select the **Print** command, type **p**. Word replaces the Edit menu with

```
PRINT: Printer Direct File Glossary Merge Options Queue Repaginate preView
```

Because this is the first time you are printing, you must tell Word which kind of printer is attached to your computer. (You only have to do this once. Word will remember which printer you choose and use it automatically in the future.)

Specifying the Printer

When you installed Word, you selected the **printer driver** (PRD) program for your printer from those on the *Utilities* disk. To make Word use your printer's program, do the following:

1. Type **o** to select Options in the Print menu. This makes Word display its print options (see Figure 2.3). Word is waiting for you to specify the name of the program that works with your printer.

```
PRINT OPTIONS printer:                setup: LPT1:
    model:                            graphics resolution:
    copies: 1                         draft: Yes(No)
    hidden text: Yes(No)              summary sheet: Yes(No)
    range: (All)Selection Pages       page numbers:
    widow/orphan control: (Yes)No     queued: Yes(No)
    paper feed: Continuous            duplex: Yes(No)
```

Figure 2.3   Print Options menu.

2. Press the F1 key to obtain a list of the available printer programs.

3. Press the arrow keys until Word highlights the program for your printer, and then press Enter.

4. Word again shows the Print menu and highlights **Printer**. Press Enter to begin printing.

If you have followed directions so far, the letter should look like Figure 2.4.

```
May 11, 1989

Dear John:

I'm writing this letter on my IBM Personal Computer! I
bought a word processing program called Word that lets me
use the PC just like a typewriter. Since this is my first
try at using it, I can't tell you how easy it actually is,
but so far so good.

Pam and I want to invite you, Saundra, and Robby to our
summer cabin by Bender Lake. To paraphrase an old joke, when
can you drop in? Write soon.

All the best,



(Type your name here)
```

Figure 2.4   Printed form of sample letter.

When the printer finishes, Word puts the Edit menu back on the screen (without any options highlighted) and assumes that you want to resume editing the letter. Now that you have a printed copy, you can check it for mistakes. If you see any, correct them and print the letter again. (Remember to press Escape to activate the Edit menu.) Once you are ready to start a new project, however, you must first clear the screen.

Clearing the Screen

To clear the screen, press Esc to return to the Edit menu, and then type **t** for Transfer. When the following menu appears,

```
TRANSFER: Load Save Clear Delete Merge Options Rename Glossary Allsave
```

type **c** for Clear. Word then wants to know how much of the screen you want to clear and shows the following menu:

```
TRANSFER CLEAR: All Window
```

Press Enter to clear all of it.

Because clearing the screen will delete your letter, which is a drastic act, Word lets you change your mind. It displays the following message on the next-to-last line:

```
Enter Y to save changes to document, N to lose changes, or Esc to cancel
```

Here, you can press Esc if you got this far by accident. But in this case you really want to delete the letter, so press **n**.

Word erases your letter and restores the screen to how it looked when you started, with the cursor and the end mark at the top left corner.

PREPARING A LIST

Now you can start a new project. This time, you will make a list of names and telephone numbers and save that list on disk. Before continuing, if you are using a dual floppy drive system, be sure your formatted data disk (i.e., the disk you want to save your documents on) is in drive B. Then enter the sample telephone list shown in Figure 2.5.

```
TELEPHONE LIST

Brown, Byron  356-7732
Chamberlain, Irv  753-6844
Edgewood, Peter  847-3896
Grayson, Dr. Leonard  931-5410
Kitsinger, Elizabeth  875-6754
Lane, Lois  557-1332
Michelle, Pam  602.5419
Raymond, Morris  705-5537
Tyner, Mavis  965-2694
```

Figure 2.5 Sample telephone list.

CHANGING LINES AND SENTENCES

Although you do not need this ability for your short letter, Word can also handle entire lines and sentences at one time. As with words, you must press a function key to indicate the size of the unit. You can also use the F6 key to extend operations over several units.

Changing Lines

The most likely occasion for changing an entire line is when you are editing a list of items, such as a recipe, telephone list, or class roster.

To insert a line, position the cursor at the beginning of the line that is currently where you want the insertion to appear, and then type the new line and press Enter. The old line moves to the right as you type; pressing Enter moves the old line down, separating it from the new line.

Try adding the local library's telephone number to your sample list. You want to put **Library 555-2738** between the entries for Lois Lane and Pam Michelle. To insert this line, move the cursor to the "M" in "Michelle," type the new line, and then press Enter.

To delete a line, first put the cursor anywhere in that line and press Shift-F9 (i.e., press the Shift and F9 keys simultaneously). The cursor widens to cover the entire line. Then press Del. Word obligingly closes the gap. You could, for example, use this method to delete Lois Lane (say she's now Lois Kent) from your telephone directory.

Changing Sentences

As with words, you can insert a sentence by moving the cursor to just beyond the point at which you want it to appear, and then simply type it. (Remember to enter the space that follows the sentence, too.) To delete a sentence, move the cursor to any character in it, press Shift-F7, and then press Del.

Pressing the Shift and F7 keys simultaneously lets you move the cursor one sentence at a time to the left. Similarly, pressing Shift-F8 moves the cursor to the next sentence to the right.

WORKING ON PARAGRAPHS

Word considers a paragraph as a block of text that ends with an Enter. (When you press the Enter key, you create an end-of-paragraph symbol in the text.) Thus, you can press the Enter key to create a new paragraph or divide one paragraph into two paragraphs. Word also lets you select (highlight) an entire paragraph by pressing the F10 key (the cursor can be positioned anywhere in the paragraph when you press F10).

Inserting and Deleting Paragraphs

To insert a paragraph, position the cursor at the end of the line where you want the insertion, and then press Enter. Word opens a one-line gap into which you can type the new paragraph. (Don't press Enter after this paragraph unless you want to insert another paragraph.)

To delete a paragraph, put the cursor anywhere in it, and then press the F10 key followed by the Del key. The entire paragraph disappears, and Word closes the gap.

Dividing Paragraphs

Pressing the Enter key tells Word to begin a new paragraph. Therefore, to divide a paragraph, simply move the cursor to the character where you want the new paragraph to begin, and then press Enter. Word moves the rest of the paragraph down one line and rearranges it to form a properly spaced new paragraph.

For example, suppose you accidentally combined two unrelated topics in a single paragraph. Perhaps you wrote the following:

Jim and Ellen stopped over for bridge last night. Jim is a mediocre player, but Ellen plays like a professional. Of course, they beat us easily, as usual. Tom had a cold, but he's almost totally recovered now. We expect to send him back to school Tuesday.

To put the two subjects (bridge and Tom's cold) into separate paragraphs, you would move the cursor to the "T" in "Tom," and then press Enter. Your text would now look like this:

Jim and Ellen stopped over for bridge last night. Jim is a mediocre player, but Ellen plays like a professional. Of course, they beat us easily, as usual.
Tom had a cold, but he's almost totally recovered now. We expect to send him back to school Tuesday.

You would press Enter again to insert a blank line between the paragraphs.

Combining Paragraphs

To combine two paragraphs, move the cursor to the space after the final sentence of the first paragraph, press the space bar to put a space between the sentences, and then press Del. The two paragraphs are now one. All you did was delete the Enter (end-of-paragraph symbol) between them.

Moving between Paragraphs

To move the cursor one paragraph forward or backward, press F10, and then press the right or left arrow key. Word puts the cursor at the beginning of the next paragraph or the end of the previous paragraph. To highlight the new paragraph, press F10 again.

Restoring Deleted Text

When you delete text, Word does not immediately discard it but instead temporarily saves it in the computer's memory, in a place called the **scrap**. Word displays the scrap — or at least part of it — between the braces { } on the bottom line of the screen, to the right of the column number. Deleted text stays in the scrap until you press Del again, at which time the newly deleted material replaces it.

To reinsert "scrapped" text back in your document, simply move the cursor to where you want the text to appear, and then press **Ins** (Insert).

As an illustration of using the scrap, suppose you absent-mindedly transposed Raymond Morris' name in the telephone list — entering **Raymond, Morris** instead of **Morris, Raymond** — and you want to reverse these names:

1. Move the cursor to the "R" in "Raymond," and then press the F8 key followed by the Del key. The bottom line now shows **{Raymond}**.

2. Move the cursor to the space after "Morris" and press the Ins key to retrieve "Raymond" from the scrap and insert it. (Note that the word is still in the scrap, so you could insert it again later if you wanted to.)

3. Press Home to move the cursor to the comma, then press F8 followed by Del to put the comma and the space following it in the scrap. (Note that the comma and space replaced "Raymond" in the scrap.)

4. Move the cursor to the "R" in "Raymond," and then press Ins to retrieve the comma and the space that follows it.

The scrap always contains only the most recently deleted material. This can be a character, word, line, sentence, paragraph, or an entire document. However, Word only has limited space between the braces on the bottom line of the screen. If you delete more, it will show just the beginning and ending characters, separated by ellipses (...). For example, suppose you delete the text "The company expects greatly improved results during the next quarter." Word's scrap displays the following:

```
{The com...arter.}
```

Undoing Changes

Suppose you change something—that is, delete the old and type the new—and then decide you were better off originally. You could, of course, simply delete the new text and retype the original, but Word saves you the trouble by providing an **Undo** command.

Undo does what its name implies: It undoes the text you have entered after a deletion and replaces it with the deleted material.

For example, suppose you end a letter with "My lawyer will contact you if you don't respond by January 15." Thinking a diplomatic approach might be more effective, you decide to replace the sentence with "Please call me before January 15 to discuss the matter." To make this replacement, first delete the original by moving the cursor to it (anywhere will do) and pressing Shift-F7 (sentence) followed by Del. Then type the new sentence.

"But," you say, "they'll never call unless I threaten them. I was better off the way it was." To restore the original, simply press Esc to move to the Edit menu (below the text area) and type **u** to select Undo. The original sentence returns from the scrap (highlighted), and its replacement vanishes.

Undo is such a nice idea you'll soon be wishing it were available for other things. If you could only unsay those last words, unsend that nasty letter, or unstep out of that mud puddle!

If you Undo again, Word undoes the undo. This option allows you to choose either the current text or what you had before the last deletion.

SAVING A DOCUMENT ON DISK

To save the telephone list on disk, activate the Edit menu by pressing Esc, and then type **t** to select **Transfer** and **s** to **Save** the document. Now Word displays

```
TRANSFER SAVE filename:
```

and waits for you to enter a name for the list. A name is necessary because eventually your disk will hold several documents, and you need some way to tell one document from another.

Document Names

Documents (**files**) on disk can have names up to eight characters long. Filenames should be meaningful, easy to read and type, and easy to tell apart. They may consist of letters, numbers (0-9), or any of the following symbols:

$ & # @ ! % ' - ( ) { } _ ' ^

You can use either uppercase or lowercase letters in naming files; Word treats them as identical. But beware of the obvious problems with O (letter) and 0 (zero), and with I (letter) and 1 (number). Those who use filenames like IO01I0 will get the fate they deserve.

Saving the Telephone List

This document is a telephone list, so type **phonelst** for its filename, and then press Enter. When you do this, Word displays a summary information form, called a **summary sheet**. This is a convenient log form that can help you keep track of your documents and will be discussed in more detail in the next chapter. For now, press Enter to continue with the Transfer Save operation.

If you have a dual floppy drive system, when you press Enter, the red light on drive B will come on, and the drive will make a whirring sound. When Word finishes (be patient, this will take a while if the document is long), it puts the Edit menu back on the screen and waits for you to resume editing.

If you have a hard disk system, you will probably see **C:\word5** before the filename, which tells you that the file will be saved in the Word5 subdirectory on your hard disk.

Note that Word also puts the name **PHONELST.DOC** in the bottom right border of the text area. Word adds **.DOC** to the name of every document file it creates, to signify that the file contains word processing documents rather than programs, numerical data, or something else.

EDITING A DOCUMENT ON DISK

Once you have documents on the disk, you will probably spend more time working on them than creating new ones. To retrieve a document from disk, press Esc to put Word in the Edit menu, **t** to select **Transfer**, and then Enter to select **Load**. When Word displays the following:

```
TRANSFER LOAD filename:
```

Type in the file's name, and then press Enter. Word reads the document into the computer and displays its name in the bottom right corner of the text border. When Word is finished loading the file, the document appears on the screen as if you had just entered it.

Removing the Telephone List

To see how this process works, you will remove the telephone list from the screen and then retrieve it from disk. To begin, press Esc to reach the Edit menu and then **q** to Quit (i.e., leave Word). Word clears the screen and shows the DOS prompt, which is usually A> or C>. Now, switch your computer off and then back on, and then start Word in the usual way.

Retrieving the List

When Word's main screen reappears, proceed as follows:

1. Press Esc to put Word in the Edit menu.

2. Press **1** to select **Transfer**, and then press Enter to select **Load**.

3. When Word asks for the filename, type **phonelst** and press Enter.

Word now copies the telephone list from the disk into the computer and displays PHONELST.DOC in the border.

It's important to note that loading a document simply *copies* it onto the screen; the original is still on the disk. This is handy to know if you ever change your mind about what you have done to the material on the screen. You can always discard the on-screen changes and revert back to the disk version.

For practice, insert **Evans, Tom 555-1348** and **Storr, Kim 489-7277** at the proper places in the alphabetical list, and then save the new list on disk. Note that Word leaves the list on the screen, ready for further editing.

Instead of continuing with the telephone list, suppose you want to work on another document on the disk but don't remember that document's name.

Finding Out What's on a Disk

To see what the data disk contains, go through the **Transfer Load** procedure, but press the F1 key when Word asks for the filename. Word displays a list of available files at the top of the screen. Here, you have only one file (PHONELST.DOC), but later you will have several.

To load the file that Word has highlighted, press Enter; to load a different file, press the arrow keys until that file's name is highlighted, and then press Enter. So to load and see the telephone list, press Enter.

Loading a Document at Startup

If you know which document you want to work on (and remember its name), you can tell Word to load it when you start. To do this, when the DOS prompt appears enter **word**, a space, and the filename. For example, you could start Word with the telephone list by entering **word phonelst** at the A> or C> prompt.

QUITTING WORD

You should always use the Quit command to leave Word, rather than just turning the computer off; that is, press Esc to reach the Edit menu, and then type **q** to select **Quit**.

If you have changed the document (even a single letter in it) since you last saved it, Word asks whether you really want to exit. It displays the following message:

```
Enter Y to save changes to document, N to lose changes, or Esc to cancel
```

If you don't want to lose the changes, press **y** to save them on disk, or press Esc to cancel the Quit command and return to editing. Otherwise, press **n** to exit; when the A> or C> prompt appears, switch the power off if you are done.

Using DOS

If you own a hard disk, DOS should be installed on it, and quitting Word will automatically return you to the DOS prompt.

If you have floppy disk drives, to use the DOS disk, put it in the left (or top) drive in place of the Word disk. If you want to format a new disk, you will need to replace the data disk in the right (or bottom) drive with the disk to be formatted.

For the procedure to format a disk, refer to the description of the FORMAT command in Appendix A, "Common DOS Operations."

Returning to Word from DOS

If you have floppy drives, to leave DOS and return to Word, replace the DOS disk with the Word disk, then type **word** (or **word** and a filename) and press Enter again.

DELETING DOCUMENTS

If you save a lot of work on disk, your data disks may end up containing some documents you no longer need. To discard, or **delete**, a document, use the following steps:

1. Press Esc to reach the Edit menu.

2. Type **t** for Transfer.

3. Type **d** for Delete. Word displays the **TRANSFER DELETE filename:** message.

4. Type the name of the document you want to delete, and then press Enter. (Note that because deleting a file is a drastic action, Word does not simply let you press Enter or do anything else that easy to complete the delete operation.)

5. When Word shows the message **Enter Y to confirm deletion of file**, type **y**.

Of course, the preceding procedure assumes that you know the name of the document you want to delete. You can also get a list of the available files (all of them, not just the document files), by pressing F1 at the **TRANSFER DELETE filename:** prompt. When the list appears, use the up and down arrow keys to highlight the file to be deleted, and press Enter.

HOW WORD DEFINES TEXT

One problem with Word is that it does not always define words, sentences, and paragraphs the way people think of them. This can produce surprising results when you delete text or move the cursor. For example, to Word a "word" can be any of the following:

- All characters between a space and a punctuation mark or symbol, such as * or $.

- All characters between two symbols.

- All characters starting after a space, up to and including the next space or spaces.

For example, try using F8 to move the cursor word-by-word through the sentence "Mr. F. Scott Fitzgerald isn't home." Word thinks that **Mr**, **.**, **F**, **.**, **Scott**, **Fitzgerald**, **isn't**, **home**, and **.** are all words. In particular, note that a "word" includes the space after it, but not a punctuation mark, which is a word all by itself. Similarly, if you have the equation "55+22=77" in your text, Word will treat **55**, **+**, **22**, **=**, and **77** as separate words.

Word defines a "sentence" as all characters from the beginning up to and including the next period, exclamation point, question mark, or quotation mark. This definition also includes any spaces following the concluding punctuation mark. For example,

Dr. George R. Hardy of Adams Ave. Clinic in St. Louis, Mo., charges only $4.50 for a house call.

is six sentences to Word because Word cannot tell the periods after **Dr**, **R**, **Ave**, **St**, or **Mo** from the period at the end of the sentence. It does recognize the **.** in **$4.50** as a decimal point, however, and extends the highlighting past it to the end of the sentence when you are in sentence selection mode.

Likewise, a "paragraph" is everything from just after the last Enter, up to and including the next Enter. What may appear as an entire paragraph will not actually be an entire paragraph if there are extra Enters because of equations, lists, or quoted material. Thus, Word may well treat one paragraph as several. And it will also think of each title, list entry, quotation, equation, or other material set off with Enters as a paragraph by itself.

The moral here is to always watch the screen when you use the word, sentence, or paragraph function keys. Sometimes the result will not be what you might expect. You may end up with leftover spaces, symbols, or punctuation. Or you might start typing on the wrong side of a space or symbol if you aren't careful. Don't just assume that Word thinks the way you do.

QUESTIONS AND ANSWERS

By now you probably have many questions, so now is a good time to stop and answer them.

How can I make Word go from the text (top of the screen) to the Edit menu (bottom of the screen) and back?
  To make Word move from the text to the Edit menu, press Esc. To make it move from the Edit menu back to the text, press Esc again.

What if I have something highlighted and decide it isn't what I want?
Press the left or right arrow key. This will move the cursor just beyond the beginning or end of the highlighted material and leave a single character highlighted.

How can I make something appear on a line all by itself?
Press Enter before and after typing it. It will then always have a line to itself.

How can I recover if I delete something unintentionally?
You can get it back from the scrap by pressing the Ins key, if you haven't deleted anything else since the last deletion.

Why is everything I type appearing as capital letters?
You probably pressed Caps Lock by accident. Check the bottom line to see if **CL** appears just to the left of "Microsoft Word." If so, press the Caps Lock key to turn the lock off.

Why does the text move when I move the cursor to the right?
You're pressing the space bar instead of the right arrow key. The space bar inserts spaces, and it pushes the text to the right just as entering any other character does.

When I try to move the cursor, Word puts a number on the screen. What's wrong?
You pressed Num Lock by accident. Check the bottom line to see if **NL** appears just to the left of "Microsoft Word." If so, press Num Lock to turn the lock off.

I just typed "rum" instead of "run." How do I correct it?
Press Backspace and then **n**. Note that the Del key won't do the job because the cursor is already to the right of "rum."

Whenever I type something, it erases what I had before. What's wrong?
You have Word in the Overtype mode (**OT** should appear on the bottom line). To put Word back in the normal (insertion) mode, press F5.

HINTS AND WARNINGS

Always be aware of the following features of Word:

1. When you just type characters without first pressing F5, the characters you enter will be added to the text; they will not replace old characters.

2. Remember to use Backspace, not Del, to delete what you just typed.

3. If you put Word in the Overtype mode, remember to return it to insert mode by pressing F5 after you finish replacing text. Other than putting **OT** on the status line, Word does not indicate that you are overtyping; hence, it is easy to write over text you meant to keep.

4. Pressing Del deletes everything covered (highlighted) by the cursor. Look before you leap, but remember that you can always leap backward with Undo.

5. Save your work often. Don't leave a large amount of work in a vulnerable state. The power could go off, someone could trip over or dislodge the power cord, or you could accidentally turn the computer off without saving the text on disk. Always save your work every ten minutes or so. Remember to occasionally ask yourself whether you would like to retype the material that is only in temporary memory (i.e., on screen); if the answer is no, stop and save your work on disk.

6. Always give your disk documents reasonable names that suggest what they contain. It's difficult to remember what **MEMO031** or **X** contains, but not so difficult to remember the contents of **SALES89** or **RESUME**.

7. If you want to retrieve a document but can't remember its name, select **Transfer** in the Edit menu and then **Load**. When Word asks for a filename, press the F1 key. Word will list the disk's filenames at the top of the screen and highlight the first one. To load that file, press Enter; to load any other file, press the arrow keys until that file's name is highlighted, and then press Enter.

8. Always use the Quit command to leave Word. Word will remind you to save your work before quitting. Unless there's a fire, resist the temptation to merely switch the computer off.

KEY POINTS

The following table summarizes the purpose of the keys and commands introduced in this chapter:

Key or key combination	Purpose
F5	Turn Overtype (replace) mode on or off
F6	Extend selection (highlighting)
F7	Preceding word
Shift-F7	Preceding sentence
F8	Next word
Shift-F8	Next sentence
F9	Preceding paragraph
Shift-F9	Current line
F10	Current paragraph
F10, left arrow	Preceding paragraph
F10, right arrow	Next paragraph
Del	Delete selected text to scrap
Esc	Move to Edit menu
Ins	Insert text from scrap

Cursor-moving key or key combination	Location moved to
Left arrow	Move to preceding character
Right arrow	Next character
Up arrow	Preceding line
Down arrow	Next line
Home	Beginning of line
End	End of line
Ctrl-Home	Top left corner of the screen
Ctrl-End	Bottom right corner of the screen

Command	Purpose
Print Options	Select print options
Print Printer	Print according to print options
Quit	Leave Word
Transfer Clear All	Clear screen for new document
Transfer Load	Copy disk document onto screen
Transfer Save	Save document on disk
Undo	Replace new text with deletion

Table 2.1   Keys and commands introduced in Chapter 2.

Following are the key points you learned in this chapter:

1. Word keeps track of the length of text lines and starts a new line automatically when necessary. You should press Enter only when you reach the end of a paragraph or want to leave a blank line.

2. You can move the cursor by pressing keys on the numeric keypad. Pressing an arrow key moves the cursor in the direction the arrow key points. Holding an arrow key down keeps the cursor moving in that direction.

3. Pressing the Home or End key moves the cursor to the beginning or end of the line. When combined with the Ctrl (Control) key, they move it to the top left corner or bottom left corner of the screen, respectively. Word always indicates the cursor's current line and column position on the status line at the bottom of the screen.

4. To move the cursor one word at a time, press F7 (word left) or F8 (word right). But you should also watch the screen to see how far the cursor moves. Remember, Word doesn't always think of words the same way you do.

5. To move the cursor to the next sentence, press Shift-F8. To move it to the preceding sentence, press Shift-F7.

6. To move the cursor to the next paragraph or the preceding one, press F10 and the right or left arrow key.

7. To insert text, move the cursor just to the right of where you want it to start, and then type it.

8. To delete the character at the cursor position, press Del. To delete the preceding character, press Backspace.

9. To delete a block of text, move the cursor to the first character, select the block, and then press Del. The following table tells you which key or key combination will select a particular unit of text:

Unit	Key or key combination
Preceding word	F7
Current word	F8
Current line	Shift-F9
Preceding sentence	Shift-F7
Next sentence	Shift-F8
Preceding paragraph	F9
Next paragraph	F10

10. You can also delete text in the Extend mode. To do this, press F6 to turn Extend mode on, move the cursor until Word highlights everything you want to delete, and then press the Del key.

11. Whenever you delete something, Word temporarily saves it in the "scrap." You can see what the scrap contains by looking between the braces on the bottom line of the screen.

    To copy deleted text back into a document, move the cursor to where you want it to appear and press the Ins key.

12. If you have already entered new text in place of a deletion, you may use the Undo command to replace the new text with the old text. To undo a deletion, press Esc (Escape) to activate the Edit menu, and then type **u** for Undo. You can even repeat the process and "undo the undo."

13. To replace text, move the cursor to where the replacement should start, press F5 to activate the Overtype mode, and then type the new material. Press F5 again when you want to return to the normal, insert mode.

14. To print a document, select **Print** in the Edit menu. When the Print menu appears, press Enter.

15. To delete the current document and start a new one, select **Transfer** in the Edit menu and **Clear** in the Transfer menu, and then press Enter.

16. To load a document from disk, select **Transfer** in the Edit menu and **Load** in the Transfer menu. Then enter a filename (up to eight characters) and press Enter (or press F1 to see a list of files on disk).

17. To save the current document on disk, select **Transfer** in the Edit menu and **Save** in the Transfer menu. Then enter a filename (up to eight characters) and press Enter.

18. To leave Word altogether, select **Quit** in the Edit menu.

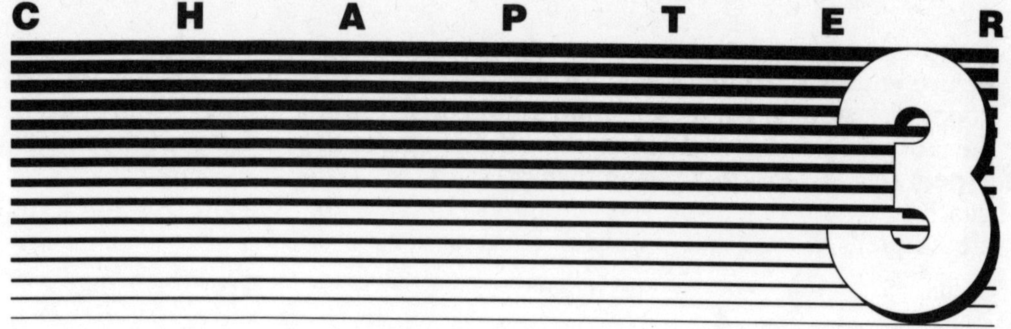

3

FORMAL CORRESPONDENCE

This chapter describes how to use Word to prepare formal business correspondence, such as requests for payment, order confirmations, and memoranda. Such correspondence usually has strict, standardized formats with precise margins and other special requirements. Furthermore, formal correspondence is often several pages long and may include repetitive names, addresses, or phrases.

This chapter also introduces the **mouse**, the optional pointing device you can use with Word. As mentioned earlier, Word shows the mouse's screen position as a "pointer" — either a blinking square or an arrow. If you move the mouse forward, backward, or sideways on your work surface, the pointer moves up, down, or across the screen. In this chapter, if you have a mouse, you will use the mouse to select menu options. If you do not have a mouse, disregard the mouse instructions and select menu items by using the keyboard.

Before entering a letter, you must restart Word. As before, if you have a dual floppy disk system, put the Program disk in drive A and the data disk in drive B; then turn the power on. The first thing the computer does is ask you for the date. Type it (e.g., type **7-20-89**), and then press Enter. When the computer asks for the time, type it (e.g., type **9:30**) and press Enter again. Finally, type **word** and press Enter. Word displays its basic blank screen.

SETTING MARGINS AND TABS

Figure 3.1 shows a typical one-page business letter. Note that the return address, complimentary closing, and the writer's name all start at the center of the page. The easiest way to place this material is to use margins and tabs.

```
                                    211 Washington Street
                                    San Diego, CA 92121
                                    July 3, 1989


Mr. Samuel Thompson
Gospel Island Computer Co.
146 Moonrise Drive
Inverness, FL 32650

Dear Mr. Thompson:

As of the close of business on 30 June 1989, your company
has outstanding invoices over 30 days old totaling
$7,350.00. We must request immediate payment of these
invoices or we will be forced to add a 1 1/2% monthly
service charge.

Until we receive payment, we cannot extend credit to your
company or process further orders. Please remit this payment
to my attention as soon as possible.

                                    Sincerely yours,



                                    Marie F. Gerard
                                    Assistant Credit Manager
```

Figure 3.1   Business letter.

Fixing the Margins

Word organizes documents into sections called **divisions**. Within a division, it gives each page the same **format** — that is, the same width and length, the same margins, and so on. Unless you tell it otherwise, Word assumes that your printer uses standard 8-1/2" by 11" paper. It also assumes that you want 1" margins at the top and bottom of each page and 1-1/4" margins on the sides. This is just what you want for your example business letter, except that you need 1" side margins.

Word keeps margin settings in its **division parameters**. To see these parameters, proceed as follows:

1. Press Esc to reach the Edit menu, and then type **f** for Format. Word displays the following Format menu:

```
FORMAT: Character Paragraph Tab Footnote Division Running-head Stylesheet
        sEarch repLace revision-Marks pOsition Annotation bookmarK
```

2. Type **d** for **Division**. Word shows the Format Division menu:

```
FORMAT DIVISION: Margins Page-numbers Layout line-Numbers
```

3. Because you are changing the margins, press Enter to select Margins. This brings up the division margins parameters shown in Figure 3.2.

```
FORMAT DIVISION MARGINS
        top: 1"              bottom: 1"
        left: 1.25"           right: 1.25:
        page length: 11"      width: 8.5"        gutter margin: 0"
        running head position from top: 0.5"     from bottom: 0.5"
        mirror margins: Yes(No)                  use as default: Yes(no)
```

Figure 3.2   Division margins parameters.

The parameters you want to change are the "left" and "right" margin settings on the second line. You can reach them by pressing the Tab key, which moves the cursor from option to option, but it's easier to use the mouse if you have one.

4. Move the mouse until its pointer is on the number following "left" (**1.25"**) and press the left button. (If you don't have a mouse, remember to use the Tab key instead.) Word highlights the number. Then type **1** (or **1"** — the quotation, or inch, mark is optional), and press the Tab key.

5. With the "right" margin value (also **1.25"**) highlighted, type **1** again, but this time press Enter to return to editing.

The double line of dots at the top of the text area indicates a **division break**, the place where a division ends. This means that Word will apply the new margin settings to text above the double line.

Before you can enter text above the break, you must open up space for that text. To do this, press the up arrow key once (Word highlights the division break), then press Enter to open a gap at the top, and press the up arrow key to move the cursor to it.

Displaying the Ruler

Word can show you the side margins and tabs at any time on a line called the **ruler**. You can also set a tab by entering it on the ruler. This is handy in situations such as the current example, where you want a tab at the center (for the return address) but don't know the actual column number of the center position.

To determine where the center is, move the cursor there by holding the Alt key down and pressing **c**. Then, to see the ruler, press Esc to reach the Edit menu, and then press **f** for **Format**. This time, when the Format menu appears, type **t** for **Tab** and press Enter to select **Set**. (The Word manual refers to a sequence like this as a single command; in this case, the **Format Tab Set** command. Thus, "perform a Format Tab Set command" means "press Esc, and then **f**, **t**, and **s**.")

Word shows the ruler at the top of the text area. It should look like this:

```
[.........1.........2.........3.........4.........5.........6....]....7
```

Each dot on the ruler represents 1/10"; the numbers are inch markers. The brackets [and] indicate the left and right margin settings. Because you have assigned 1" margins, the text is 6-1/2" wide, and the right margin marker has replaced the fifth ("five-tenths") dot beyond 6.

Setting Tabs with the Mouse

To set a tab at the center, move the mouse pointer to the dot directly above the cursor, and then press the left mouse button. Word marks the tab position with an **L** .

If you did everything correctly, the L should be in column 32, the second dot to the right of 3. Press Enter to put Word back in the editing mode. If you put the tab in the wrong place, move the mouse pointer to it and press both buttons to clear it. Now move the pointer to column 32 and press the left button, and then press Enter. Finally, move the cursor back to the beginning of the line by holding Alt down and typing the letter **l** (for left).

Setting Tabs from the Keyboard

You can also set tabs from the keyboard, which is what you will need to do if you don't have a mouse. To do this, first display the ruler. When it appears, Word shows the following menu

```
FORMAT TAB SET position:
        alignment: (Left)Center Right Decimal Vertical leader char: (Blank).-_
```

below the text area and **Enter measurement** on the message line. Word wants you to enter a tab position of the form *n*, where *n* is the distance in inches from the left margin. To set a tab 2-1/2" right of the margin, for example, you would type **2.5** and then press Enter. Using the keyboard method, you must set each tab individually, whereas the mouse lets you set all the tabs at once.

To clear a tab from the keyboard, select **Clear** from the Format Tab choices; that is, press Esc to reach the Edit menu, type **f** for **Format**, **t** for **Tab**, and **c** for **Clear**. Then type the position of the tab you want to clear (e.g., **2.5**) and press Enter. You can also clear all tabs by pressing **r** (for **Reset-all**) instead of **c**.

If you are using the keyboard to set a center tab for the business letter, do so now.

ENTERING THE BUSINESS LETTER

Now that you have set the margins and tabs, you can enter the letter from Figure 3.1. Press Tab (the key with the left and right arrows, on the left side of your keyboard) before typing the return address because you want to start the address at the center. Also press Tab to reach the place where the date belongs. With Word, you needn't type the date because you can tell Word to insert it.

Inserting the Date

To insert the date, simply type **date**, press the F3 key, and then press Enter. Word replaces **date** with today's date, which is determined by the date you enter when you start up Word.

This didn't happen by magic. In fact, **date** is a code that Word has in a list called a "glossary" in memory. The glossary holds, among other things, the expanded form of **date** and some useful codes. When you press F3, Word assumes that the preceding word is a glossary code. Hence, it looks up that code in the glossary and inserts its expanded form in your document. You will learn more about the glossary later.

Completing the Letter

Finally, enter the body of the letter normally, but press Tab before typing **Sincerely yours,** and the writer's name and title.   Remember to press Enter whenever you want to skip a line.

SAVING AND PRINTING THE LETTER

To save the completed letter on disk, perform a **Transfer Save** command. (That is, press Esc to reach the Edit menu, then type **t** for **Transfer**, and, when the Transfer menu appears, type **s** for **Save**.) Because this letter is addressed to someone named Thompson, enter **thompson** for the filename and press Enter.

To print the letter, set your printer to "on-line," and then select **Print** in the Edit menu. When the Print menu appears, press Enter.

JUSTIFYING TEXT

Many people like their correspondence to have an even, or **justified**, right margin. You can produce justified text by changing a **paragraph format** parameter. The paragraph format parameters tell Word the following:

- How to arrange lines (ragged right, centered, ragged left, or justified)

- How far to indent from the side margins

- What kind of line spacing to use (single-spacing, double-spacing, etc.)

- How to split a paragraph when it crosses a page boundary

Note that paragraph formats stay in effect until you change them.

Now you will learn how to justify the body of your business letter. To begin, move the cursor anywhere on the top line of the first paragraph, and then select **Format** in the Edit menu. When the Format menu appears, type **p** for **Paragraph**. Word displays the paragraph parameters shown in Figure 3.3.

```
FORMAT PARAGRAPH alignment: Left Centered Right Justified
    left indent: 0"          first line: 0"        right indent: 0"
    line spacing: 1 li       space before: 0 li    space after: 0 li
    keep together: Yes(No)   keep follow: Yes(No)  side by side: Yes(No)
```

Figure 3.3   Paragraph parameters.

The top line specifies the alignment. To justify the letter's first paragraph, type **j** for **Justified**, and then press Enter. Word rearranges the paragraph to justify it. Then move the cursor to the top line of the second paragraph and do the same thing. (That is, press Esc, **f** for **Format**, **p** for **Paragraph**, and so on.) The letter should now look like Figure 3.4.

```
                                    211 Washington Street
                                    San Diego, CA 92121
                                    July 3, 1989

     Mr. Samuel Thompson
     Gospel Island Computer Co.
     146 Moonrise Drive
     Inverness, FL 32650

     Dear Mr. Thompson:

     As of the close of business on 30 June 1989, your company has
     outstanding invoices over 30 days old totaling $7,350.00. We
     must request immediate payment of these invoices or we will
     be forced to add a 1 1/2% monthly service charge.

     Until we receive payment, we cannot extend credit to your
     company or process further orders. Please remit this payment
     to my attention as soon as possible.

                                    Sincerely yours,



                                    Marie F. Gerard
                                    Assistant Credit Manager
```

Figure 3.4   Justified business letter.

You needed to justify each paragraph individually because you had already entered them. To justify new text, simply change the paragraph alignment to **Justified** *before* typing. Word will then justify lines automatically as you enter them.

MULTIPAGE LETTERS

So far, you have prepared only one-page letters. However, formal correspondence is often longer — sometimes *much* longer. For example, Figure 3.5 shows a two-page memorandum summarizing a company's regional sales for the second quarter of 1989.

<pre>
                    This material is on the first page:

Date: July 15, 1989

To: Gloria A. Powell, National Sales Manager

From: Frank P. Hall, Southeast Regional Sales Manager

Subject: Second Quarter Sales

Attached are the second quarter sales figures for my region.
As you can see, Cynthia Chamber continues to lead, but Jerry
Leonard is gaining ground on her. Dick Morris is still at
the bottom of the list; he blames that on the recent
cancellation by the Wilson & Sons account.

In all, second quarter sales are 15 percent higher than
those of last quarter.

Enclosure

                    This material is on the second page:

Southeast Region Sales, Second Quarter, 1989

State   Sales Rep.   Units Sold   Revenues ($)

Alabama   Adams, Jason   500   215,000
N. Carolina   Holmes, James   550   236,500
S. Carolina   Jackson, Charles   490   210,700
Florida   Chamber, Cynthia   640   275,200
Georgia   Grogan, Phyllis   420   180,600
Louisiana   Leonard, Jerome   610   262,300
Mississippi   Morris, Richard   320   137,600
Tennessee   Baker, Thomas   540   232,200
Virginia   Nelson, Patricia   480   206,400
                                     ───────   ─────────
                         Totals   4,550   1,956,500
</pre>

Figure 3.5   Two-page memorandum.

To enter this memorandum, create a new document. When Word's blank screen appears, enter the first page. After typing the final word (**Enclosure**), press Enter.

Starting a New Page

To start a new page, hold both Ctrl and Shift down and simultaneously press Enter (Ctrl-Shift-Enter). When you do this, Word puts a line of dots across the screen to mark the **page break** and moves the cursor below it. The status line notation **Pg2** indicates that the cursor is now on a new page.

Creating a Table

The second page consists of a title and a table. Start by entering the title, and then skip a line to reach the place where the table belongs.

You could enter the table, using spaces to separate the columns, but it's more efficient to separate them using tabs. If you know where the tab stops belong, you can simply set them and then enter the table. However, you often don't know the tab settings ahead of time.

Not knowing where the tab stops belong ahead of time isn't really a problem, though. You can simply type your table, using whatever tab stops are active, and then change the tab settings to what you want. As you change the tabs, Word will shift the text to show the effects of your new tab stops. This is certainly better than tabs on a typewriter, where tabbed text retains whatever tab stops you used to type it.

Defining a Table as a Single Paragraph

When you change tabs within existing text, Word always applies them to the current paragraph and reverts back to the original tab settings for anything that follows that paragraph. As you may recall, Word considers a "paragraph" as text preceded and followed by an Enter. Thus, if you type a table as you would on a typewriter, by pressing Enter at the end of each line, Word will treat each line as a separate paragraph and will only apply any new tabs to the line in which you set them, which would require you to set new tabs individually for each line in the table.

Fortunately, there is a way to define an entire table as a single paragraph: Simply press **Shift** and **Enter** simultaneously (rather than Enter alone) at the end of each line but the last one. Shift-Enter tells Word to start a new line but not a new paragraph.

Entering the Sales Table

To enter the sales table for the memorandum, do the following:

1. Type the table headings, and press the Tab key after each heading except the last one.

2. Press Enter *twice* to reach the line where the table begins.

3. Type the **Alabama** line, and press Tab after each column entry, but press Shift-Enter (rather than Enter alone) at the end of the line.

4. Similary, type the next seven lines (**N. Carolina** through **Tennessee**), pressing the Tab key after each column entry, and press Shift-Enter at the end of each line.

5. Type the **Virginia** line, pressing the Tab key in the appropriate places, but press Enter at the end of the line to tell Word that this ends the "paragraph."

If you created the table, using Word's default 1/2" tab settings, it should look like Figure 3.6.

```
State          Sales Rep.      Units Sold       Revenues ($)

Alabama     Adams, Jason    500  215,000
N. Carolina     Holmes, James  550  236,500
S. Carolina     Jackson, Charles    490  210,700
Florida     Chamber, Cynthia    640  275,200
Georgia     Grogan, Phyllis     420  180,600
Louisiana   Leonard, Jerome    610  262,300
Mississippi     Morris, Richard     320  137,600
Tennessee   Baker, Thomas 540  232,200
Virginia    Nelson, Patricia    480  206,400
```

Figure 3.6   Table entered with default tab settings.

Now you must adjust the column spacing by setting tabs for both the headings and the table itself. You must set the heading and table tabs separately because the third and fourth columns in the table start at different places from their headings. If the columns and headings had the same spacing, you could have defined all the text from the headings to the end of the "Virginia" line as a single paragraph.

As it is, you must set tabs for the headings and table paragraphs separately with a series of Format Tab Set operations. Note that Word has put five spaces between each heading. That's not exactly what you want, but the headings are certainly in better shape than the data columns, so you will probably want to work on the data first, and then adjust the headings as needed. Do this as follows (note: if you do not have a mouse, refer back to the section "Setting Tabs from the keyboard" to set up this table):

1. Move the cursor to the beginning of the data (i.e., to the "A" in "Alabama").

2. Press Esc, and then type **f**, **t**, and **s** to issue a Format Tab Set command.

Your first job is to put three spaces between the longest item in the first column ("N. Carolina") and the column of Sales Rep. names.

3. When the Format Tab Set form appears, move the mouse pointer to the fourth dot past **1** on the ruler and press the left button. Word puts an **L** on the ruler and aligns the column of names below it.

4. Press Enter to hide the ruler.

   You must now align the "Sales Rep." title with the names.

5. Move the cursor to the "S" in "State" and issue another Format Tab Set command.

6. Move the mouse pointer to the fourth dot past **1** on the ruler and press the left button. Word puts an **L** on the ruler for the headings and aligns the "Sales Rep." heading below it.

Now you must move the "Units Sold" heading three spaces to the right of the longest Sales Rep. name ("Jackson, Charles").

7. Move the mouse pointer to the third dot past **3** and press the left button. Word puts another **L** on the ruler and aligns "Units Sold" below it.

8. Move the mouse pointer to the sixth dot past **4** and press the left button. Word puts another **L** on the ruler and aligns "Revenues" below it.

9. Press Enter to hide the ruler.

The headings are now in place, and you must align the third and fourth data columns. The third column must be aligned with the "t" in "Units"; the fourth column must be aligned with the "u" in "Revenues."

10. Move the cursor to the "A" in "Alabama" and issue another Format Tab Set command.

11. Place a tab above the "t" in "Units" and another above the "u" in "Revenues," and then press Enter.

12. Enter the **Totals** line.

You are finished. Save the memorandum on disk. Name it **salesq2**.

WORKING WITH PAGES

In the preceding memorandum, you knew exactly where to end the first page and begin the second. However, you normally don't know ahead of time where page breaks will occur.

If you are using standard 11" paper, one page can hold 54 single-spaced lines. When Word prints the document, it automatically starts a new page when it encounters the 55th line. However, like most professional typists, it will not leave the first line of a paragraph alone at the bottom of a page (called a "widow"), nor put the last line at the top of a new page (called an "orphan"). It always keeps the first and last two lines of a paragraph together on a page.

Keeping Paragraphs Together

Sometimes you may want to keep a paragraph all on one page, for example, if the split would come at the end of a chapter or some other awkward position.

The paragraph parameter list in Figure 3.3 shows a "keep together" option that forces Word to keep all the lines in a paragraph together on a page. Word initially sets this option to **No** (it shows **No** in parentheses), meaning it will split paragraphs. To change "keep together" to **Yes**, position the cursor anywhere in the paragraph you want to keep together, and then issue a Format Paragraph command. When the paragraph parameters appear, press Tab to reach "keep together," type **y**, and then press Enter. If there isn't enough room on a page for a paragraph, however, Word will move the entire paragraph to the next page.

Moving between Pages

Sometimes changes or corrections on one page will require changes on another page. Or you may suddenly think of an error or omission on some other page. Word lets you move quickly to any page in a document.

Moving is easiest if you want to reach the beginning or end of the document: Press Ctrl-PgUp (beginning) or Ctrl-PgDn (end).

You can move the cursor to any other page by using a **Jump Page** command. Press Alt-F5, type the number of the page you want to jump to, and then press Enter. Pressing Alt-F5 and then Enter instead of entering a page number moves the cursor to the beginning of the current page.

Finding Page Breaks

Because Jump Page moves the cursor to the beginning of a page, you can use it to find page breaks. Word marks where each new page begins by displaying a line of dots across the screen.

UNDERLINING

Writers use underlining for emphasis, or to indicate a new term, a book title, or a magazine name. You can also use it to create mathematical symbols such as $\geq$ or $\pm$.

To underline material, simply extend the cursor to cover it, and then hold down the Alt key and simultaneously press **u** (Alt-U). Remember, you can select a word with F8, a line with Shift-F9, a sentence with F9, or a paragraph with F10. You can also use F6 to extend the cursor over several units. For example, if your sales letter says

We must reduce the inventories of bedspreads this month.

you may want to underline "must" for emphasis. To do this, move the cursor to "m," and then press F8 to select "must" and Alt-U to underline it. Note that F8 selects "must" and the space after it, but Word underlines only "must."

Removing Underlining

You can remove underlining with **Alt-Spacebar**. For example, to remove the underline from "must" in the preceding example, move the cursor to the "m," press F8 to select the word, and then press Alt-Spacebar to erase the underline.

To operate on a single character, hold the Alt key down and press the other key (U or the Spacebar) *twice*. For example, if you accidentally underline the space after "must," move the cursor to that space, and then hold the Alt key down and press the Spacebar twice.

CENTERING

Tables usually require centered titles. You can produce one by simultaneously pressing Alt and **c**.

Center the title on page 2 of the memorandum in Figure 3.5. Load **salesq2** into the computer from disk, using the Transfer Load command. Move the cursor to the title and center it with Alt-C. Issue a Transfer Save command to save the memorandum with the centered title.

USING THE GLOSSARY

One way to save on typing and reduce the number of errors is by abbreviating common names, addresses, or phrases. For example, a letter might have repeated references to the National Aeronautics and Space Administration, University of Florida, United States Steel Corporation, or the law firm of Parker, Gillespie, Monk, and Mingus. You might also be continually mentioning "the party of the first part," "the cooperating investigative agencies," or "the three major television networks."

Wouldn't it be nice if you only needed to type in abbreviations such as NASA for National Aeronautics and Space Administration, USSC for United States Steel Corporation, and pfp for "party of the first part" and have Word enter the full name or phrase for you? Word lets you do this by defining abbreviations in a **glossary.**

Adding Entries to the Glossary

To put something in the glossary, just type it the first time, select it (i.e., extend the cursor to cover it), and issue the Copy command. When Word displays

```
COPY to: {}
```

type the abbreviation (up to eight characters), and then press Enter. Do this for as many abbreviations as you want. Word will add each one to the glossary.

Of course, the Copy command leaves the original text on the screen. If you are simply building a glossary in preparation for using it later within a document, you may want to remove the entries from the screen as you insert them in the glossary. To do this, type the text you want to abbreviate and go through the same procedure, but use **Delete** instead of Copy. Delete puts the text in the glossary but erases it from the screen.

For example, suppose you prepare a letter that includes many references to Acme International Corporation. To abbreviate the name as **AIC**, do the following:

1. Type **Acme International Corporation**.

2. Select all three words. (If they are at the beginning of a line, you can press Shift-F7 to highlight the previous "sentence.")

3. Execute a Delete operation; that is, press Esc, and then press **d**.

4. Type **AIC** (or **aic**, Word is not particular) as the destination, and then press Enter.

This puts **Acme International Corporation** in the glossary, gives it the abbreviation AIC, and erases it from the screen.

Now, whenever you want "Acme International Corporation" inserted in a document, simply type **aic** and press F3. Word will expand the abbreviation.

Finding Out What's in the Glossary

But what if you don't remember the abbreviation? Then press Esc to reach the Edit menu, press **i** for **Insert**, and then press F1 when Word requests the source of the insertion. Word will provide a list of the glossary abbreviations. You can then select the one you want by highlighting it and pressing Enter.

If you try this, you will see the abbreviation you're looking for (e.g., **aic**), **date**, and some other entries that can be useful in your documents, as follows:

<table>
<tr><th>This glossary entry</th><th>Inserts this in your document</th></tr>
<tr><td>page</td><td>(page) code</td></tr>
<tr><td>nextpage</td><td>(nextpage) code</td></tr>
<tr><td>date</td><td>Current date as text</td></tr>
<tr><td>dateprint</td><td>(dateprint) code</td></tr>
<tr><td>time</td><td>Current time as text</td></tr>
<tr><td>timeprint</td><td>(timeprint) code</td></tr>
<tr><td>footnote</td><td>Footnote reference mark</td></tr>
</table>

The four codes here are markers that Word will replace with specific material when you print the document. At print time, Word replaces *(page)* with the current page number, *(nextpage)* with the number of the page that follows the current page, *(dateprint)* with the date on which you are printing, and *(timeprint)* with the time of day at which you are printing. The *(dateprint)* and *(timeprint)* codes are particularly useful in form letters because they make your printed copies current without you having to do anything.

Note that the glossary also contains names with **.mac** at the end, usually followed by the abbreviation **Ctrl** and a letter in angular brackets, and then another letter. One such entry is

Annot_merge.mac < Ctrl A > M

These types of entries are **macros**, which will be discussed in Chapter 10.

Saving the Glossary on Disk

You can even save the glossary on disk so the abbreviations don't disappear each time you leave Word. To save the glossary, issue a **Transfer Glossary Save** command. On a computer with a hard disk, Word shows

```
TRANSFER GLOSSARY SAVE filename: C:\WORD5\NORMAL.GLY
```

where **NORMAL.GLY** is a glossary that Word uses automatically for every new document you create. You now have three choices:

1. To insert your abbreviations in NORMAL.GLY and use them everywhere thereafter, press Enter.

2. To put your abbreviations in a separate glossary (say, you only use those abbreviations for some projects), type a name of up to eight characters for this particular list of abbreviations, and then press Enter.

    For example, if the glossary contains abbreviations for Acme International Corporation and your name, you could enter **names** as the filename.

3. To return to editing without saving the glossary, press Esc.

To put abbreviations into the active glossary, issue a **Transfer Glossary Merge** command. As with document files, press the F1 key if you need a list of what's available. Note that Word automatically puts the extension **.GLY** on glossary files. (For example, it would list the file you called "names" as **NAMES.GLY**.) However, you don't need to type the extension when you enter the filename.

Preserving the Glossary between Documents

To use the current glossary entries in a new document, preserve them by clearing the screen, using **Transfer Clear Window** instead of Transfer Clear All. Word also preserves the glossary when you load a document from disk without clearing the screen.

Switching Glossaries

NORMAL.GLY is the **default** glossary, the one Word assumes you want to use when you start. However, it also provides two other glossaries: CON-TRACT.GLY and MACRO.GLY.

CONTRACT.GLY contains abbreviations that expand into "boilerplate" text that you can use to create a business contract. For example, the abbreviation "60days" expands into a five-paragraph section of a contract that sets forth the terms of the contract, and allows either party to terminate it with 60 days notice.

The other built-in glossary, MACRO.GLY, contains mostly macros (see Chapter 10).

To switch from NORMAL.GLY to CONTRACT.GLY, MACRO.GLY, or a glossary *you* created, issue a **Transfer Glossary Load** command. When

```
TRANSFER GLOSSARY LOAD filename:
```

appears, type the name of the glossary file you want (e.g., type **contract.gly**) and press Enter. To see a list of the available glossaries, press F1 at the prompt, highlight the file you want, and press Enter.

NUMBERING PAGES

If your letter is longer than two pages, you may want to number the pages. To do this, move the cursor to the page where you want numbering to start (usually the first page), and then issue a **Format Division Page-numbers** command. Word shows its list of page number parameters (see Figure 3.7).

```
FORMAT DIVISION PAGE-NUMBERS: Yes(No)  from top: 0.5"   from left: 7.25"
       numbering:(Continuous)Start     at:            number format:(1)I i A a
```

Figure 3.7   Page number parameters.

The initial (or default) settings are as follows:

- **No** for no page numbers. Change it to **Yes** (by typing **y**) to make Word print page numbers on your document.

- The "from top" and "from left" values are set to **0.5"** and **7.25"**, respectively. This makes Word print page numbers at the top right corner of each page and start them at the right margin.

- On a page with 1.25" side margins (Word's standard setting), the text ends 7.25" from the left edge — and that's where **from left: 7.25"** puts the page number. You can change either or both of these numbers to print page numbers somewhere else. For example, you could set "from top" to **10.5"** to print pages numbers 1/2" from the bottom of an 11" page.

- The "numbering" parameter is set to **Continuous** to make Word start numbering pages from this point on and to make the current page **1**. To start with some other number, type **s** for **Start** and type your starting page number in the "at" field.

- The "numbering format" parameter determines whether Word will use Arabic numbers (1, 2, 3), uppercase Roman numbers (I, II, III), lowercase Roman numbers (i, ii, iii), uppercase letters (A, B, C), or lowercase letters (a, b, c) to number the pages.

When you finish setting up the page numbering, press Enter to return to your document. If you changed the number with the **Start** setting, Word will put your new number at the bottom left corner of the screen.

SUMMARY SHEETS

When you save a document on disk, Word lets you create a convenient log form, called a **summary sheet**, for it. The summary sheet, shown in Figure 3.8, displays the dates when the document was created and last revised.

```
SUMMARY INFORMATION
   title:                        version number:
   author:                       creation date: 5/15/89
   operator:                     revision date: 5/15/89
   keywords:
   comments:
```

Figure 3.8   Document summary sheet.

It also provides space for you to enter the following:

- A title and revision number

- The names of the author and operator

- Keywords for searching for this summary (more about this shortly)

- Comments about the document (perhaps why you wrote it or references to other letters to this person)

Printing Summary Sheets

Although the document summary is part of the document, Word does not normally print it. To make Word print the summary sheet along with a document, issue a **Print Options** command and type **y** for **Yes** in the "summary sheet" field.

Changing Summary Sheets

Once you enter anything in a document's summary sheet, Word will stop showing the sheet when you save the document. To change the contents of a summary sheet, you must issue a **Library Document-retrieval Update** command.

When you select **Library** and then **Document-retrieval**, Word displays **Path: C:\WORD5** (where C is the letter that identifies a hard disk drive — note that the drive letter will be different if you are using a dual floppy disk system) at the top of the screen, followed by a list of the documents in the WORD5 directory. Word shows these document names in the form DOS uses them: as a drive letter, a directory path, and a filename. For example, it shows the file ADDRESS.DOC in the WORD5 directory on drive C as follows:

```
C:\WORD5\ADDRESS.DOC
```

The **Library Document-retrieval** command also produces the following menu at the bottom of the screen:

```
DOCUMENT-RETRIEVAL: Query Exit Load Print Update View Copy Delete
```

To change a summary sheet, move the selection bar to the document's name, and type **u** for Update. The summary sheet appears in the form of an UPDATE SUMMARY, with the document's DOS path and filename at the top. Make your changes, and then press Enter to save them.

SEARCHING THROUGH DOCUMENTS AND SUMMARY SHEETS

Word lets you search documents and their summary sheets for words that you specify. To begin, issue a **Library Document-retrieval** command. When the list of files appears, you can select the files to be searched by marking them, using one of the following two methods:

- To mark an individual file, highlight its name and press the Spacebar. (Word precedes the filename with an asterisk, *.)

- To mark all the files, press Ctrl-Spacebar. (Word puts an * in front of every name.)

Here, if a file is already marked, pressing the Spacebar unmarks them. Similarly, Ctrl-Spacebar unmarks all files.

These two key commands are useful for excluding just a few files from the search. Start by pressing Ctrl-Spacebar to mark every file, and then press the Spacebar on each file you want to exclude.

Now, to begin the search procedure, type **q** to select **Query** from the Document-retrieval menu. This produces the Query form shown in Figure 3.9.

```
QUERY path: C:\WORD5
  author:
  operator:
  keywords:
  creation date:              revision date:
  document text:
  case: Yes(No)               marked files only: Yes(No)
```

Figure 3.9   Query form.

As you can see, the first six entries on this form ("author" through "revision date") are fields on the summary sheet. The "document text" field and "case" parameter refer to text *within* the documents. The "marked files only" parameter lets you tell Word whether to search every file (No) or just the ones you marked (Yes).

Filling Out the Query Form

It is easiest to search for just one item: Type that item in the appropriate field, and press Enter. Word displays the message **Searching documents. . .** at the bottom of the screen and then displays a list of the files that meet that criteria and shows the Document-retrieval menu at the bottom. For example, if you type **Smith** in the Query form's "author" field, Word produces a list of files written by someone named Smith.

You can also be more explicit. For example, you could search for "Joan Smith" to find only the documents she wrote — and disregard those written by, say, Tom Smith. You can also narrow the search by typing entries in several fields. For example, if you type **Joan Smith** for "author" and **memo** for "keywords," Word will locate documents whose summary sheets contain both of those entries.

Searching for Document Text

As mentioned previously, the Query form's "document text" and "case" fields let you search for text within documents, as opposed to entries on summary sheets. For "document text," you can type any string of text, up to 80 characters. Word will produce a list of all documents that contain that string of text. For example, you can search for all occurrences of the phrase, "party of the first part."

The "case" parameter lets you tell Word whether to search for exact matches of your "document text" string (Yes) or any form of it (No). For example, searching for **International** with case set to Yes makes Word find only "International," not "international" or "INTERNATIONAL."

Operating on a Document List

When Word finishes a Query search, it lists all documents that match your criteria and shows the Document-retrieval menu at the bottom of the screen:

```
DOCUMENT-RETRIEVAL: Query Exit Load Print Update View Copy Delete
```

You can then do one of the following:

- Query again, to narrow the search even further.

- Exit back to your document.

- Select a document and Load it, Print it, or Update its summary sheet information.

- Change the way you View the document list. View's **Short** option lists the files in two columns; **Long** uses one column for the filenames and other columns to display the author and title for documents that have summary sheets; and **Full** gives a Short listing, but with the highlighted document's summary sheet at the end of the list.

- Copy or Delete marked files.

Using Logical Operators

Word also lets you search for multiple entries in a single field. For example, you can search for documents having summary sheets that list either Smith or Jones as the operator. Or you can search for summary sheets containing the keywords "memo" and "sales" (i.e., all memos that discuss sales). To search for multiple entries, you must use the **logical operators** listed in Table 3.1 (see next page).

Use this character	To do this
, (comma)	Find either of two items.
Example:	**Smith,Jones** tells Word to search for either Smith or Jones.
& or space	Find occurrences of both items.
Example:	**memos&sales** tells Word to search for documents or summary sheets containing both memos and sales. Similarly, **John Jacobs** tells Word to search for both John and Jacobs.
~ (tilde)	Disregard files containing this item.
Example:	**~Smith** tells Word to accept any item but Smith. Similarly, **national~international** tells Word to locate national, but not international.
<	Search for earlier dates.
Example:	**<5/15/88** tells Word to locate dates earlier than May 15, 1988.
>	Search for later dates.
Example:	**>5/2/87** tells Word to locate dates later than May 2, 1987.

Table 3.1   Logical operators for use with a Query.

QUESTIONS AND ANSWERS

I keep reaching for the Tab key and nothing happens.   What's the problem?
Look where you're reaching.   You are probably pressing Ctrl or some other key instead of Tab.

I tried to move a table to a new location, but Word would only pick up one line at a time. Why?

You ended each line with Enter instead of Shift-Enter. Shift-Enter starts a new line without starting a new paragraph. If you end a line with Enter alone, Word thinks of that line as a paragraph.

How can I force Word to start a new page?

Hold both Ctrl and Shift down and simultaneously press Enter.

How can I make sure that Word doesn't split a table between two pages?

Change the paragraph parameter list's "keep together" option to **Yes** before entering the table. Then, after you type each line, press Shift-Enter to move to the next line.

While working on page 7 of a long letter, I decided to change some terms that I mentioned on page 2. How do I get back and forth?

Issue a Jump Page command (Alt-F5) and enter 2. Then make your changes and do a Jump Page back to page 7. If page 7 is as far as you have typed, you can use Ctrl-PgDn to return to it.

I only want to underline words, not the spaces between them. How can I do this?

You must underline each word individually, using F8 to select it, left arrow to deselect the space after it, and Alt-U to underline it.

I went to use my glossary abbreviations in a new letter, but they didn't work. What happened to them?

You probably used a Transfer Clear All operation to erase the old letter. That erases the glossary as well as the text. Next time, use Transfer Clear *Window*, which erases the screen but not the glossary.

I issued a Format Division Page-numbers command and told Word to print page numbers at the bottom. Why isn't it printing them?

You forgot to turn on the page numbering by setting the first parameter to **Yes.** Go back to the beginning of your document and issue your **Format Division Page-numbers** command again.

HINTS AND WARNINGS

1. Word automatically provides tabs at every fifth column position, although it doesn't show these tab stops on the ruler. However, when you set a tab, Word

clears the automatic ones to the left of that tab. For example, setting a tab in column 22 clears the automatic tabs in columns 5, 10, 15, and 20.

2. To see what the tab settings are, display the ruler as follows: (A) Move the mouse pointer to the upper right corner of the text border and (B) press the left button. To erase the ruler, do the same thing, except press both buttons. From the keyboard, issue the Format Tab Set command.

3. To force Word to start a new line, but not a new paragraph, press Shift and Enter together. Use this technique to enter the lines of a table so Word will treat all lines as a single paragraph. Remember to end the last line with Enter alone.

4. To force Word to start a new page, hold both Ctrl and Shift down and simultaneously press Enter. Word marks page breaks by displaying a line of dots across the screen.

5. When adding or removing underlining, be sure that the cursor covers exactly the material you want Word to operate on. In particular, remember that Word considers a word and the space after it as a single unit. Remember also Word's strange handling of words with apostrophes, sentences with periods or decimal points in them, and numbers.

6. To underline (or remove underlining from) a single character, position the cursor on that character, and then hold the Alt key down and press **u** twice.

7. When you name glossary entries, Word warns you if you accidentally use the same abbreviation twice. You can then replace the entry with the new text (by typing **y**), retype the abbreviation (**n**), or return to editing (**Esc**).

8. When you name or use glossary entries, remember that Word does not differentiate between lowercase and uppercase letters. Thus, you can refer to the National Aeronautics and Space Administration as either NASA or nasa, but you cannot use names differing only in case as separate abbreviations.

9. If you forget which glossary files are on a disk, use Transfer Glossary Merge and press the F1 key when Word asks for a filename. If you forget which glossary entries are in memory, issue an Insert command and press F1 when Word asks for the source.

10. Remember that Word reverts to NORMAL.GLY (the "normal" glossary) when you Quit or issue a Transfer Clear All command.

11. Don't confuse the glossary entries **date** and **dateprint** or **time** and **timeprint**. The **date** and **time** entries insert text in your document on the screen, whereas

dateprint and **timeprint** insert codes that Word replaces with the correct information when you print the document.

KEY POINTS

Table 3.2 summarizes the keys and commands introduced in this chapter.

Key or key Combination	Purpose
F3	Insert specified glossary entry
Alt-C	Center current line
Alt-L	Move to left margin
Alt-U	Underline highlighted text
Alt-Spacebar	Remove underlining
Ctrl-Shift-Enter	Start a new page
Shift-Enter	Start a new line, but not a new paragraph
Ctrl-PgUp	Move to beginning of document
Ctrl-PgDn	Move to end of document
Command	**Purpose**
Copy	Copy text to scrap ({}) or glossary (specify name)
Delete	Delete text to scrap ({}) or glossary (specify name)
Format Division	Change division parameters
Format Division Page-numbers	Print page numbers
Format Paragraph Justified	Right-justify text
Format Tab Clear	Clear a tab
Format Tab Reset-all	Clear all tabs
Format Tab Set	Set tabs
Insert	Insert text from scrap ({}) or glossary (specify name)
Jump Page	Move to specified page
Library Document-retrieval Update	Change a summary sheet
Library Document-retrieval Query	Search documents for text or summary sheet information
Transfer Clear Window	Erase the screen, but not the glossary
Transfer Glossary Load	Activate a different glossary
Transfer Glossary Merge	Transfer glossary file from disk to glossary
Transfer Glossary Save	Save glossary on disk

Table 3.2   Keys and commands introduced in Chapter 3.

1. Word automatically provides 1" margins at the top and bottom of each page and 1-1/4" margins along the sides. You can use the **Format Division Margins** command to change these settings.

2. The **Format Tab Set** command lets you set tabs, using the mouse or the keyboard. It displays tab stops on a "ruler" at the top of the text area.

   To set a tab with the mouse, move the mouse pointer to the ruler position and press the left button. To clear a tab, position the mouse pointer on the ruler's **L** marker and press both buttons.

3. To set a tab from the keyboard, type its distance from the right margin (in inches) and press Enter.

   To clear a tab from the keyboard, issue a **Format Tab Clear** command, type the position of the tab (in inches), and press Enter. To clear all tabs, issue a **Format Tab Reset-all** command.

4. Word normally gives text a ragged right margin. To produce an even right margin, select the Format Paragraph command's **Justified** option.

5. Word automatically divides single-spaced text into 54-line pages. However, you can force Word to start a new page anywhere by holding Ctrl and Shift down and simultaneously pressing Enter (Ctrl-Shift-Enter).

6. If the first line of a paragraph occurs at the bottom of a page, Word moves it to the next page. Likewise, if the last line of a paragraph occurs at the top of a page, Word moves the preceding line along with it to that page. You can force Word to keep a paragraph intact on one page by changing the Format Paragraph command's "keep together" setting to **Yes**.

7. The **Jump Page** command (Alt-F5) lets you move the cursor to another page

8. To underline material, extend the cursor to cover it, and then press Alt-U. To remove underlining, do the same thing, but press Alt-Spacebar.

9. To center a line, make sure the cursor is somewhere in that line, and press Alt-C.

10. You can save text in the glossary by highlighting it with the cursor, performing a **Delete** or **Copy**, and giving that text a name—usually an abbreviation. (Delete erases the block; Copy does not.) To insert the text in a document, type its abbreviation, and press F3.

11. To see a list of entries in the glossary, issue an **Insert** command and press F1. To insert one of the glossary entries in your document, highlight it and press Enter.

12. You can save the glossary contents on disk with a **Transfer Glossary Save** command and retrieve them later with a **Transfer Glossary Merge** command.

13. To start a new document and use the current glossary with it, clear the screen with a **Transfer Clear Window** command, as opposed to a Transfer Clear All command.

14. Word's default glossary is called NORMAL.GLY, but it also provides two other glossaries, called CONTRACT.GLY and MACRO.GLY. To switch to a different glossary, issue a **Transfer Glossary Load** command.

15. All three built-in glossaries contain seven entries that insert something in your text. The entries **date, time,** and **footnote** insert date text, time-of-day text, or a footnote reference mark. The entries **page, nextpage, dateprint,** and **timeprint** insert codes that Word will replace with the current information whenever you print the document.

16. Word will number the pages in your document if you issue the **Format Division Page-numbers** command.

17. When you save a document on disk, Word lets you fill in a **summary sheet** for it. The summary sheet includes the creation and revision dates and provides space for you to fill in a title, revision number, the names of the author and operator, keywords that can be used for searching, and comments.

18. To change the information in a summary sheet, issue a **Library Document-retrieval Update** command.

19. The **Library Document-retrieval Query** command lets you search documents for text strings or summary sheet information. You can use logical operators to specify the search conditions.

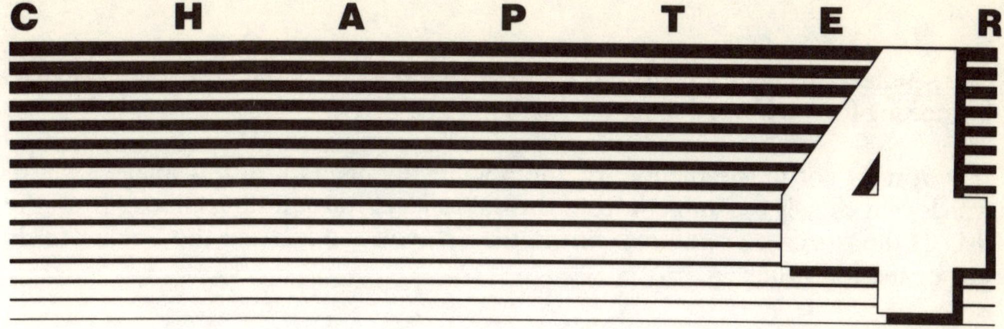

SPELLER AND THESAURUS

Word includes a Speller and Thesaurus that can help improve the quality of your work. This chapter discusses these useful features and provides examples of how to use them.

The **Speller** can check an entire document, or a portion of one, for spelling errors by looking for each word in its dictionary.

If a word is not in the dictionary, the Speller highlights it and displays a list of words that closely resemble it from the dictionary; you can then choose from the list. If the word you're after is not in the list, you can instruct the Speller to do any of the following:

- Ignore it (e.g., it is a proper name or part of a book title).

- Add it to a supplemental dictionary (e.g., it is a technical term not found in most dictionaries).

- Let you correct it manually.

The Speller also marks duplicated words (as in "All the the students got good grades.") and misplaced punctuation (as in "wri;ter") and tells how many words it checked.

The **Thesaurus** is similar to a book thesaurus but is much faster because the synonyms appear on the screen almost instantaneously. To obtain a list of synonyms, you simply move the cursor to the word in question, and then start the Thesaurus.

The Thesaurus displays a list of nouns, verbs, adverbs, prepositions, and adjectives appropriate to the word in question. You can then choose a replacement from the list, display more synonyms, or return to your document without replacing the word.

STARTING THE SPELLER

Word can spell-check an entire document or a portion of it. To spell-check a document, perform the following steps:

1. Position the cursor where you want Word to start spell-checking (usually at the beginning of the document).

2. Select **Library** from the Edit menu.

3. When the following menu appears at the bottom of the screen,

```
LIBRARY: Autosort Document-retrieval Hyphenate Index Link Number Run Spell
         Table thEsaurus
```

type **s** for **Spell**. Word replaces the Library menu with Library Spell and displays the message **Loading dictionary...** while it reads its dictionary into the computer's memory. Then it briefly displays the messages **Checking document** and **Checking dictionaries** while it starts spell-checking.

4. If the Speller can't find a word in its dictionary, it highlights the word, displays a list of possible replacements (if it has any) and a message of the form **word Not found** at the bottom of the text area. It also shows the following menu at the bottom of the screen:

```
SPELL: Correct Add Exit Ignore Options Undo
```

5. If the word you want appears in the list, highlight it and then press Enter. Otherwise, if the word is not listed, choose from the following menu options:

- **Correct** lets you enter a replacement word manually. When CORRECT: appears, type the word you want. You can do one of the following:

    a. Press **F1** to make the Speller look up the word you typed.

    b. Press **Enter** to make the Speller replace the original with your word and verify the new spelling.

- **Add** makes the Speller add the word to a supplemental dictionary (discussed later in this chapter).

- **Exit** makes Word leave spell-checking and return to editing.

- **Ignore** tells the Speller to skip this word and any subsequent occurrences of it, which lets you disregard a word you don't use often enough to add to the dictionary.

- **Options** lets you change the Speller's spell-checking criteria. This topic will be discussed in more detail later in this chapter.

- **Undo** returns the last word you corrected to its original form and puts the Spell list and menu back on the screen.

6. If you started spell checking somewhere other than at the beginning of the document, when the Speller finishes spell-checking, it displays the following message:

```
Enter Y to continue spelling from top of document or Esc to exit
```

7. Then, when you finally exit, the following message appears on the message line:

```
x words checked, y unknown
```

Duplicated Words

The Speller will also check for duplicated words, as in "I drove the the car." If it encounters dublicated words, it highlights the second occurrence and displays a message in the form

```
word is repeated
```

below an empty Spell list, where *word* is the duplicated word. Here, you can press Enter to delete the second instance or type **i** to **Ignore** the repetition (e.g., with a sentence such as "I had had that experience before.").

Other Checks

The Speller also stops on the following items:

- Numbers mixed with letters, as in "P230" (number within a word). These instances produce an **Invalid character** message.

- Words with embedded punctuation marks (such as ".the" and "res;ponse") or two words separated by only a punctuation mark (e.g., "this.word"), which produces an **Improper punctuation** message.

- Words that include capital letters, such as "corPoration," which generate an **Improper capitalization** message.

Unfortunately, the Speller does not find double punctuation, as in "cars,, trucks, and sleds!!" You will have to look for them yourself.

Leaving Spell-Checking

You can leave spell-checking at any time by selecting **Exit** from Word's Spell menu. Here, the last word to be spell-checked remains highlighted.

If you perform another **Library Spell** operation immediately, Word will spell-check only the highlighted word. Otherwise, to remove the highlighting, press an arrow key.

SPELLING CORRECTION EXAMPLE

As an example of using the Speller, consider the letter in Figure 4.1, which contains several spelling errors. If you try this example on your own, don't be restricted by the mistakes in Figure 4.1 (see next page); surely you can make bigger, better, or different ones.

Once you have entered the letter, position the cursor at the start of it and press Esc to reach the Edit menu. Then select **Library** and **Spell**.

The program proceeds to search the document for words that it cannot find in its dictionary. As mentioned previously, in addition to misspellings, these "incorrect" words may include proper names, abbreviations, and technical terms. In this case, the program finds ten unmatched words (starting with "reqqest" in the first paragraph), and displays the Spell list and menu each time.

```
                                    2211 Washington Street
                                    San Diego, CA 92121
                                    May 16, 1989


Mr. Carl Johnson
1236 Summit Drive
San Diego, CA 92121

Dear Mr. Johnson:

In response to your recent reqqest, we need the following
information to cunsider a credit applivdation:

     1)  Name and adddress of your bank, along with your
         account number.
     2)  Three credit references.
     3)  A    signed    corprate    resullution    indicating
         trepponsabillity for payment.

You may either use our enclosed form or sumbit a standard one
of your own. Please indicate any ratings you may have from
credit burows.

                                    Sincerely yours,



                                    Marie F. Gerard
                                    Assistant Credit Manager

Enclosure
```

Figure 4.1 Credit application letter with misspellings.

Dealing with Unmatched Words

For the sample letter, you can deal with the unmatched words as follows:

- The words **reqqest**, **adddress**, **corprate**, **resullution**, and **sumbit** are so close to words in the dictionary that the Speller is able to produce a list that includes the correct form, so you can highlight the correct spellings and press Enter to make the replacement. For **reqqest**, for example, the Speller shows the following list of possible corrections:

```
request        requests       requested
requester      requestor      retest
Ernest         rennets        retests
repeats        reseats        Eries
Erses
```

In this case, you can press Enter because **request** is already highlighted.

- You can select "Add" to add **Gerard** to a supplemental dictionary. (Surprisingly, the Speller already has **San Diego, CA, Carl, Johnson, Marie,** and **F.** in its main dictionary.)

- Select "Correct" to manually replace **cunsider** with **consider, trepponsabillity** with **responsabillity** (intentional misspelling again), and **burows** with **bureaus.** In the case of "responsabillity," however, pressing F1 after entering **responsabillity** shows that it is still misspelled but produces a list that includes the correct spelling, so you are home free.

SPELL-CHECKING A BLOCK OF TEXT

You can also spell-check a word, sentence, paragraph, or any other selected portion of a document. To do this, position the cursor where you want to start and then highlight the words to be checked. Finally, start the Speller as usual, with **Library Spell**.

Changing Word's Spell-Checking Criteria

The Spell menu's **Options** selection lets you change Word's spell-checking criteria, using the parameter list shown in Figure 4.2. Note that Word assumes you want to use a file called SPECIALS.CMP to hold your supplemental dictionary.

```
OPTIONS  user dictionary: C:\WORD5\SPECIALS.CMP
         lookup:(Quick)Complete        ignore all caps: Yes(No)
         alternatives:(Auto)Manual     check punctuation:(Yes)No
```

Figure 4.2   Spell Options parameters.

The other parameters are as follows:

- **lookup** is set to Quick to make Word suggest replacement words from a list of common words in the main dictionary. To make it use the entire dictionary, type **c** for Complete.

- **ignore all caps** is set to No, (check every word). Typing **y** for Yes makes Word ignore words that are entirely capitalized, such as DOCUMENT, but it is just as easy to misspell words that are entirely capitalized as it is to misspell other words, so you will probably want to keep the No setting.

- **alternatives** is set to Auto, which displays a list of possible replacements immediately. Manual requires you to press F1 to obtain the list.

- **check punctuation** makes Word stop on (Yes) or ignore (No) words that are improperly preceded or followed by punctuation marks.

SUPPLEMENTAL DICTIONARIES

When the Speller stops on a word, and you select **Add** from the Spell menu, Word displays the following at the bottom of the screen:

```
ADD word to: Standard User Document
```

The three options here are types of supplemental dictionaries to which you can add the highlighted word.

Standard Dictionary

The "standard" supplemental dictionary, which is stored in a file called UPDAT-AM.CMP, is the dictionary you should use for most of your work. Unless you tell Word otherwise, it will check UPDAT-AM.CMP and its regular dictionary (SPELL-AM.LEX) whenever you perform a Library Spell operation.

User Dictionary

A user dictionary is useful for storing words that you use with a specific project. For example, if you are writing a science fiction book and use character names and place names such as "Arkt" or "Broog," you should store these words in a user dictionary. Then, once you have finished the project, you can simply delete that dictionary file.

Word provides a default user dictionary called SPECIALS.CMP and adds your word to it when you select **User** from the ADD menu. To create a new user dictionary, do the following:

1. Issue a **Library Spell** command.

2. When the Speller stops on a word, choose **Options**.

3. In the "user dictionary" field, type the name you want to give the new user dictionary (up to eight characters), and then press Enter.

Word creates your user dictionary file (and gives it the extension **.CMP**) and then continues spell-checking.

Document Dictionary

A document dictionary is a supplemental dictionary that the Speller uses with a particular document. When you choose **Document** from the ADD menu, Word creates (if necessary) a document dictionary with the current document's name and the extension **.CMP** and then adds the highlighted word to that dictionary. From then on, whenever you perform a Library Spell operation, the Speller will search that dictionary as well as its standard dictionary and any other supplemental dictionaries.

USING THE THESAURUS

Word's Thesaurus can display synonyms for a word on the screen and replace that word with any word in its list.

To look up a word, put the cursor anywhere in it (or just past it), press Esc to reach the Edit menu, type l for **Library**, and type **e** for **thEsaurus**. Note that these selections aren't very intuitive; you probably wouldn't guess that Library is the starting point to get to the thesaurus, nor would you expect to type an E once you are in the Library menu. Fortunately, you can also issue a Library thEsaurus command by pressing Ctrl-F6.

To begin, the Thesaurus reads your word and then does one of two things:

1. If your word is one the Thesaurus recognizes, Word shows a **Word Finder Thesaurus** window that lists the synonyms (nouns, verbs, adverbs, preposi-
    tions, and adjectives) and highlights the first one. Your options are as follows:

    - Press Enter to replace the word in your text with the highlighted word from the Thesaurus.

    - Press Ctrl-F6 to look up synonyms for the highlighted word.

    - Press an arrow key to highlight a different word in the list and then press Enter.

    - Press Esc to get back to editing without looking anything up.

2. If the Thesaurus does not contain your word, it displays a half-screen list of similarly spelled words and puts the cursor on the word that is at the position where your word *would* have been. It also displays the message **The word was not found. Choose another word to look up.** at the top of the list. You can then do one of the following:

    - Press Enter or Ctrl-F6 to look up the highlighted word.

    - Press an arrow key to highlight a different word in the list.

    - Press Esc to get back to editing without looking anything up.

QUESTIONS AND ANSWERS

I corrected the spelling in a four-page letter but have since made changes to page 2. How can I correct just that page?

Move the cursor to page 2 and select (highlight) the entire page. Then start the Speller as usual, with Library Spell. Word will spell-check only that page.

The Speller marked the name of my company as misspelled, so I added it to the Standard dictionary. However, there are more mentions of the company in my letter. Will it ask me to correct them, too?

No. Once you select a replacement from the dictionary (by highlighting it and pressing Enter) and **Add** it to the dictionary or **Correct** the spelling from the keyboard, the Speller will change all subsequent occurrences of the word throughout your document. If you **Ignore** a word, Word will disregard it throughout the rest of your document.

HINTS AND WARNINGS

1. Word's Speller always works forward through a document, but if you start from somewhere within a document, it will offer to check from the beginning when it finishes.

2. The Speller acts as a proofreader as well as a spelling checker. Many of the errors it finds are really typing mistakes.

3. Even if you're reasonably sure of a correction, you might as well have the Speller look it up. This takes only a few seconds and verifies the spelling.

4. In practice, you should add abbreviations, proper names, and technical terms to the dictionary rather than just ignore them. If you skip them, the Speller will find them every time it spell-checks a document, which is both time-consuming and annoying.

5. The Speller will not locate double punctuation (e.g., "Bill,, that's the best thing you ever said."). You must correct these mistakes yourself.

6. The Speller "remembers" all your **Ignore** commands for as long as you keep a document active. Hence, if you check your document, make some changes, and then spell-check again, the Speller will skip all the words you told it to ignore.

7. The Speller counts words as it spell-checks a document and displays the total when it finishes. This feature is handy for writers sand students who must prepare an article, short story, report, or term paper of a specific length.

8. To stop a spell-check operation before it finishes, press Esc to reach the Spell menu and type **e** for **Exit**.

9. If you start the Thesaurus on a non-word such as a space or a number, it always looks up the preceding word. For example, if you start with the cursor on **32** in the sentence **We shipped your order in 32 cartons**, you will get synonyms for the word **in**.

10. With the Word Finder Thesaurus window on the screen, you can return to your document by pressing Esc.

KEY POINTS

Table 4.1 summarizes the keys and commands introduced in this chapter.

Key Combination	**Function**
Alt-F6	Speller
Ctrl-F6	Thesaurus
Command	**Function**
Library Spell	Speller
Library thEsaurus	Thesaurus

Table 4.1   Keys and commands introduced in Chapter 4.

1. Word can spell-check a highlighted block of text or (if you didn't highlight anything) the rest of the document.

2. To start spell-checking, issue a **Library Spell** command or press Alt-F6.

3. If the Speller can't find a word in its dictionary, it highlights the word and displays a list of closely related words (if any). If the correct word appears in the list, move the cursor to it and press Enter; otherwise, press Esc to reach the Spell menu.

4. The Spell menu's options let you **Correct** the word by entering replacement text, **Add** the word to a supplemental dictionary, **Exit** spell-checking, **Ignore**

this word (and any remaining occurrences of it), or **Undo** the preceding correction. It can also provide **Options** that let you use a different supplemental dictionary, do a Quick or Complete lookup, ignore capitalized words, or ignore punctuation.

5. You can **Add** a word to three kinds of supplementary dictionaries: Standard, User (for a group of documents) or Document (for the current document). Word provides default standard and user dictionaries, called UPDAT-AM.CMP and SPECIALS.CMP, respectively.

6. When the Speller finishes, it shows a count of the number of words it checked and how many "unknown" words it stopped on.

7. Word's Thesaurus can look up synonyms for a word and replace it with a word from an on-screen list.

8. To start the Thesaurus, issue a **Library thEsaurus** command or press Ctrl-F6.

9. The Thesaurus lists synonyms (nouns, verbs, adverbs, prepositions, and adjectives) for the word you specified, and positions the cursor on the first word in its list. To replace your word with the highlighted word, press Enter. Otherwise, press an arrow key to move through the Thesaurus's list, press Esc to get back to your text, or press Ctrl-F6 to look up synonyms for the highlighted word.

10. If the Thesaurus does *not* contain the word you requested, it assumes you misspelled the word. Thus, it displays an alphabetized list of words, with the cursor on your word or the Thesaurus word that's closest to your word (e.g., if you ask for "creating," it highlights "creation"). You can then use the arrow keys to highlight a different word, press Enter or Ctrl-F6 to look up the highlighted word, or press Esc to get back to your text.

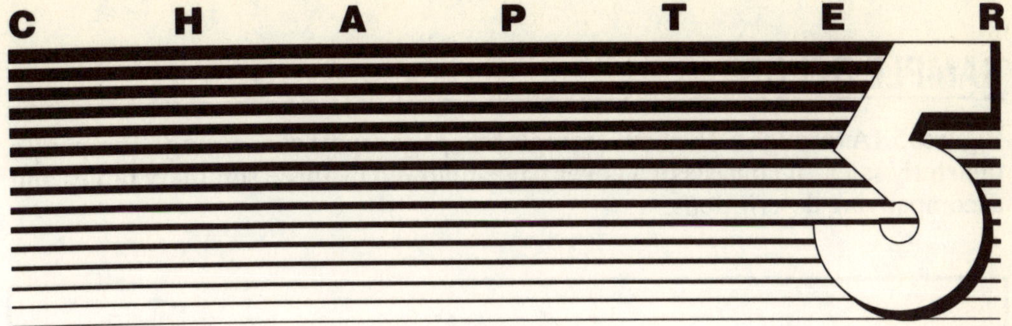

REPORTS

To write a report with Word, you will need features not yet discussed. For example, you may want the pages numbered. You may also want a heading on the top of each page and the chapter number, section title, or report title at the bottom of each page.

Furthermore, you may want the report double-spaced, but with single-spaced lists or tables. You may also want titles in bold print, and you may want to use subscripts or superscripts in references, equations, and formulas. These features will be discussed in this chapter within the context of a five-page sample report.

SAMPLE REPORT

Figures 5.1A through 5.1E show a sample five-page report concerning a company's quarterly sales. It consists of a cover page, followed by three summary tables and accompanying descriptions.

```
                          ACME CORPORATION

                        National Sales Report

                        Second Quarter, 1989


















   Gloria A. Powell
   National Sales Manager
   July 19, 1989

   cc: P.M. Cornell, President
       J.R. Johnson, Vice-President
       Regional Sales Managers
```

Figure 5.1A   Sample report, cover page.

This report summarizes national sales for the second quarter of 1989. Table 1 lists the sales figures for the six regions and compares them to the second quarter of 1988. As the table shows, sales are moderately better than last year in every region except the Southwest.

The Southeast region tops the list with a 9.9 percent gain, due in part to large orders from Jenco in Florida and Symtech in Georgia. Although the Southwest region continues to lead in volume, its sales are slightly below last year's. This reflects decreased orders from Winicon Corp. in Nevada, which has been troubled by economic conditions. In all, this quarter's sales are <u>5.7 percent higher</u> than those of the second quarter of 1988.

Table 2 lists the leading sales representatives in each region. These are the same people listed on last year's report, with one exception: Doris Kim, who joined Acme in January, closed a 290-unit order with Pacifico to put her on top in the Northwest. Our sales force continues to be among the best in the business, but I am especially proud of the exceptional individuals listed here.

-2- (Second Quarter Report/1989)

Figure 5.1B   Sample report, second page.

Table 1.   Second Quarter Sales

Region	Units Sold	Revenues ($)	% Change from 1988
Northeast	5,770	2,481,100	+6.7
Southeast	4,550	1,956,500	+9.9
Midwest	6,430	2,764,900	+8.8
Mountain	4,300	1,849,000	+4.7
Northwest	5,130	2,205,900	+7.4
Southwest	6,780	2,915,400	−0.3
Totals	32,960	14,172,800	+5.7

Table 2.   Top Sales Representatives

Region	Sales Rep.	Units Sold	% Increase from 1988
Northeast	R. Roberts	790	22.4
Southeast	C. Chamber	640	16.3
Midwest	J. Wilkes	730	19.1
Mountain	P. Wallach	620	20.6
Northwest	D. Kim	590	--
Southwest	B. Lloyd	710	17.7

-3- (Second Quarter Report/1989)

Figure 5.1C   Sample report, third page.

Table 3 lists the orders that were placed by key accounts during the quarter. Most significant of these is the 510-unit order by Chicago Gear, whose orders appeared to have leveled off at about 400 units per quarter during the past two years. The Wilburg Sons and Storr Brothers accounts also show notable increases; both orders are about 19 percent higher than in recent quarters.

-4- (Second Quarter Report/1989)

Figure 5.1D   Sample report, fourth page.

Table 3. Orders by Key Accounts

<u>Region</u>	<u>Account</u>	<u>State</u>	<u>Sales Rep.</u>	<u>Order</u>
Northeast	Wilburg Sons	New York	R. Roberts	430
Southeast	Jenco	Florida	C. Chamber	390
	Symtech	Georgia	P. Grogan	240
Midwest	Chicago Gear	Illinois	J. Wilkes	510
Mountain	Hart Foods	Montana	P. Wallach	420
Northwest	Pacifico	Oregon	D. Kim	290
Southwest	Storr Bros.	California	B. Lloyd	470

-5- (Second Quarter Report/1989)

Figure 5.1E   Sample report, fifth page.

Note the following formatting conventions used in the report:

- All titles are in bold print.
- Descriptive text is double-spaced and has a ragged right-hand margin.
- Tables are centered.

The page number and report title appear at the bottom of every page except on the cover. These features will be discussed as you would encounter them in the course of preparing the report. To begin, start Word as usual.

RUNNING HEADS

In this example, you will instruct Word to print the following line at the bottom of pages 2 through 5,

```
-n- (Second Quarter Report/1989)
```

where n is the page number. The Word manual calls text that appears on every page a "running head," even if it appears at the bottom of the page. (Text at the bottom of a page is often called a "footer" in other programs.)

When you create a running head, you must tell Word when and where to print it. You can specify up to six different running heads. For example, you can have a section title at the top of right-hand pages, the report title at the bottom of left-hand pages, and the page number at the bottom of every page.

Creating a Running Head

To create a running head, you simply enter it at the beginning of the division, select it, and then tell Word where to print it. The procedure is as follows:

1. Type the text for the running head and press Enter at the end of the final line. You can center or underline it using standard methods.

To make Word print the page number in a running head, type **page** where you want it to appear, and then press F3. Word puts parentheses around **page** to distinguish it from literal text.

2. Highlight the running head text.

3. Select **Format** in the Edit menu.

4. Type **r** for **Running-head**. Word displays the running head parameter list (see Figure 5.2).

```
FORMAT RUNNING-HEAD position: Top Bottom None
       odd pages:(Yes)No  even pages:(Yes)No  first page: Yes(No)
       alignment:(Left-margin)Edge-of-paper
```

Figure 5.2   Running head parameters.

5. Type **t** or **b** to put the head at the **Top** or **Bottom**, respectively.

6. Press Tab to reach the second line. This line lets you select the pages on which the running head will appear. (Note that Word assumes you want to print the running head on every page but the first one.)

7. Proceed through the page options with the Tab key.

8. With "alignment" set to **Left-margin** on the third line, Word assumes you want the running head to start at the left margin. However, you can select **Edge-of-paper** by typing **e**.

9. Press Enter to exit.

Word puts a caret (^) in the left margin of each running head line to remind you that it is not just ordinary text.

Running Head for the Sample Report

To enter the running head for the sample report, follow these steps:

1. Press Alt-C to center the text you are about to type.

2. Type **-page** and press F3. Word changes **page** to **(page)** to indicate where it will print the page number.

3. Type another **-** and press the spacebar, and then type (**Second Quarter Report/1989**) and press Enter.

4. Press the up arrow key to move up to the running head.

5. To tell Word where to print the running head, select **Format** in the Edit menu and then **Running-head** in the Format menu.

6. When the Edit menu reappears, press the down arrow key to move past the running head.

Editing and Deleting Running Heads

You can edit a running head just as you would edit regular text: move the cursor to the running head and make your changes. If you accidentally specified the wrong print position (e.g., you intended to make position **Bottom** but left it as **None**), highlight the running head text and issue a new Format Running-head command. To delete a running head, highlight it, and then press Del.

ENTERING THE COVER PAGE

As Figure 5.1A shows, the cover has a centered, bold title and the author's name and title, date, and distribution list ("cc" means carbon copy) in the lower left corner. Here, the title starts three inches from the top.

Word automatically provides a one-inch top margin, so you must move the cursor two inches down the page before entering the title. To do this, press Enter 12 times (Word's built-in, or "default," spacing is six lines per inch), and then press Alt-C to issue a Center command. This moves the cursor to the center of the screen.

Bold Print

To make something print in **bold** type, select it and press **Alt-B**. The text is bolded on the screen, although on some displays bold print is difficult to distinguish from ordinary text. Note the following about bold print:

- To make a single character bold, position the cursor on it and then hold the Alt key down and press **b** *twice*.

- If you accidentally apply the bold format to too many characters or to the wrong characters, simply select the characters you do not want to appear as bold, and press **Alt-Spacebar**. Press it twice to remove bold formatting from a single character.

To make ACME CORPORATION bold on the cover page, do the following:

1. Press Shift-F9 to select the line.

2. Press Alt-B to make the title bold.

To reach the line where **National Sales Report** belongs, press the down arrow key and then press Enter. Use the procedure just described to enter this line and the **Second Quarter, 1989** line.

Finishing the Cover Page

To complete the page, you must press Enter to reach the line where the author's name goes. Because you want seven lines (including a blank line) at the bottom of a 54-line page, the author's name belongs on line 48. However, although Word tells which page and column you're on (with the **Pg** and **Col** indicators on the bottom line), it does not give the current line number. But that's not really a problem.

Because you know that the author's name and the other six lines should appear at the bottom of the page, you can simply type them at the current position and then move them as a group to the bottom of the page. Follow these steps:

1. Enter the lines for the author's name and title.

2. Insert the date (issue an Insert command and enter **date**).

3. Enter the distribution list.

This completes the material you want to move to the bottom of the page.

4. Move the cursor back up to the beginning of the line that contains the author's name and press Enter until the **Regional Sales Managers** line is just below Word's dotted page break line.

5. Press the up arrow key (to reach the line that precedes the author's name) and press Del. The seven lines of material are now just above the page break — which is where Word will print them.

6. Move the cursor just past the page break, to the beginning of the second page.

ENTERING THE SECOND PAGE

To double-space the second page, you must change the "line spacing" value in Word's paragraph parameter list. This is the list you used in Chapter 3 to give paragraphs even right margins.

To switch to double-spacing, follow these steps:

1. Obtain the paragraph parameter list with a Format Paragraph command. Note that "line spacing" is set to **1 li**, where **li** means line.

2. Position the mouse pointer on **1 li** and press the left button (or use the Tab key from the keyboard).

3. Type **2** (for double-spacing), and press Enter.

Now Word will both display and print text with double-spacing.

Now enter the text for the second page, as shown in Figure 5.1B. When you finish, hold Ctrl and Shift down while you press Enter. This Ctrl-Shift-Enter combination creates a page break and moves the cursor to the top of the third page.

ENTERING THE THIRD PAGE

As Figure 5.1C shows, the third page consists of two tables. Before entering them, note the following:

- You must change the line spacing back to single-spaced (**1 li**).

- You need different tabs for each table because the columns are spaced differently.

- The tables and titles are centered.

To begin, use the same procedure as before to switch Word back to single-spacing. Then press Alt-C and enter the centered title for Table 1. Move the cursor back to the title line. Press Shift-F9 to select it and Alt-B to make it bold. Press the down arrow key once, and then press Enter twice to move the cursor down to where the table begins.

Centering a Table

Now you must create tabs for the table. The easiest way to determine where the tabs belong is to enter the table headings and the data, adjust the spacing, and then center the headings and move the data under them. The starting points of the data will tell you where to set tabs. This is the same procedure you followed in Chapter 3 except that here you need to center the headings with Alt-C.

As Figure 5.1C shows, the leftmost data column starts directly below the "R" in "Region." Instead of shifting each data line right manually, you can simply have Word indent the table.

The paragraph parameter list controls indentation. To display this list, position the cursor on the first data line and then issue a Format Paragraph command. The second line of the list shows the following,

```
left indent: 0"          first line: 0"          right indent: 0"
```

where "first line" tells Word how much to indent the first line from the "left indent" value.

Note that Word displays the ruler at the top of the screen with the paragraph parameters. This lets you see the current indent settings. The opening bracket ([) represents left; the closing bracket (]) represents right.

To change "left indent," move the mouse pointer to its value and then press the left-hand button to highlight it. (From the keyboard, tab through the menu settings.) You want the new value to be the position of "R" in "Region" (below the ruler's fifth dot). Type **.5"**, and then press Enter. Word moves the entire data line right and shows the two lines as follows:

```
Region     Units Sold   Revenues ($)    % Change from 1988
Northeast  5,770    2,481,100    +6.7
```

After setting the tabs, you can use them on every line except "Totals" because some data starts ahead of the tab positions.

You can enter Table 2 in much the same way as Table 1, except you must use different tabs for Table 2. When you finish, press Ctrl-Shift-Enter to begin page 4.

ENTERING THE FOURTH PAGE

Like the second page of the report, the fourth page (shown in Figure 5.1D) is double-spaced. Use the Format Paragraph command to change the line spacing to **2 li.**

Now enter the text. When you finish, press Ctrl-Shift-Enter to begin the final page.

ENTERING THE FIFTH PAGE

Page 5 is much like page 3. Once again, you must change the line spacing back to **1 li**. You must also create a centered table and change "left indent."

PRINTING AND SAVING A REPORT

After entering the final page, you can print the report. The Print Printer command will print only one copy. To get multiple copies, you must change Word's **print options.** For example, you can get nine copies as follows:

1. Obtain the print options list by issuing a Print command and then pressing **o** for **Options.**

2. When the list appears, put the mouse pointer on the "1" that follows "copies", type **9**, and press Enter. (From the keyboard, use the Tab key to move through the menu selections.)

3. When Word displays the Print menu again, press Enter to select **Printer**.

4. When the Edit menu reappears, save the report on disk under the name **rptq289**.

Printing Selected Pages

Word also lets you print selected pages in a document. To do this, change the Print Options form's "range" parameter to **Pages**, and then press Tab to reach the "page numbers" field. Type the numbers of the pages you want printed, separated by commas. Then press Enter twice, once to reach the Print menu and again to print.

You can also print consecutive pages by entering the starting and ending numbers separated by a colon in the "page numbers" field. For example, to print pages 23 through 32, enter **23:32**. To print page 19 as well, enter **19,23:32**.

If you aren't sure exactly how long the document is and want to print from, say, page 30 to the end of the document, although you can't tell Word to simply print the rest of the document, you can trick it by entering an overly large value for the ending page number. For example, you could enter **100** as the final page for a document that is only about 40 pages long. Word will simply stop printing when it comes to the end of the document.

Word saves the latest "range" setting, so you must change it back to **All** before printing an entire document. Otherwise, Word will simply ignore your next Print Printer command.

Printing Disk Documents

So far, printing documents from the screen, using the Print command's **Printer** option has been discussed. You needn't load a document into Word to print it, however. If you saved it on disk, you can simply tell Word to print from disk, using Print's **File** option and then entering the name of the disk file you want to print.

Stopping a Print Operation

Sometimes you may want to stop a print operation to fix a problem (say, the printer has run out of paper) or answer the telephone, or you may want to cancel printing entirely. To do this, press Esc. When Word shows the message

```
Enter Y to continue or Esc to cancel
```

you can do whatever you need to do and then type y, or you can press Esc again to cancel.

CONTROLLING PAGE NUMBERING

For the sample report, you let Word number the pages from the beginning, with the title page **1**, the second page **2**, and so on. However, some documents begin with a title page, table of contents, and an introduction or preface. This front material is usually numbered separately — typically with Roman numerals (i, ii, iii, etc.) — and numbering restarts on the first page of regular text.

As you may recall from "Numbering Pages" in Chapter 3, Word's **Format Division Page-numbers** command produces a form that has a "numbering" parameter with a **Start** option that lets you restart the page numbering (by putting the new page number in the "at" field). It also has a "number format" option that lets you select the numbering style.

SPECIAL CHARACTER FORMATS

In addition to underlining and bold print, Word can also produce italics, double-underlines, small caps, hidden text (which shows up on screen but does not print), subscripts, superscripts, and strikethroughs — lines through text (lawyers and legislators often use strikethroughs to indicate what has been deleted in a legal contract).

As with underlining and bold print, you get these character formats by pressing Alt and another key (see Table 5.1).

To get this format:	Press Alt and	Example
Bold	B	But **don't** press the red button.
Hidden	H	
Italic	I	He starred in *Gone with the Wind*.
Small caps	K	F5 THROUGH F10 are function keys.
Underline	U	Use <u>underline</u> for emphasis.
Double-underline	D	You can also use a <u>double-underline.</u>
Strikethrough	S	Legal contracts often use ~~strikethroughs~~ to indicate deletions.
Superscript	+ or =	$E = mc^2$
Subscript	- (hyphen)	U_{235}

Table 5.1   Character formats

As before, keep the following in mind:

- If you press Alt-*key* (where *key* represents a character format key) after selecting a block of text, Word will apply that format to the entire block.

- To apply a format to the character at the cursor position, hold the Alt key down and press the other key *twice*.

- If you press Alt-*key* during regular editing (with nothing selected), Word will apply the format to whatever you type next.

You can also select these formats from the **Format Character** menu.

Word shows the special formats if you have a color screen but simply underlines them on a green or amber "monochrome" screen.

Mixing Formats

You can also apply several formats to a given piece of text. For example, you can embolden an underlined title or a subscript or superscript number. To do this, simply apply the first format and then the second. For example, to produce a title that's both bold and underlined, highlight it and press Alt-B followed by Alt-U.

Removing Character Formats

You can also remove formats from text, or "unstyle" it. To turn off all active character formatting, highlight the text and press **Alt-Spacebar** (hold the Alt key down and simultaneously press the spacebar). To turn off only the last format you used, press Alt-Z.

FOOTNOTES AND ENDNOTES

Word lets you add footnotes to any page. Once you create a footnote, Word automatically numbers it and "attaches" it to the text that refers to it. (You can also mark a footnote reference with a character such as *.) That is, if changes move the reference to a different page, Word moves the footnote along with it. Similarly, if you delete a footnote reference number (or mark), Word deletes its corresponding footnote text as well.

Endnotes are the same as footnotes, except Word puts them at the end of the document instead of on each page. You can have footnotes and endnotes in the same document.

Creating Footnotes

To create a footnote, do the following:

1. Position the cursor on the character that's currently where you want the footnote number to appear in the text.

2. Issue a **Format Footnote** command (press **Esc**, **F**, **F**). Word replaces the Format menu with

```
FORMAT FOOTNOTE reference mark:
```

and shows **Enter text** on the message line.

3. If you want Word to number the footnote, press Enter. Otherwise, type your reference mark, and then press Enter.

   Word displays the area at the end of the document where it stores footnotes. (It won't print them at the end, however, unless you tell it to.) Here, it shows a new line that starts with the number or reference mark.

4. Type the footnote text.

5. Issue a **Jump Footnote** command (press **Esc, J, F**) to return to editing. Word positions the cursor on the reference mark.

Printing Footnotes as Endnotes

Word assumes you want to print footnotes on the pages where the references occur. To make it print footnotes at the end of the division, as endnotes, issue a **Format Division Layout** command. When the form (Figure 5.3) appears, change the "footnotes" setting from **Same-page** to **End**.

```
FORMAT DIVISION LAYOUT footnotes:(Same-page)End
         number of columns: 1        space between columns: 0.5"
            division break:(Page)Continuous Column Even Odd
```

Figure 5.3   Format Division Layout form.

Footnote Example

Suppose you're writing a term paper on Alaskan explorers that includes the sentence, "Their journey took them through the Shelikov Strait." Suppose you want "Shelikov Strait" to refer to the following footnote:

A strait 30 miles wide between the Alaskan Peninsula and the Kodiak and Afognak Islands.

To put this footnote at the bottom of the page, proceed as follows:

1. Position the cursor on the space that follows the sentence.

2. Issue a Format command, and then press **f** for **Footnote**.

3. When Word shows **FORMAT FOOTNOTE reference mark:**, press Enter to tell it to number the reference. Word shows the footnote text area and displays a new line that begins with **1** (the number for this footnote).

4. Enter **A strait 30 miles wide between the Alaskan peninsula and Afognak islands.** and then press Esc to return to the Edit menu.

5. Type **j** for **Jump** and **f** for **Footnote**, and then press Enter. The main text reappears with the cursor on the footnote reference.

When you print the document, Word will put the footnote at the bottom of the reference page with a line above it, as follows:

---

[1]A strait 30 miles wide between the Alaskan Peninsula and the Kodiak and Afognak Islands.

(Of course, the superscript **1** here assumes that this is the first footnote in the term paper. If other footnotes precede it, the number will be higher.)

Locating Footnote References

Word's Jump Footnote command moves the cursor to the next footnote reference in a document. To move on, press the right arrow key, and then issue another Jump Footnote command. If there are no more footnote references, Word displays **No more footnote references** on the message line.

Editing Footnotes

You can edit footnotes in the same way you edit regular text. To do this, position the cursor on the footnote's number, and then issue the Jump Footnote command. This moves the cursor to the beginning of the footnote area. Make your changes, and then issue Jump Footnote again to return to the main text.

Deleting Footnotes

To delete a footnote, position the cursor on its reference number in the text and press Del. Word erases the footnote text as well and, if the footnotes have been numbered automatically, renumbers the rest of the references in the division.

ALIGNING DECIMAL NUMBERS

Word lets you use tabs to mark the position of the decimal point in a column of numbers. When you move the cursor to one of these **decimal tabs**, Word automatically aligns the number you enter there; that is, it shifts everything you type to the left. When you type a decimal point, Word stops shifting text and puts anything else you type to the right. When you press Enter, Word stops aligning and moves the cursor to the next line.

You can set decimal tabs for a table as follows:

1. Position the cursor on the line where the table starts.

2. Select the Format command, and then type **t** for **Tab** and **s** for **Set**. Word displays the ruler and the following list:

```
FORMAT TAB SET position:
        alignment: (Left)Center Right Decimal Vertical leader char: (Blank).-_
```

3. Press Tab to reach "alignment," and then type **d** for **Decimal.**

4. Move the mouse pointer to the ruler position where you want the tab, and then press the left button. (From the keyboard, use the Tab key and enter the position.) Word puts a **D** there.

5. Press Enter to get back to editing.

As with other tabs, you can move to a decimal tab with the Tab key.

For example, suppose your organization is raising money for a charity and you want a list, such as the following, of how much each member has collected:

```
Member             Collections

Brown, John        $1,504.36
Carlson, Ray          965.77
Decker, Patricia    1,668.43
Garnett, Vance        769.03
Evans, Sue            779.56
Gerard, Roy         1,056.90
Morton, Mary          800.00
Stevens, George       863.96
```

You must set a tab directly below the "t" in "Collections." Then you simply press Tab after each name, and type the amount. Word will align the amount around the tab position. (Assuming you want to keep the table together when Word prints your document, remember to press Shift-Enter at the end of each line. This makes Word treat the table as a single paragraph.)

For example, as you type **$1,504** on the first line, Word puts each character at the tab position and shifts all preceding characters to the left. Then, when you type the decimal point, Word stops shifting and puts the next two digits (**36**) to the right of the decimal point.

INDENTING LISTS

When people type a list of items, they often indent them and set them off with numbers, dashes, or "bullets." For example, suppose you want to indent three numbered items in a letter, like this:

```
In response to your recent request, we need the following information
to complete a credit application:

   1)  Name and address of your bank, along with your account
       number.
   2)  Three credit references.
   3)  A signed corporate resolution indicating responsibility
       for payment.
```

When you reach the line where the first indented item belongs, change Word's "left indent" and "first line" values. You need the following values:

- The second line of items in points 1) and 3) starts eight characters beyond the left margin, so you should type **.8"** for "left indent."

- The first line starts four characters to the left of this position, so you should type **-.4"** for "first line."

To obtain the paragraph parameter list, issue a Format command and type **p** for **Paragraph**. When the list appears, change "left indent" to **.8"** and "first line" to **-.4"**. Then press Enter.

Word will keep this indentation until you change it. When you finish entering the numbered items, obtain the paragraph parameter list again and change both "left indent" and "first line" back to **0**.

Indenting Paragraphs

You can also make Word indent a paragraph that you entered earlier. To do this, position the cursor anywhere in that paragraph, and then change the "indent" values, using the approach just described. When you leave the paragraph parameter list, Word reformats the paragraph. This affects only the current paragraph.

MULTICOLUMN MATERIAL

Newspaper and magazine articles, newsletters, dramatic scripts, and some legal documents are printed with several columns on a page. Word lets you arrange text in two column styles, newspaper-style or side-by-side paragraphs.

Newspaper-style columns are designed for text that continues from the bottom of one column to the top of the next, in winding fashion. You may want to use this style for a newsletter.

Side-by-side paragraphs are useful for scripts, side-by-side translations, inventory lists, and other documents where information is arranged left-to-right across the page. For example, an inventory list may have four columns—for the product name, part number, quantity in stock, and comments.

Word normally displays only a single column on the screen. However, if you issue a **Show Layout** command (by pressing Alt-F4), it will show the columns next to each other, just as they will be printed. When Show Layout mode is active, Word displays the abbreviation **LY** on the status line.

Newspaper-Style Columns vs. Side-by-Side Paragraphs

In this chapter, arranging text in newspaper-style columns will be covered rather than side-by-side paragraphs because newspaper-style columns are more commonly used and fairly easy to do. You simply set up the format at the beginning of your text; Word will use that format until you say otherwise. By contrast, producing side-by-side paragraphs is a tedious and error-prone process that involves specifying the format for every paragraph you enter.

Fortunately, Word provides a "macro" called **sidebyside.mac** that sets up a two- or three-column side-by-side format to your specifications. (A macro is a mini-program that you can run by entering its name or inserting it by selecting from a list.) If you need side-by-side text, you should use that macro. Macros are discussed in Chapter 10.

Creating Newspaper-Style Columns

To create newspaper-style documents, you must change the "number of columns" value in Word's **Format Division Layout** parameter list (shown earlier in Figure 5.3). Word sets this value to **1** initially.

Word divides the text into equal-sized columns by assuming a "space between columns" of **0.5"**. If you are printing two columns on standard 8.5" paper with 1.25" side margins, this spacing value makes each column 2.75" wide.

Once you have set up the columns, you can begin entering your columnar text. Word proceeds to the next column when the current one is full and starts a new page when the last column is full. If Show Layout (Alt-F4) is on, Word displays all your columns on the screen.

Headlines

You may also want to switch back to single-column format temporarily to create a headline or "banner" across several columns. To do that, issue another **Format Division Layout** command and change "number of columns" back to **1**. Enter your headline, and then reestablish the multicolumn format.

Moving between Columns

You can use the standard cursor-moving keys (left arrow, right arrow, Home, PgDn, etc.) to move within a column. To make editing changes in a different column, move the cursor as follows:

- To reach the preceding column, hold down Ctrl and press 5, and then press the left arrow key.

- To reach the next column, hold down Ctrl and press 5, and then press the right arrow key.

EDITING WITH A MOUSE

Until now, you have been using keys to move the cursor and select (highlight) text. You can also use the mouse if you have one. The mouse is sometimes handier than the keyboard because it lets you move the cursor rapidly in any direction. Here are the fundamentals of selecting material with the mouse:

- Pressing the mouse's left button moves the cursor to the **character** indicated by the mouse pointer.

- Pressing the right button selects the **word** in which the pointer is positioned.

- Pressing both buttons selects the **sentence** in which the pointer is positioned.

If the pointer is on a space, Word selects the word or sentence to the left of it.

Selecting Lines and Paragraphs

If you move the mouse pointer to the gap between the text's left margin and the border, you can use the buttons to select a line or paragraph. Pressing the left button selects the current *line*, while pressing the right button selects the current *paragraph*.

Scrolling

You can also use the mouse to move, or **scroll**, through a document. To do this, put the mouse pointer on the left border. Pressing the left button moves the text down (backward), while pressing the right button moves it up (forward). The text moves by the number of lines the mouse pointer is positioned below the top border.

Word does not move the cursor when it scrolls, so the cursor may disappear. However, pressing the down arrow key makes Word return to where the cursor is. (This is useful for examining text far from where you are working.) Otherwise, to move the cursor to where you have scrolled, position the mouse pointer there, and then press the left mouse button.

HANDLING LONG REPORTS

Hard disks can hold millions of characters (i.e., thousands of pages), so hard disk users rarely run out of space for their documents. However, floppy disk users can run out of storage space by filling the data disk.

If you try to save a document on a full disk, Word displays **Disk full** on the message line. At this point, you may either insert a new (formatted) disk or delete something from the full disk and then save it again. For details on how to remove document files from a disk, see "Deleting Documents" in Chapter 2.

Organizing Long Reports

The most efficient way to organize long reports is to create a separate document for each section or chapter. This not only gives you logical stopping points if you need to switch to a new disk but lets you make changes to one section without affecting others.

PRODUCING BACKUPS

When you issue a Transfer Save command, or confirm that you want to save changes during a Quit or Transfer Clear operation, Word saves a new version of your document that includes any changes you made. It's good practice to save your work frequently. That way, you won't lose as many changes if the power goes off, if someone dislodges the power cord, or if someone turns off your computer.

BAK Files

When you revise an existing document and issue a Transfer Save command, Word converts the original into a "backup" file. It gives the backup the same name as the original, but with the extension **.BAK** (instead of .DOC). For example, when you edit and save a document called **roster**, Word saves the new version as ROSTER.DOC and the original as ROSTER.BAK.

Because the BAK file occupies disk space, you may want to delete it. However, it can come in handy if you want to save the original for future comparison or even go back and work on the original. To reinstate the original document (say, ROSTER), do the following:

1. Use the Transfer Load command to load ROSTER.BAK into memory. Note that you must type the entire filename (ROSTER.BAK). BAK files do not appear in Word's directory except when you issue Transfer Delete commands.

2. Use a Transfer Delete command to erase ROSTER.DOC.

3. Use a Transfer Rename command to change ROSTER.BAK to ROSTER.DOC.

You can also use the Transfer Load/Transfer Rename sequence to save the backup file under a new name, such as OLDROST.DOC.

Backing Up Automatically

A possible disadvantage to Transfer Save is that you must *remember* to do it every so often. Fortunately, Word will also back up your work at regular intervals, if you tell it to. To make Word automatically save your work, you must activate the **autosave** feature.

To turn on autosave, follow these steps:

1. Activate the Edit menu and type **o** for Options. This makes an Options form appear. As Figure 5.4 shows, this form has two parts, with **window options** at the top and **general options** at the bottom.

```
    WINDOW OPTIONS for window number: 1        show hidden text:(Yes)No
              show ruler: Yes(No)     show non-printing symbols:(None)Partial All
              show layout: Yes(No)              show line breaks: Yes(No)
              show outline: Yes(No)              show style bar: Yes(No)


    GENERAL OPTIONS mute: Yes(No)               summary sheet:(Yes)No
                measure:(In)Cm P10 P12 Pt        display mode: 1
                paginate:(Auto)Manual                 colors:
                autosave:                     autosave confirm: Yes(No)
                show menu:(Yes)No                show borders:(Yes)No
              date format:(MDY)DMY          decimal character:(.),
              time format:(12)24            default tab width: 0.5"
              line numbers: Yes(No)          count blank space: Yes(No)
              cursor speed: 3               linedraw character: (¦)
              speller path: WORD5\SPELL-AM.LEX
```

Figure 5.4   Options form.

2. Move the cursor to the "autosave" field under GENERAL OPTIONS.

3. Specify (in minutes) how often you want Word to save your work, and then press Enter. For example, to save every 15 minutes, type **15** and press Enter.

Word will then save your changes at the interval you specified. During the first autosave operation, Word will save your entire document. In subsequent autosaves, it will save only the changes you made since the preceding autosave.

Turning Autosave Off

If you ever want to turn autosave off, you can use the same procedure you used to turn it on, but when the Options form appears, delete the "autosave" value or replace it with **0** (zero).

Restoring Autosaved Material

If the power goes off for any reason while you are working, you can restart Word and recover the autosaved changes. When you start Word, it will tell you that "Autosave backup files exist." You can then do one of the following:

- Type **y** (for Yes) to recover the autosaved material.
- Press Esc to discard it.

You *must* respond to this prompt; if you press any other key, the computer just beeps.

MERGING DOCUMENTS

If you use some text (such as a disclaimer, list of instructions, product or price list, or standard contractual or financial terms) in many documents, you may want to make it a document by itself. Then you can copy or **merge** it into other documents when you need it, using Word's **Transfer Merge** command. To do this, you simply move the cursor to where you want the text to appear, select **Transfer** and **Merge**, and then enter the document's name (or press F1 and select it from the directory).

For example, suppose you often need the following Proprietary Information notice:

> **This document contains information of a proprietary nature. All information contained herein shall be kept in confidence. None of this information shall be divulged to persons, other than Acme employees authorized to receive such information, or individuals or organizations authorized by Acme Information Development in accordance with existing policy regarding release of company information.**

Assuming you don't want to type that long paragraph in every document you prepare, enter it once, and save it as **PROPINFO**. Then, when you need it (say, on the cover page of a report), issue a Transfer Merge command with PROPINFO as the filename. All that fine, deathless prose will appear at once in your current document.

Merging While Printing

Word's INCLUDE instruction lets you combine documents at print time. The general form is as follows:

«INCLUDE filename»

where the chevrons « and » tell Word that INCLUDE is an instruction, not just ordinary text.

These chevrons do not appear on the keyboard, so you must press Ctrl-[(opening bracket) to produce « and Ctrl-] (closing bracket) to produce ».

When you use INCLUDE, the only restriction is that the file must be on the current data disk. If Word encounters a name it cannot find, it displays **Not a valid file** on the message line.

For example, suppose you want to produce a quarterly sales report on five departments in a company. Each manager prepares a document summarizing the activities of his or her department, which you copy onto your data disk. To make Word print them after your overall report, you would put the sequence shown in Figure 5.5 at the end of the document.

```
SALES
«INCLUDE SALES.DOC»
MARKETING
«INCLUDE MARKET.DOC»
ENGINEERING
«INCLUDE ENG.DOC»
MANUFACTURING
«INCLUDE MANUF.DOC»
PERSONNEL
«INCLUDE PERS.DOC»
```

Figure 5.5   INCLUDE instructions to create a report.

Note the difference between compiling a document with INCLUDEs and with Transfer Merge:

- INCLUDE makes Word simply *print* the new document as if it were part of the current one.

- Transfer Merge makes Word *insert* the new document in the current one.

PREVIEWING DOCUMENTS

Word's regular editing screen shows only the main text of a document; it does not show margins, footnotes, headers, footers, page numbers, or right justification. For informal writing projects and most business correspondence, you are probably willing to accept whatever the printer produces. However, for documents where the layout and appearance are critical, you may want to see how the pages will look before you print them.

Word's Print command has a **preView** option that lets you preview pages. (Note that the capital "V" is the selection letter here. Word couldn't use "P" because it is already designated to select **Printer**.) For each page, preView inserts blank space to reflect the top and bottom margins; shows footnotes, headers, and footers; and displays page numbers and right justification, if appropriate. You also need preView to see graphics in your document; this is described shortly.

Obtaining a Preview

To preview a Word document, choose **Print** from the Edit menu, and then **preView** from the Print menu. Word shows a miniaturized display of the current page and the next one (if any) with the following menu at the bottom:

```
PRINT PREVIEW: Exit Jump Options Print
```

As the following message line prompt indicates,

```
Use PgUp and PgDn to scroll through document
```

you can press the PgUp or PgDn key to move backward or forward through the document. You can also select **Jump** to move directly to a specific page. Word shows **Pg** numbers at the bottom of the screen to indicate which pages you are viewing.

Word normally shows two consecutive pages on the screen, the current page and the next one. However, the Print Preview menu's **Options** selection produces a menu that lets you view only "1-page" (the current one) or two "Facing-pages" (even-numbered on the left, odd-numbered on the right) by typing **1** or **f**, respectively. Viewing facing pages is useful for coordinating graphics or text on one page with references to it on the other page.

Leaving the Preview Screen

To leave the preview screen and return to your document, type **e** to issue an **Exit** command.

GRAPHICS

So far the focus of this book has been on text within documents. However, you may also want to include **graphic images** in your reports. A graphic image may be a picture or drawing that was created using a commercial drawing program or one that a scanner has converted to a computer-displayable image.

Microsoft Word can insert graphics from disk files in a variety of types, or **formats**, including the following:

- Lotus 1-2-3 graph (**PIC**) files

- PC Paintbrush **PCX** files

- Files using the **HPGL** instruction set supported by the Hewlett-Packard ColorPro printer (for example, Microsoft Chart **HPG** files)

- Microsoft Pageview bitmap files

- Microsoft Windows bitmap (**BIT**) files

- PostScript files, including Encapsulated PostScript (**EPS**)

- Scanned material, in either **TIFF B** (black-and-white) format or uncompressed **TIFF G** (gray scale) format

To insert a graphic image in a document, you must tell Word two things: the name of the disk file that contains the image and the image's format. When you have done this, Word automatically sets up an invisible box, or **frame**, to hold the image. It makes the frame as wide as the current column (left margin to right margin, if you only have one column) and sizes the frame's height proportionally.

To make the image appear smaller or larger in your document, you can simply increase or decrease the size of its frame. Word also assumes you want the image centered within the frame, but you can align it with the left or right border instead.

Once an image is in place, Word surrounds it with regular text, giving your document the professional look you find in newspapers and books. Following are the details.

Importing Graphics

To insert, or **import**, a graphic disk file into your text, move the cursor to where the graphic's top left corner belongs, and do the following:

1. Select **Library** from the Edit menu and **Link** from the Library menu. Word shows the following menu:

```
LIBRARY LINK: Document Graphics Spreadsheet
```

2. Select **Graphics**. Word displays the graphics parameters shown in Figure 5.6.

```
LIBRARY LINK GRAPHICS filename:
        file format:                    alignment in frame: Centered
        graphics width: 6"              graphics height: 6"
        space before: 0"                space after: 0"
```

Figure 5.6   Graphics parameters.

3. For "filename," type the path — drive and subdirectory — (if necessary), filename, and extension of the disk file that contains the image.

   If you don't remember the name of the file, obtain a list of available files by pressing F1. (Word lists *every* file. It's your job to know which ones contain graphics.)

4. In the "file format" field, press F1 to see a list of the supported formats, highlight the correct one, and press Enter to select it.

5. Word assumes you want the graphic as wide as the current column or text. To specify its size, type a width or height in "graphics width" or "graphics height," respectively.

6. Press Enter.

Word inserts the graphic but doesn't show it. Instead, the graphic is represented with a hidden text paragraph that gives the graphic's pathname (disk directory, filename, and extension), dimensions, and file format. For example,

```
.G.C:\WORD5\DEMO\CHART.MC;6",4.411",HPGL
```

represents a graphic image (as indicated by **.G.**) contained in file **CHART.MC** that Word imported from the **DEMO** subdirectory of **WORD5** on drive **C.** Word has set up the graphic in a frame that is **6"** wide and **4.411"** high. This particular graphic is in **HPGL** format.

Viewing Graphics

To see how the graphic actually looks on the page, issue a Print preView command. Based on how the graphic looks, you may want to change its size or move it somewhere else on the page. You may also want to draw a border around it or add a caption.

Sizing Graphics

The Library Link Graphics form has "graphics width" and "graphics height" parameters that let you specify the dimensions of a graphic image on the page. In the form, Word assumes you want the frame as wide as the current column (left margin to right margin, if you only have one column) and a height appropriate to that width. If you want some other size, you can change either or both dimensions.

You can make these changes when you import the graphic, or you can change them later. To resize a graphic that you have already imported, position the cursor anywhere in the ".G." paragraph and issue a Library Link Graphics command. When the form appears, change "graphics width" and/or "graphics height" to the size you want, and then press Enter.

Positioning Graphics

Word always assumes that you want to center a graphic frame within the current column (or margins, if you have only one column) and sets the "alignment in frame" parameter to **Centered** on the Library Link Graphics form. You can change it to **Left** or **Right** to align the frame with the left or right edge of the column. Of course, the frame alignment only has an effect if you have made the frame narrower than the column.

Word also includes a **Format pOsition** command that lets you move a graphic frame anywhere on the page and specify its distance from surrounding text. When you issue a Format pOsition command, Word displays the form shown in Figure 5.7. Its parameters need some explanation:

```
FORMAT POSITION
        horizontal frame position: Left      relative to:(Column)Margins Page
        vertical frame position: In line      relative to:(Margins)Page
        frame width: Single Column            distance from text: 0.167"
```

Figure 5.7   Format pOsition form.

The "horizontal frame position" and "relative to" parameters let you specify a frame's horizontal alignment and the portion of the page to which it applies. The valid position options are **Left**, **Centered**, **Right**, **Outside**, and **Inside**.

The last two options pertain to bound documents with double-sided pages. **Outside** aligns frames toward the outside on facing pages. On odd-numbered (right) pages, it aligns frames along the right edge of the column, the right margin, or the right edge of the page — depending on the "relative to" setting. On even-numbered (left) pages, it left-aligns frames. The **Inside** option is similar, but it aligns frames toward the inside on facing pages.

You can also type a **number** in "horizontal frame position" to tell Word how many inches to put between the frame's left edge and the left edge of the column, the left margin, or the left edge of the page.

The "vertical frame position" and "relative to" parameters let you specify a frame's vertical alignment and the portion of the page to which it applies. The valid position options are **In line** (current position in text), **Top**, **Centered**, and **Bottom**. Here, "relative to" tells Word whether Top, Centered, or Bottom refers to the area between the margins or the entire page.

You can also type a number in "vertical frame position" to tell Word how many inches to put between the top of the frame and the top margin or the top of the page.

The "frame width" parameter lets you tell Word whether to make the frame as wide as a **Single Column** (margin to margin, on a one-column page) or the same as the **Width of Graphic**.

Word assumes you want one-sixth of an inch (0.167") of white space between a frame and its surrounding text, but you can specify a different amount in the "distance from text" option.

Borders and Shading

To add a border to a graphic or print with shading, position the cursor in the .G. paragraph and issue a **Format Border** command to obtain the form shown in Figure 5.8.

```
FORMAT BORDER type:(None)Box Lines     line style: Normal     color: Black
   left: Yes(No)     right: Yes(No)    above: Yes(No)         below: Yes(No)
   background shading: 0               shading color: Black
```

Figure 5.8   Format Border form.

To create a border, you can use the following options:

- Tell Word to make its "type" either a **Box** or **Lines**. Word always keeps Boxes on a single page (and moves one to the next page if it doesn't fit on the current one), whereas borders drawn with Lines can be split between pages.

- Specify the "line style" of the border as **Normal**, **Bold**, **Double**, or **Thick**.

- If you have a color printer, fill in "color" with the color you want, or press F1 to select from a list of colors.

- Tell Word to draw a border at the "left," "right," "above" (top), or "below" (bottom). Of course, normally you would set all four values to **Yes**.

For shading, you can type a "background shading" value from **0** (no shading) to **100** (solid) and select a "shading color," provided you have a color printer (otherwise, the color will be black).

QUESTIONS AND ANSWERS

How can I make Word print something both bold and underlined?
If you haven't yet typed the text you want to be bold and underlined, press Alt-B (for Bold) and Alt-U (for Underline), type the text, and then press Alt-Spacebar to turn off both formats. If the text already exists, highlight it and press Alt-B and then Alt-U.

I set up a running head to print my name and the page number at the bottom of each page, but Word only starts printing them on the second page. What happened?
You probably forgot to change the Format Running-head form's "first page" setting to **Yes**. Word assumes you want to bypass the first page (because it's often a cover page or a cover letter) and start printing running heads on the second page.

I typed "(page)" in my running head to make Word supply the page number, but that didn't work. What am I doing wrong?
Instead of typing (**page**), type **page** and then press F3. Word will add the parentheses; you shouldn't type them in yourself.

I printed pages 9 and 10 of a report, and now I want to print the whole thing. But Word just ignores my Print Printer command. Why?

The "range" field in the Print Options list is still set to **Pages**. Change it to **All**, and then try Print Printer again.

I want to print from page 30 to the end of my report, but I don't remember the number of the last page. What should I do?

Enter a page number you know is much larger than the last page number. For example, if your report is about 60 pages long, enter **30:100** for "page numbers."

How can I indent a paragraph on both sides?

Move the cursor to the beginning of the paragraph and issue a Format Paragraph command. When the paragraph parameters appear, change "left indent" and "right indent." For example, to indent your paragraph six spaces on the left and seven on the right, type **6** for "left indent" and **7** for "right indent."

HINTS AND WARNINGS

1. Set up all running heads at the beginning of a division (generally, this is the beginning of the document), preceding ordinary text. Word will ignore any running heads you put elsewhere.

2. You can stop a print operation at any time by pressing Esc.

3. When using a character format such as Bold, Underline, Subscript, or Superscript, be sure to turn the format off at the end of the affected material. For example, to type a word in bold, press Alt-B, type the word, and then press Alt-Spacebar.

4. When applying a character format to (or removing one from) existing text, be sure you have the correct material selected. Word will affect everything that is highlighted.

5. Be careful when using more than one character format at a time. Alt-Spacebar will remove all of them.

6. To apply a character format to a single character, you must hold the Alt key down, and then press the other key (such as "U" for "underline") *twice*.

7. If you print selected pages of a document, Word leaves the "range" setting in the Print Options list set to **Pages**. Before you can print the entire document, you must change "range" to **All**. If you don't, Word will ignore your Print Printer command.

8. Word does not tell you how much space is left on a disk. If you fill a disk, it simply displays a **Disk full** message.

9. If you import a graphic file into a document, Word represents it with a line that starts with **.G.** To see how the graphic actually looks before you print it, issue a Print preView command.

10. Word provides "macros" called **table.mac**, **tabs.mac**, and **tabs2.mac** that set tabs for a table. It also provides a macro called **bulleted_list.mac** that indents paragraphs and precedes them with hyphens to form a list. See Chapter 10 for details.

11. Word can insert reviewers' comments and notes you have written to yourself as footnote-like "annotations." See Chapter 12 for details.

KEY POINTS

Table 5.2 summarizes the keys and commands introduced in this chapter.

1. To create a running head for a division, enter the text, highlight it, and then issue a Format Running-head command. When the parameter list appears, tell Word where to position the head (top or bottom), which pages to print it on (odd or even), and whether to align it with the left margin or the edge of the paper.

2. To include the page number in a running head, type **page** and then press F3.

3. To double-space text, issue a Format Paragraph command and change "line spacing" to **2 li**.

4. To print selected pages of a document, issue a Print Options command. When the form appears, change "range" to **Pages**. Then, in the "page numbers" field, specify the page numbers; separate them with a comma (to indicate individual pages) or a colon (to indicate a range).

5. Word offers a variety of character formats that you can obtain by pressing Alt and another key. For example, Alt-B produces bold text; Alt-U produces underlining; and Alt-D produces double-underlining. You can also press Alt-Z to remove the last character format or press Alt-Spacebar to remove all character formats.

6. Word can produce both footnotes and endnotes. It prints each footnote on the same page as its reference number, and prints endnotes at the end of the division.

Key or key combination	Function
Alt-+	Superscript
Alt-hyphen	Subscript
Alt-B	Bold print
Alt-D	Double-underline
Alt-H	Hidden text
Alt-I	Italic
Alt-K	Small caps
Alt-S	Strikethrough
Alt-U	Underline
Alt-Z	Remove last character format
Alt-Spacebar	Remove all character formatting
Alt-F4	Show Layout (of multicolumn material)
Ctrl-5, left arrow	Move to preceding column
Ctrl-5, right arrow	Move to next column

Command	Function
Format Border	Add a border or shading to graphic frame
Format Division Layout	Print footnotes as endnotes or arrange text in newspaper-style columns
Format Footnote	Create a footnote
Format Paragraph	Change paragraph parameters (e.g., line spacing and indents)
Format pOsition	Move graphic
Format Running-head	Create header or footer
Jump Footnote	Move to next footnote reference
Library Link Graphics	Import graphic file
Print Options	Change print options (e.g., print selected pages or multiple copies)
Print preView	Show current document as it will be printed
Transfer Merge	Insert another document on disk

Table 5.2   Keys and commands introduced in Chapter 5.

7. To create a footnote, enter the reference text and issue a Format Footnote command. To make Word number the footnote, press Enter; otherwise, type your reference mark (say, *), and then press Enter. Finally, enter your footnote, and then issue a Jump Footnote command to return to editing.

8. To make Word print footnotes as endnotes at the end of the division, issue a Format Division Layout command, and change the "footnotes" setting from **Same-page** to **End**.

9. Decimal tabs allow you to align columns of numbers around a decimal point. Create them as you would regular tabs, but change the Format Tab Set "alignment" option to **Decimal**.

10. You can change the paragraph margins by indenting them. You do this by issuing a Format Paragraph command and changing the "indent" values.

11. Word can arrange text on a page as newspaper-style columns that continue from the bottom of one column to the top of the next, in winding fashion. To put Word into column mode, issue a Format Division Layout command and specify the "number of columns" and the "space between columns" (in inches).

12. To see multiple columns on the screen, issue a Show Layout command by pressing Alt-F4.

13. You can move between columns by holding down Ctrl and then pressing **5** and pressing left arrow (preceding column) or right arrow (next column).

14. You can use the mouse to move the cursor. Table 5.3 summarizes the mouse commands introduced in this chapter.

Operation	Mouse pointer location	Button(s) to press
Select character	Character in text	Left
Select word	Character in a word	Right
Select sentence	Character in a sentence	Both
Select line	Gap left of line	Left
Select paragraph	Gap left of paragraph	Right
Scroll text down	Left border	Left
Scroll text up	Left border	Right

Table 5.3   Mouse editing operations.

15. When you issue a Transfer Save command, Word always copies the previous version of your document to a file with the same name, but with the extension **.BAK**. To discard your latest changes and reinstate the previous version, use Transfer Load to load the .BAK file into Word; use Transfer Delete to erase its .DOC file counterpart; and use Transfer Rename to change the file's .BAK extension to .DOC.

16. You can also make Word save your changes at prescribed intervals to guard against data loss during power outages. To do this, issue an Options command and specify the interval (i.e., how often you want Word to automatically save your changes) in minutes in the "autosave" field. When you start Word, it will prompt you if there is autosaved material that hasn't been saved in a document.

17. To insert a disk document into your current document, issue a Transfer Merge command. You can also make Word merge a document at print time by using an «INCLUDE» instruction. To produce the left or right chevron, press Ctrl-[or Ctrl-], respectively.

18. Word's Print preView command shows the current document as it will be printed, with graphics, footnotes, running heads, page numbers, and so on in place. With the preview on the screen, you can press PgDn or PgUp to move forward or backward through the document.

19. Word's Library Link Graphics command can import a variety of graphic files into your documents. Word represents the graphic with a graphic image (.G.) paragraph; to view the graphic, you must use Print preView.

20. The Format pOsition command lets you move a graphic on the page. You can also add a border or shading by issuing a Format Border command.

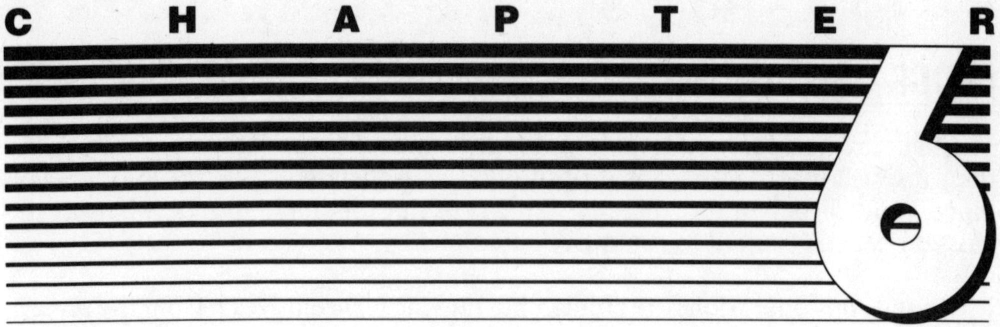

REVISING

In the preceding chapters, you learned how to change and correct characters, words, lines, sentences, and paragraphs. However, formal correspondence, reports, and large projects often require more extensive revisions.

For example, you may want to move material to improve continuity, combine related ideas or separate distinct ones, change emphasis, or balance the length of sections. Or you may need the same legal or technical terminology, table or figure headings, addresses, equations, or sets of instructions in several places. You may also want to find occurrences of certain words, phrases, or sequences in a document and perhaps change them to correct spelling, improve grammar, standardize terminology, or change dates, names, places, numbers, or titles. These types of revisions are discussed in this chapter.

BLOCK OPERATIONS

In Chapter 3 you learned how to put text such as a name into the glossary and then insert it where you want it positioned in a document. Word also lets you **move, copy,** or **delete** text directly. This is useful for single moves, whereas the glossary is better suited to repetitive situations.

Move and copy operations are similar, but moving text removes it from the screen, while copying text simply makes a copy of it and leaves the original intact. In both cases, you "paste" the moved or copied material in its new location by moving the cursor to that location and then **inserting** the text.

Like a move operation, a delete operation removes text from the screen. But you normally delete something when you want to discard it rather than use it somewhere else.

Moving Text

To move text, select it (using either function keys or the mouse), and then press Del to put it in the scrap. Next, move the cursor to where you want the block to be inserted, and press Ins.

Copying Text

If you want to leave the original text in place, select **Copy** in the Edit menu, and press Enter instead of Del. For example, suppose you are typing in the following text:

Our firm specializes in tax-advantaged investments such as oil and gas exploration and development, equipment leasing, and real estate.
    Our background in oil and gas exploration and development includes over 50 projects during the last ten years.

When you start the second paragraph, you notice the repetition of "oil and gas exploration and development." Rather than typing it again, move the cursor up to it, select it, press Esc and **c** (Esc-C) to perform a **Copy** operation, and press Enter to move it to the scrap. Now move the cursor back where it was previously positioned (after "in") and press Ins.

The original phrase is still in place and a copy of it appears in the text. Note that the phrase also appears in the scrap in case you need it again. If you are likely to need it repeatedly, however, you should put it in the glossary.

COLUMN OPERATIONS

In earlier chapters tables were discussed. As you may recall, to construct a table in a Word document, you press Tab between the column entries and press Shift-Enter at the end of each line except the last one. Pressing Shift-Enter tells Word to start a new line, but not a new paragraph. Thus, Word treats your entire table as a single paragraph and applies any tab changes to every line.

Word also lets you move, copy, or delete a column. These operations can save a lot of time when you want to manipulate tables.

Operating on a column requires the same steps as operating on regular text in that you first select what you want to operate on (the column items, in this case) and then do one of the following:

- Press Del to start a move or delete operation.
- Issue a **Copy** command to start a copy operation.

However, column operations involve tabs as well as text. Specifically, to move, copy, or delete a column, you must select the text in the column *and* the tabs that either follow the text (for the first column) or precede the text (for any other column).

The following descriptions assume that you are operating on the first column. Thus, they tell you to select text and the tabs that follow it. To operate on any other column, start at the tab that *precedes* the first text item.

Moving and Deleting

To move or delete a column, perform the following steps:

1. Position the cursor on the character at the top left corner of the column.

2. Press Shift-F6 to put Word in the **Column Select** mode. The abbreviation **CS** appears on the status line, just to the left of "Microsoft Word."

3. Move the cursor to the bottom line of the column. Word highlights each starting character.

4. Move the cursor to the right, to the space that precedes the next column. Word highlights every line in the column and the tabs that follow it.

5. Press Del to delete the column. Word puts that column of text in the scrap.

6. If you are moving a column, position the cursor where you want the column and press Ins to copy it from the scrap.

Copying

To copy a column, use the same procedure as for moving or deleting, but for step 5, press Esc and then press Enter (instead of Del). This makes Word **Copy** the column to the scrap but leave the original text on the screen.

Inserting

You may also want to insert a new column into an existing table, in which case you should follow these steps:

1. Insert the heading for the column.

2. Obtain the ruler.

3. Change the tabs to reflect an additional column; that is, set a tab for the new column and move the remaining tabs to the right to provide a space for the insertion. (To move a tab to the right, delete it and then set it at its new location.) Finally, return to editing.

4. Position the cursor on the first data line, and then move it to where the new column should start.

5. Type the first data item in the new column, and then press Tab to shift the remaining columns to the right.

6. Enter the rest of the data items in the new column by repeating steps 4 and 5.

Column Insert Example

As an example, suppose you have prepared a list of your company's major customers, as shown in Figure 6.1. As usual, you used tabs at the beginning of each column to enter the data. In this example, the tabs are at columns 15 and 32.

```
Account        Buyer             Sales Rep.

Wilburg Sons   Paul Wilkinson    R. Roberts
Jenco          Carrie Black      C. Chamber
Symtech        Wayne Beck        P. Grogan
Chicago Gear   Morris Daley      J. Wilkes
Hart Foods     Sandy Karras      P. Wallach
Pacifico       Bill Anderson     D. Kim
Storr Bros.    Lee Walters       B. Lloyd
```

Figure 6.1   Customer list before column insertion.

Suppose that, after finishing the list, you decide to insert a column for the buyer's telephone number between "Buyer" and "Sales Rep." Each number is 12 characters long, and you want three spaces between the number and the next column, so the new column must be 15 characters wide. To insert the new column, proceed as follows:

1. Position the cursor on the heading line and issue a **Format Tab Set** command.

2. On the ruler, set a new tab at column 47. This is where the Sales Rep. column will move after the insertion.

3. On the heading line, move to the **S** in **Sales Rep.**, type **Phone #**, and then press Tab. Pressing Tab makes **Sales Rep.** shift to the right.

4. Move to each data line, and insert the telephone number. Then press the Tab key.

The final list should look similar to Figure 6.2.

Account	Buyer	Phone #	Sales Rep.
Wilburg Sons	Paul Wilkinson	212-555-3589	R. Roberts
Jenco	Carrie Black	904-388-6743	C. Chamber
Symtech	Wayne Beck	404-783-8832	P. Grogan
Chicago Gear	Morris Daley	312-395-1904	J. Wilkes
Hart Foods	Sandy Karras	406-184-5683	P. Wallach
Pacifico	Bill Anderson	503-438-9532	D. Kim
Storr Bros.	Lee Walters	213-679-4260	B. Lloyd

Figure 6.2   Customer list with inserted column.

SEARCH AND REPLACE OPERATIONS

Word has a Search command that searches forward or backward through a document, looking for a **string** (any sequence of characters). It also has a Replace command that both searches for a string and then replaces it with the correct text. You can use these features to do the following:

- Locate a customer's name in a mailing list.

- Correct a common misspelling throughout a document.

- Update a document to account for changes in names, titles, dates, or locations.

- Change prices, rates, or terms in an invoice or contract.

- Change a part number or order number in a technical manual.

- Replace an overused or inappropriate phrase throughout a report.

- Check for occurrences of obsolete or revised names, titles, dates, or terms.

Searching

The procedure to search for a string is as follows:

1. Move the cursor to where you want the search to begin.

2. Press Esc to reach the Edit menu, and then press s to select **Search**. Word shows the following menu:

```
SEARCH text:
       direction: Up(Down) case: Yes(No) whole word: Yes(No)
```

3. Enter the string you want to find. The options on the second line let you determine the following:

- The search's direction: **Down** (toward the end) or **Up** (toward the beginning).

- Whether you are concerned with case. **No** makes Word find every form of the string — uppercase or lowercase, in any combination. You would use No, for example, to find **First Quarter 1989**, **FIRST QUARTER 1989**, or **First quarter 1989**, when revising a first quarter sales report to produce the second quarter or first half sales report.

- Whether you want to consider embedded occurrences of the search string. You would make "whole word" **No**, for example, if you were looking for every instance of "color." Here, you would want Word to find not only the word "color," but also "colored," "coloring," "color," and "discolored."

To change an option, press Tab to reach it, and then type the first letter of the new choice. Press Enter when you have made all the changes. Note that Word will make all your choices (including the string itself) its new defaults for the next search.

4. When Word finds an instance of the string, it highlights it. When you are finished with that instance, you can make Word search for the next one by pressing Shift-F4. If Word cannot find a match, the computer makes a beeping sound and displays **Search text not found** on the message line.

For example, return to the sample text on page 136, where it states, "oil and gas exploration and development." To search for the phrase "oil and gas," you would proceed as follows:

1. Issue a Search command.

2. Type the phrase **oil and gas** and press Tab.

3. Make "direction" **Down**, "case" **No** (you also want to find instances at the start of a sentence), and "whole word" **Yes** (to avoid matches such as "oil and gasohol").

4. Press Enter.

Word will highlight the first occurrence of the phrase. If, because of a series of dry holes and investor lawsuits, you have decided to insert "research and development," press Del to delete the phrase "oil and gas," then replace "exploration" with "research," and finally press Shift-F4 to move ahead to the next occurrence.

Replacing

If you have a specific replacement in mind and are sure there are no exceptions, you should use Word's **Replace** command to make all the changes automatically. You can make Word search and replace as follows:

1. Move the cursor to where you want the search to start.

2. Select **Replace** in the Edit menu. Word displays the following:

```
REPLACE text:                           with text:
        confirm:(Yes)No  case: Yes(No) whole word: Yes(No)
```

3. For "text," type the string you want to search for, and then press Tab to move the cursor to "with text."

4. Type the replacement text, and then press Tab to move the cursor to the "confirm" option.

    Note that you can press Tab at "with text" to delete the search string; that is, you can replace it with nothing. You might do this, for example, to update someone's title from **Assistant Vice-President** to **Vice-President** throughout a report or interview. Here, you would have Word search for **Assistant**.

5. The second line of the REPLACE form has three options. The "confirm" option lets Word either replace automatically (**No**) or stop and ask each time (**Yes**). The "case" and "whole word" options mean the same as in the Search command. Note that there is no "direction" option here; Word always proceeds forward when replacing.

6. Press Enter.

Word begins searching when you press Enter. If "confirm" is set for **Yes**, Word stops at each instance of the search string and asks whether you want to do any of the following:

- Replace it (type **y**)

- Skip this occurrence and look for the next one (type **n**)

- Stop searching (press Esc)

At the end of the replace operation, Word's message tells you how many replacements were made or, if Replace never found a matching string, displays **Search text not found.**

Like the Search command, Replace always assumes that you want to do the same thing the next time and fills in the REPLACE form with your previous values. However, "confirm" is the exception; it always defaults to **Yes**. This is Word's way of trying to keep you out of trouble. It will never replace without asking unless you explicitly switch "confirm" to **No**.

Replace Example

Figure 6.3 (see next page) shows a document that illustrates the use of the Replace options.

NOTICE OF STOCKHOLDERS' MEETING

The 1988 Annual Stockholders' Meeting for International Consolidated Industries will be held at company headquarters, 19880 Pine Street, Des Moines, Iowa on Friday, June 3, 1988. The following matters will be considered:

1) Election of the Board of Directors for the 1988-89 fiscal year.
2) Designation of Smith, Brown, and Little as the company's independent auditors for the 1988-89 fiscal year.
3) Amendments to the Employees' Qualified Stock Ownership Plan (ESOP) in accordance with new regulations.
4) Other amendments and matters as they may be brought to the attention of the Secretary of the Corporation.

Anyone wishing to have matters considered at that meeting must notify the Secretary by registered mail on or before May 15, 1988. In accordance with regulations adopted at the annual meeting of June 11, 1982, such notifications must be presented on forms provided by the Secretary and must contain notarized signatures representing no fewer than 1% of the common stock of the Corporation of record May 15th, 1988. In accordance with guidelines adopted at a special Board of Directors meeting on February 1, 1988, the board has the final authority on whether to accept notifications that are presented after May 17th, 1988 or that contain an insufficient number of signatures.

Figure 6.3   Original search document.

You want to update this notice for the 1989 annual meeting to be held at the same place on Friday, June 2, 1989. To do this, you will perform the following operations:

1. Replace automatically each occurrence of **1988-89** with **1989-90**.

2. Replace automatically each occurrence of **June 3** with **June 2.**

3. Find all occurrences of **1988** and replace them with **1989**. You must be careful here to avoid changing historical dates accidentally.

To replace **1988-89** automatically with **1989-90**, do the following:

1. Position the cursor at the beginning of the first line of the text, and then issue the **Replace** command.

2. For the "REPLACE text:" option, type **1988-89** and then press Tab.

3. For the "with text:" option, type **1989-90** and press Tab again.

4. For the "confirm:" option, type **n** to replace automatically.

5. Press Enter to start the search-and-replace operation.

Word immediately makes the replacements but does not move the cursor.

To replace **June 3** with **June 2**, get the REPLACE form back, enter the strings, change "confirm" to **No**, and press Enter. Now the meeting notice should look like Figure 6.4.

```
                NOTICE OF STOCKHOLDERS' MEETING

    The 1988 Annual Stockholders' Meeting for International
Consolidated Industries will be held at company headquarters,
19880 Pine Street, Des Moines, Iowa on Friday, June 2, 1988. The
following matters will be considered:

    1)   Election of the Board of Directors for the 1989-90
         fiscal year.
    2)   Designation of Smith, Brown, and Little as the company's
         independent auditors for the 1989-90 fiscal year.
    3)   Amendments to the Employees' Qualified Stock Ownership
         Plan (ESOP) in accordance with new regulations.
    4)   Other amendments and matters as they may be brought to
         the attention of the Secretary of the Corporation.

    Anyone wishing to have matters considered at that meeting
must notify the Secretary by registered mail on or before May 15,
1988. In accordance with regulations adopted at the annual
meeting of June 11, 1982, such notifications must be presented on
forms provided by the Secretary and must contain notarized
signatures representing no fewer than 1% of the common stock of
the Corporation of record May 15th, 1988. In accordance with
guidelines adopted at a special Board of Directors meeting on
February 1, 1988, the board has the final authority on whether to
accept notifications that are presented after May 17th, 1988 or
that contain an insufficient number of signatures.
```

Figure 6.4   Revised document after automatic replacements.

To replace **1988** with **1989** selectively, proceed as follows:

1. Obtain the REPLACE form.
2. For the "REPLACE text:" option, type **1988** and then press Tab.
3. For the "with text:" option, type **1989**.
4. Press Enter to start searching.

Word will immediately find a match in the second word. You must press **y** to make the replacement.

The next match is unexpected. Word finds **1988** at the beginning of the company's address. You could have avoided this match by setting the "whole word:" option to **Yes**. But here you must press **n** to make Word continue forward without replacing. You must do this again later when Word finds **1988** as part of "a special Board of Directors meeting on February 1, 1988." That is a historical date, and you must not change it.

When Word finishes, the document should look like Figure 6.5.

Wild Card Searches

Sometimes you may want to search for any of several similarly spelled words. You can do this by typing a question mark (**?**) in the search string for each character that may differ from one occurrence to another. To Word, **?** is a **wild card** character that acts as shorthand for "any single character." You can compare it with the Joker in popular card games, a free number in Bingo, or a blank tile in Scrabble.

For example, to find every mention of dates in the 1980s, you could perform a Search command using **198?** as the search string. This makes Word stop on 1980, 1981, 1982, and so on.

NOTICE OF STOCKHOLDERS' MEETING

The 1989 Annual Stockholders' Meeting for International Consolidated Industries will be held at company headquarters, 19880 Pine Street, Des Moines, Iowa on Friday, June 2, 1989. The following matters will be considered:

1) Election of the Board of Directors for the 1989-90 fiscal year.
2) Designation of Smith, Brown, and Little as the company's independent auditors for the 1989-90 fiscal year.
3) Amendments to the Employees' Qualified Stock Ownership Plan (ESOP) in accordance with new regulations.
4) Other amendments and matters as they may be brought to the attention of the Secretary of the Corporation.

Anyone wishing to have matters considered at that meeting must notify the Secretary by registered mail on or before May 15, 1989. In accordance with regulations adopted at the annual meeting of June 11, 1982, such notifications must be presented on forms provided by the Secretary and must contain notarized signatures representing no fewer than 1% of the common stock of the Corporation of record May 15th, 1989. In accordance with guidelines adopted at a special Board of Directors meeting on February 1, 1988, the board has the final authority on whether to accept notifications that are presented after May 17th, 1989 or that contain an insufficient number of signatures.

Figure 6.5   Final form of search-and-replace document.

You can put **?** (the question mark) anywhere in a search string—even several times. For example, you could use **???ember** to find mentions of either November or December. Here, you should also make "whole word" **Yes** to keep Word from accepting spaces, as in "a member." As another example, you could use **19-??-3657** to find all mentions of part numbers that start with 19 and end with 3657.

You can also include **?**s in the search ("SEARCH text:") string of a Replace command, but not in its replacement ("with text:") string. Of course, if you use them, you should always make "confirm" **Yes.**

Sometimes you may want to search for a string that actually includes a question mark. This requires telling Word that **?** is a regular character, not a wild card. To make the distinction, type a caret (^) character ahead of the **?**. (Caret is the uppercase symbol on the 6 key at the top of the regular keyboard.) In other words, put ^? in your search string. For example, searching for **who**^? finds only "who?," while searching for **who?** locates "whom," "who," or "whoa."

Word also provides a number of other wild cards that are useful in searches, as follows:

Wild card code	Searches for
^d	Division mark or manual page break
^n	Newline character
^p	Paragraph mark
^s	Nonbreaking space
^t	Tab character
^w	White space (any number and combination of spaces, tab and newline characters, paragraph and division marks, manual page breaks, and nonbreaking spaces)
^-	Optional hyphen

Abbreviations

Replace also lets you use abbreviations when typing a document. This is similar to the common practice in note-taking of jotting down UN for "United Nations" or DoD for "Department of Defense."

For example, if you are writing a report on European sales, you may simply type "UK" for "United Kingdom," "WG" (West Germany) for "Federal Republic of Germany," and "US" for "United States." Then, when you have finished, perform replace operations to expand the abbreviations. Be sure that your abbreviations are distinct (note, for instance, that you will find "US" in "USSR") and do not conflict with each other (such as using "UN" for "United Nations" and "University of Nebraska").

Replace and the Glossary

In Chapter 3 you learned how to use the **glossary** to replace abbreviations. Replace has the advantage of making Word (not you) replace the abbreviations. On the other hand, you must issue a Replace command every time you want to expand the abbreviations. There is no dedicated function key or storage (in memory or on disk) as there is with the glossary.

Replace and the glossary are not competitive. In fact, if you use a glossary, you should probably perform a Replace at the end to catch abbreviations you accidentally left unexpanded.

Searching for Formats

Sometimes you may want to search for a formatting change, such as the start of underlining or a switch to double-spacing, to perhaps insert some additional material there. Word's **Search** command, which lets you locate a text string, has already been discussed. However, Word has a separate search command that lets you search for bold, underlines, subscripts, and other "character" formats, as well as line spacing and other "paragraph" formats.

This search-for-format command is a Format menu option called **sEarch**. Thus, to start searching for a format, select **Format** from the Edit menu, and then select **sEarch** from the Format menu. This makes Word display the following:

```
FORMAT SEARCH: Character Paragraph Style
```

For now you will concentrate on Character and Paragraph searches. Style searches will be discussed in Chapter 8.

The Format command also provides a **repLace** option for formats, which is discussed later in this chapter.

Character Formats

To search for a character format, select **Character** from the Format Search menu. This brings up the character format search form shown in Figure 6.6.

```
FORMAT SEARCH CHARACTER direction: Up Down
        bold: Yes No               italic: Yes No          underline: Yes No
        strikethrough: Yes No      uppercase: Yes No       small caps: Yes No
        double underline: Yes No   position: Normal Superscript Subscript
        font name:                 font size:              font color:
        hidden: Yes No
```

Figure 6.6   Character format search form.

As with a text search, Word assumes that you want to search in the same direction
as last time, or search **Down** (forward) if this is your first search operation.
However, it does not make any other guesses about what you want to locate. It
shows choices in most fields, but does not place any of them in parthentheses.

To search for a particular character format, tab to its field on the form and fill in
the field or enter a selection letter. By filling in two or more fields, you can even
make Word limit the search to format changes that meet several criteria . For
example, to find a character that is both bold and italicized, type **y** for both "bold"
and "italic." When you finish selecting the direction and specifying the formats,
press Enter to begin searching.

Word highlights the next occurrence of text that has the format you specified. If
it can't find any text that satisfies your search criteria, Word leaves the cursor
where you started searching and displays **Search format not found** on the message
line.

Paragraph Formats

To search for a paragraph format, select **Paragraph** from the Format Search
menu. This brings up the paragraph format search form shown in Figure 6.7.

As with a text search, Word assumes that you want to search in the same direction
as last time, or search **Down** (forward) if this is your first search operation.
However, Word does not make any other guesses about what you want to locate.
It shows choices for "alignment" and the fields on the bottom line but does not
enclose any of them in parentheses.

```
FORMAT SEARCH PARAGRAPH direction: Up Down
        alignment: Left Centered Right Justified
        left indent:           first line:
        line spacing:          space before:
        keep together: Yes No  keep follow: Yes No    side by side: Yes No
```

Figure 6.7   Paragraph format search form.

To search for a particular paragraph format, tab to its field on the form and fill it in or enter a selection letter. By filling in two or more fields, you can even make Word limit the search to format changes that meet several criteria. When you finish selecting the direction and specifying the formats, press Enter to begin searching.

Word highlights the next occurrence of text that has the format you specified. If it can't find any text that satisfies your search criteria, it leaves the cursor where you started searching and shows **Search format not found** on the message line.

Repeating a Search

As with a text **Search** command, you can repeat the preceding **Format sEarch** command by pressing Shift-F4. Word remembers which kind of search you performed last (and, for a format search, whether it was a Character or Paragraph search), and starts the search again.

REPLACING FORMATS

Just as Word has a **Format sEarch** command that is the format counterpart of a text **Search**, it has a **Format repLace** command that is the format equivalent of a text **Replace**. This is handy for replacing one format with another. You could use it to change bold text to underline or switch from single-spacing to double-spacing.

To start searching and replacing a format, select **Format** from the Edit menu, and then select **repLace** from the Format menu. This makes Word display the following:

```
FORMAT REPLACE: Character Paragraph Style
```

For now, you will concentrate on Character and Paragraph replace operations. Style replace operations are covered in Chapter 8.

Character Formats

To replace a character format, do the following:

1. Select **Character** from the Format Replace menu. This brings up the Format Replace Character form shown in Figure 6.8.

```
FORMAT REPLACE CHARACTER confirm: Yes No
        bold: Yes No               italic: Yes No          underline: Yes No
        strikethrough: Yes No      uppercase: Yes No       small caps: Yes No
        double underline: Yes No   position: Normal Superscript Subscript
        font name:                 font size:              font color:
        hidden: Yes No
```

Figure 6.8   Format Replace Character form.

Note that this form is similar to the character format search form displayed earlier in Figure 6.6. But here, the top line asks you to choose whether you want to "confirm" the replacement each time rather than indicate the direction. (As with text, you can only proceed forward when replacing formats.)

2. Word always assumes that you want to confirm the replacement, but makes no other guesses about what you want to locate. To search for and replace a particular format, tab to its field on the form and fill it in or enter a selection letter.

    By filling in two or more fields, you can even make Word limit the search to format changes that meet several criteria. For example, to find text that is bold and italicized, type y for both the "bold:" and "italic:" options.

3. When you finish specifying the formats, press Enter. Word displays a similar Replace With Character Format form, and positions the cursor in the "bold" field.

4. Specify your replacement format(s), and then press Enter to begin the search-and-replace operation.

Word begins searching when you press Enter. If "confirm" is set to **Yes**, Word stops at each instance of the search string and asks whether you want to do any of the following:

- Replace it (type **y**)
- Skip this occurrence and look for the next one (type **n**)
- Stop searching (press Esc)

At the end of the replace operation, the message line tells you how many replacements were made or, if Word never found a matching string, displays **Search format not found**.

Paragraph Formats

To replace a paragraph format, do the following:

1. Select **Paragraph** from the Format Replace menu. This brings up the Format Replace Paragraph form shown in Figure 6.9.

```
FORMAT REPLACE PARAGRAPH confirm: Yes No
        alignment: Left Centered Right Justified
        left indent:           first line:
        line spacing:          space before:
        keep together: Yes No  keep follow: Yes No    side by side: Yes No
```

Figure 6.9   Format Replace Paragraph form.

Note that this form is similar to the character format search form shown previously in Figure 6.7. But here, the top line asks you to choose whether you want to "confirm" the replacement each time rather than indicate the direction. (As with text, you can only proceed forward when replacing formats.)

2. Word always assumes that you want to confirm the replacement. However, it does not make any other guesses about what you want to locate. It shows choices for "alignment" and the fields on the bottom line but does not put any of them in parentheses.

   To search for a particular format, tab to its field on the form and fill it in or enter a selection letter. By filling in two or more fields, you can even make Word limit the search to format changes that meet several criteria.

3. When you finish specifying the formats, press Enter. Word displays a similar Replace With Paragraph Format form, and positions the cursor in the "alignment" field.

4. Specify your replacement format(s), and then press Enter to begin the search-and-replace operation.

Word begins searching when you press Enter. If "confirm" is set to **Yes**, Word stops at each instance of the search string and asks whether you want to do any of the following:

- Replace it (type **y**)
- Skip this occurrence and look for the next one (type **n**)
- Stop searching (press Esc)

At the end of the replace operation, the message line tells you how many replacements were made or, if Word never found a matching string, displays **Search format not found**.

Reformatting Entire Documents

Note that **Format repLace** is only useful for documents that contain format changes. If you want to reformat an entire document (say, single-space a report that you have double-spaced so you could edit it easily), you can simply highlight everything and issue a **Format Character**, **Paragraph**, or **Division** command. Use the following steps:

1. Move the cursor to the beginning of the document by pressing Ctrl-PgUp.

2. Select the entire document by pressing Shift-F10.

3. Perform one or more Format operations to specify your new settings.

For example, to single-space a document, highlight it, issue a **Format Paragraph** command, type **1** in the "line spacing" field, and press Enter.

QUESTIONS AND ANSWERS

I need the same table heading several times in a report. How can I avoid retyping it?

Highlight the heading and then issue a Copy command. When Word asks where you want the copy to go, press Enter to put it in the scrap. Then move the cursor to each place where you want to insert that heading and press Ins. The heading will stay in the scrap until you issue another Copy or Move command, or press the Del key.

I searched for a phrase that I know is in my report, but Word couldn't find it. Why not?

The most likely reason is that you positioned the cursor past where the phrase occurred and issued a Search forward (**Down**), or you positioned the cursor ahead of the phrase and issued a Search backward (**Up**). Try searching in the other direction. Also, check the spelling and the "case" option. If you misspelled the phrase, Word surely won't find it. If you have "case" set on (**Yes**) and the phrase is in lowercase, Word won't find it if it's at the beginning of a sentence.

I just finished my monthly sales report when the Northwest sales office called with some corrections. How can I find all the places where I might have mentioned their figures?

Press Ctrl-PgUp to move the cursor to the beginning of the report, and then issue a Search command. When the search form appears, type **Northwest** for "SEARCH text:" and then set "direction" to **Down**, "case" to **No** (you may have left "Northwest" capitalized somewhere), and "whole word" to **No** (you may have referred to "Northwestern"). Press Enter to begin the search.

Word will stop the first time it finds "Northwest." To find the next occurrence, press Shift-F4.

I misspelled "principle" as "principal" throughout a term paper. How can I correct it?

Move the cursor to the beginning of the document, and then issue a Replace operation. In the replace form, type **principal** for "REPLACE text:" and **principle** for "with text:," and then set both "confirm" and "case" to **No**. Make "whole word" **No** so Word will also catch variations such as "principals."

Our company's statement of qualifications always refers to us as "Smith, Brown, Jones, and Associates, Inc." Unfortunately, after a minor argument and a small lawsuit, Brown left and is now our chief competitor. How do I change the name to "Smith, Jones, and Associates, Inc." and make sure Brown isn't mentioned anywhere?

You can remove Brown from the company name by issuing a Replace command. Use **Smith, Brown** as the search string and **Smith** (no comma) as the replacement. Make "confirm" **No** so the replacement is automatic. Then search the entire statement for "Brown" and change the text as required.

You should even issue a final search for "Brown" just to make sure you haven't missed any mentions. Better to be safe than to worry about a few keystrokes and some computer time.

HINTS AND WARNINGS

1. Watch the distinction between moving and copying text. Pressing Del deletes text from its old position (and puts it in the scrap), while the Copy command simply makes a copy and leaves the original alone.

2. When moving text, insert it at its destination immediately. If the telephone rings or a visitor drops in, finish moving the text before acknowledging the interruption. Otherwise, you may not remember what you were doing when you return to it.

3. Remember that the scrap keeps anything you move, copy, or delete until you perform another of these operations or leave Word. You can insert scrap material over and over by pressing Ins wherever you want it.

4. When you first start Word, it sets the Search command's "direction" option to **Down**, the Replace command's "confirm" option to **Yes**, and their "case" and "whole word" options to **No**. If you change "direction," "case," or "whole word," Word will remember the new settings, and use them as its defaults. However, it will always keep **No** as its default setting for "confirm."

5. Note that **Search** and **Format sEarch** can go forward or backward, while **Replace** and **Format repLace** always go forward.

6. Be careful about using automatic replacement. Word does not indicate what it replaced. If you aren't absolutely sure you want to make the replacement each time, keep the "confirm" option set to **Yes**.

    This may take some time, but it can avoid errors that are almost impossible to find. Presumably, the danger of automatic replacement is what made Word's designers keep the "confirm" option's default at **Yes**, regardless of how many times you change it.

7. You can cancel a selective replace operation at any time by pressing Esc.

8. Word provides "macros" called **move_text.mac** and **copy_text.mac** that move or copy a block of text you select. See Chapter 10 for details.

KEY POINTS

Table 6.1 summarizes the keys and commands introduced in this chapter.

Key combination	Function
Shift-F4	Repeat last Search or Format sEarch command
Shift-F6	Column Select mode
Shift-F10	Select entire document
Command	**Function**
Search	Search for specified string
Replace	Search for specified string and replace it
Format sEarch	Search for specified formats
Format repLace	Search for specified formats, and replace them

Table 6.1   Keys and commands introduced in Chapter 6.

1. To move text, highlight it and then press Del to put it in the scrap. To "paste" it in the new location, move the cursor there and then press Ins. (Deleting text is the same as moving it, except you never paste it.)

2. To copy text, highlight it, and then issue a Copy command. When the **COPY to:** prompt appears, press Enter to put the text in the scrap. To "paste" the text in the new location, move the cursor there, and then press Ins.

3. To move, delete, or copy a column of text or numbers, operate on it as you would regular text, but press Shift-F6 (for **Column Select**) before you highlight it.

   If the column is the first one in a table, you must highlight the text and the tabs that *follow* it. For any other column, you must highlight the text and the tabs that *precede* it.

4. To insert a column, set a tab for it and move the remaining tabs to the right. Then put the cursor where you want the insertion and enter the new data items. Press Tab at the end of each one to move the existing material to the right.

5. Word's Search command searches through a document or a specified **string** (a sequence of characters).

6. Before beginning a search, Word displays a search form in which you enter the string and set the following options:

   - "direction" tells Word whether to search backward (**Up**) or forward (**Down**).

   - "case" tells Word whether to locate only exact instances of the string (**Yes**) or accept any combination of uppercase or lowercase letters (**No**).

   - "whole word" tells Word whether to locate stand-alone occurrences of the string (**Yes**) or locate embedded mentions as well (**No**).

7. Word's Replace command can search a document for a string and replace it with another string of your choice. The replacement can be nothing, in which case the string is simply deleted.

8. Before starting a replace operation, Word displays a replace form in which you type the string and its replacement. There are three options. The first, "confirm," makes Word ask whether to replace each occurrence (**Yes**) or replace all occurrences automatically (**No**). The other options, "case" and "whole word," are the same as for the Search command.

9. Replace lets you use abbreviations while typing. It provides automatic replacement but does not remember the abbreviations the way the glossary does. You may want to use Replace to confirm that you have expanded all glossary abbreviations.

10. Both Search and Replace let you use **?** as a wild card character to find similarly spelled words.

11. Word also has a **Format sEarch** command that lets you locate format changes. This command has a Character option that lets you find bold, underlining, and the like. It also has a Paragraph option that lets you locate changes to line spacing and other paragraph formats.

12. Similarly, Word has a **Format repLace** command that lets you search for formats and replace or remove them.

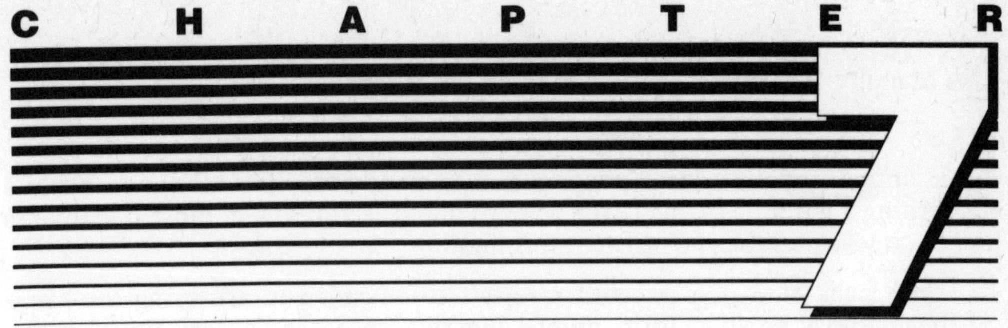

WINDOWS

Word can divide the screen in up to eight areas or **windows**, where each can display a different document or a different part of a document. Once you have set up the windows, you can work in any of them. This chapter teaches you how to divide the screen into windows and discusses both the advantages and the complications of doing so.

Use of multiple windows allows you to do the following:

1. Examine previous correspondence, a contract, or other documents while writing a letter. You may even want to quote sections from those documents or, at least, establish consistent terminology.

2. Look back at earlier parts of a report to be sure you are using the same terminology, spelling, form, numbering, references, or figures. You can also avoid repetitions and — even worse — contradictions.

3. See a table, chart, or quotation while preparing a description of it.

4. Examine an outline while you write, and check off sections as you finish them.

5. Keep footnotes, references, figure and table numbers, problem sets, and summary material on the screen as you write.

6. Move text a long distance without misplacing it, making errors along the way, or leaving part of it behind.

7. Take formats, figures, tables, or terminology from old versions of a document, partial or extended versions, or standard forms. Thus, you could use part of last year's report or the last project's contract in a new report or contract, combine weekly reports into a monthly report, or excerpt a brief synopsis from a complete project report.

Word's main area is itself a window (window #1, as indicated in the upper left corner). Word will number subsequent windows consecutively. Figure 7.1 shows an example of the screen split into two windows horizontally (a) and vertically (b).

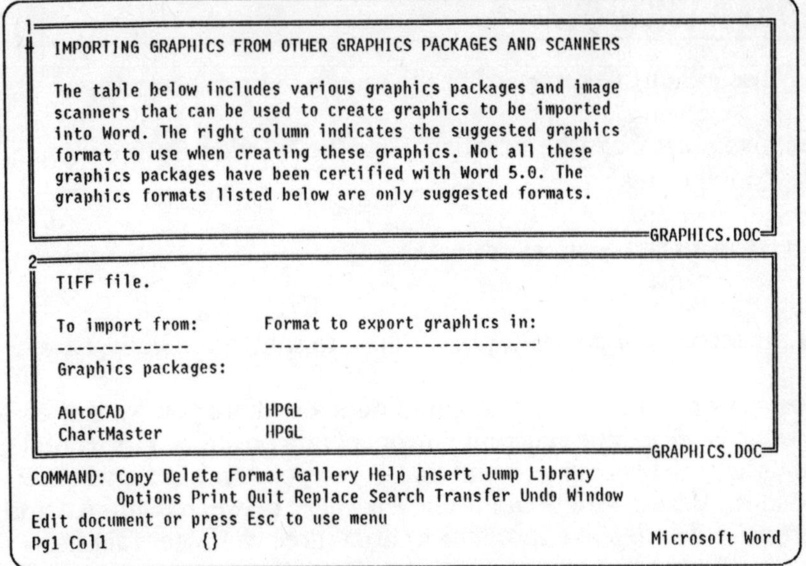

```
1
  IMPORTING GRAPHICS FROM OTHER GRAPHICS PACKAGES AND SCANNERS

  The table below includes various graphics packages and image
  scanners that can be used to create graphics to be imported
  into Word. The right column indicates the suggested graphics
  format to use when creating these graphics. Not all these
  graphics packages have been certified with Word 5.0. The
  graphics formats listed below are only suggested formats.

                                                        GRAPHICS.DOC
2
  TIFF file.

  To import from:          Format to export graphics in:
  --------------           -----------------------------
  Graphics packages:

  AutoCAD                  HPGL
  ChartMaster              HPGL
                                                        GRAPHICS.DOC
COMMAND: Copy Delete Format Gallery Help Insert Jump Library
         Options Print Quit Replace Search Transfer Undo Window
Edit document or press Esc to use menu
Pg1 Col1           {}                             Microsoft Word
```

Figure 7.1a   Window split horizontally.

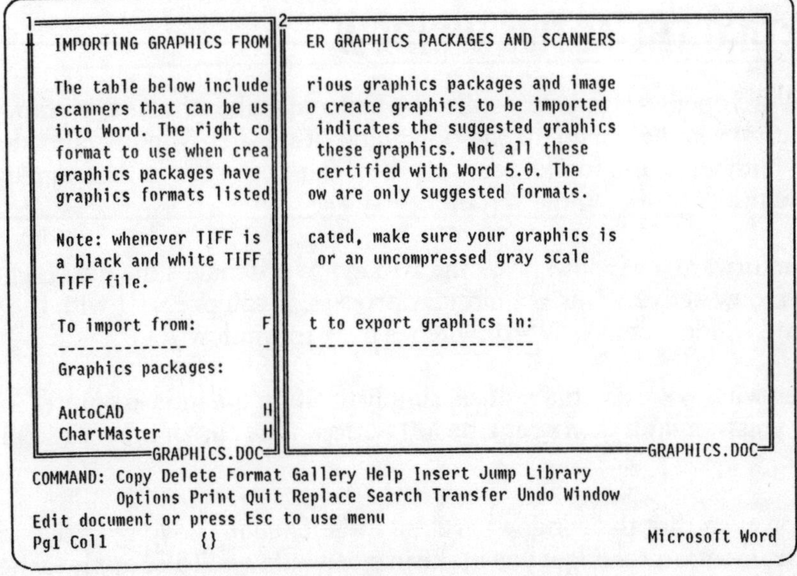

```
1                             2
  IMPORTING GRAPHICS FROM      ER GRAPHICS PACKAGES AND SCANNERS

  The table below include      rious graphics packages and image
  scanners that can be us      o create graphics to be imported
  into Word. The right co       indicates the suggested graphics
  format to use when crea      these graphics. Not all these
  graphics packages have       certified with Word 5.0. The
  graphics formats listed      ow are only suggested formats.

  Note: whenever TIFF is       cated, make sure your graphics is
  a black and white TIFF        or an uncompressed gray scale
  TIFF file.

  To import from:        F     t to export graphics in:
  --------------         -     ------------------------
  Graphics packages:

  AutoCAD                H
  ChartMaster            H
            GRAPHICS.DOC                            GRAPHICS.DOC
COMMAND: Copy Delete Format Gallery Help Insert Jump Library
         Options Print Quit Replace Search Transfer Undo Window
Edit document or press Esc to use menu
Pg1 Col1           {}                             Microsoft Word
```

Figure 7.1b   Window split vertically.

OPENING A WINDOW

You may use either the keyboard or the mouse to open a window.

To open a window from the keyboard, use the **Window Split** command. Word displays the following:

```
WINDOW SPLIT: Horizontal Vertical Footnote
```

To split the screen horizontally, press Enter; to split it vertically, type **v**.

You must now enter the line or column number where you want the split. The default value is the cursor's current line or column position. Horizontal splits can occur anywhere between line 3 and line 18, so you can have a window with just one line in it. Vertical splits can occur anywhere between column 4 and column 71 and require you to leave room for at least three characters across.

To open a window with the mouse, move the pointer to the place on the right border (horizontal) or top border (vertical) where you want the split. Then press the left button.

SELECTING THE ACTIVE WINDOW

When Word opens a window, it splits the text and makes the new window "active"; that is, it moves the cursor to the beginning of the new window and shades the window number in the top left corner. You can now work in that window just as if it were the only one on the screen.

To move forward a window, press the F1 key. Word makes the next higher-numbered window active. This is a circular process; if you press F1 with the highest-numbered window active, Word switches back to window #1.

To switch windows using the mouse, simply position the mouse pointer inside the window you want and then press the left button. The cursor moves to the pointer location.

Note, however, that the windows are not independent. As long as they show the same document, any changes you make in one window will also apply to the others. The result is eerie if a line appears in more than one window. Then, any changes you make on that line will appear in all the windows simultaneously. The effect is like standing in front of a trick mirror and watching your movements appear in all the reflections.

Creating Independent Windows

To create an independent window, you must either load a disk document into it (using Transfer Load) or clear it. You can clear the active window with a Transfer Clear Window command. Note that you must do this even if the new window is empty; otherwise, Word will think of it as a different view of the original document; that is, unless you clear the active window with a Transfer Clear Window command, any text you put in the new window will appear in the original document as well.

Once you have cleared a window or loaded a document into it, that window is a separate entity. You can then work on it without affecting documents in other windows.

Be sure to use Transfer Clear *Window* to clear the active window, not Transfer Clear All. Transfer Clear All clears everything and returns the screen to its original state, with a single window.

CLOSING A WINDOW

To close a window from the keyboard, issue a Window Close command. Word displays a prompt such as the following,

```
WINDOW CLOSE window number: n
```

where *n* is the currently active window. To close the window, press Enter. To close a different window, type its number and then press Enter.

If the window is independent and you have not saved its contents, Word will ask you to confirm the loss of changes. If you confirm, Word then erases the window and fills the area with text from adjacent windows. Note that Word also renumbers any windows that have numbers above the one you closed (e.g., if you close window #1, what was previously window #2 becomes #1 and what was previously window #3 becomes #2, etc.).

To close a window by using the mouse, position the pointer on the window's right border and press both buttons.

OPERATING ON WINDOWS

Word treats the active window the same way it treats the full screen. You can edit, move the cursor, load or save a document, issue commands, and so on. Of course, a vertical window may not be wide enough to show an entire line. In that case, you must press an appropriate arrow key to view text off the screen.

Moving Text between Windows

The only special part of moving text to another window is that you must remember to switch active windows. That is, you go through the usual process of highlighting the text and using the Del or Copy command to put that text in the scrap, but you must then press F1 until Word selects the destination window. Once the correct destination window is selected, you can finish the task by moving the cursor to the text location you want and pressing Ins.

This approach is convenient when you are moving text a long distance. Say, for example, you want to move a paragraph from page 2 to page 5 of a report. You would perform the following steps:

1. Position the cursor in the paragraph. Divide the screen into two equal windows at that point.

2. The lower window is now active. Issue a Jump Page command to reach page 5 and move the cursor where you want to insert the paragraph.

3. Switch windows, select the paragraph, and use Del to put it in the scrap.

4. Switch windows again and use Ins to insert the paragraph in the proper position.

For the following reasons, this approach is better than just putting the paragraph in the scrap and moving it:

- You can see the original position and the destination at the same time. This lets you determine whether the move is appropriate.

- You can easily go back and get more text if you need it. It is also more obvious how much text you need to move and what adjustments you must make.

- You are less likely to make mistakes during the move. While moving the cursor to the destination, you could accidentally change what is in the scrap or reach the wrong position. Using windows allows you to move the cursor before you do anything to the text.

- You can make adjustments and other minor changes in both places. This ensures consistency and continuity.

- You can proceed from either position in the text by closing the other window.

Zooming Windows

If you're working in a particular window, you can temporarily make it fill the screen by pressing Ctrl-F1. Ctrl-F1 is Word's "zoom" command. It zooms the active window to full-screen size and hides any other windows. To return the window to its original size and position, press Ctrl-F1 again.

Saving Documents in Windows

You can save a document in any window by issuing the usual Transfer Save command, but Word provides another Transfer option called **Allsave** that saves the documents in every window. When you're working with multiple windows, it's much more convenient to issue a single Transfer Allsave command than to issue separate Transfer Save commands for each document.

WINDOW EXAMPLE

As a simple application of windows, use the quarterly report you created in Chapter 5. Suppose you now want to produce a semiannual sales report combining the first and second quarters. Rather than retype Table 1 showing Second Quarter Sales, you can simply copy it into the semiannual report.

Start Word with a blank screen. Now divide it in two with a Window Split Horizontal command. When Word asks for the line number, type **10** and press Enter. Word will divide the screen into two parts and make window #2 (the bottom half) active.

To obtain the table, proceed as follows:

1. Issue a Transfer Load command, entering **rptq289** as the file to be loaded. Even if the window had material in it, Transfer Load would clear it out.

2. Issue a Jump Page command, entering **3** as the destination page.

3. Select the table. All you must do is press F10 if the table is a single paragraph. If you pressed Enter instead of Shift-Enter while entering the table, you must extend the cursor to cover the entire table.

4. Issue a Copy command and press Enter to put the table in the scrap.

To move the table to the semiannual report, press F1 to switch windows and then press Ins to insert the table. Finally, to remove the second quarter's report from the screen, issue a Window Close command, type **2**, and press Enter. You now have the second quarter's sales table for use in the semiannual report.

FOOTNOTE WINDOWS

As mentioned in Chapter 5, Word stores footnotes at the end of the division. You can examine or edit a footnote's text by positioning the cursor on the footnote's reference number in the text and then selecting the Jump Footnote command. However, Word displays only the footnote area—your text disappears. An alternative is to display footnotes and references in a special **footnote window** at the bottom of the screen. You can then change a footnote by editing in that window.

Displaying the Footnote Window

To display the footnote window, position the cursor on the line where the footnote should start and select a Window Split Footnote command. When Word shows the following prompt,

```
WINDOW SPLIT FOOTNOTE at line: n
```

where *n* is the cursor's vertical position, press Enter.

You can also use the mouse to display the footnote window. Position the mouse pointer at the place on the right border where the window should start, and then press the right button.

Word numbers the footnote window just like a regular window but draws its top border with a dashed line rather than with two solid lines. Furthermore, Word assumes that you simply want to look at the footnotes, so it makes that window inactive. To change a footnote, you must first press F1 to activate the footnote window. When you are finished with the footnotes, close the footnote window just as you would close any other window.

Because a footnote window always displays part of another document, any changes you make in it will be entered automatically into the original. You don't need to save the revised text or move the changes.

HINTS AND WARNINGS

1. Use as few windows as possible; the more windows you have, the less text you can see in each one. Three or four windows is generally the practical limit on a standard PC.

2. Always clear a new window (using a Transfer Clear Window command) if you intend to use it for a new document. Otherwise, Word treats the new window as a different view of the original document.

3. Remember that you must clear a new window or load a document into it if you want it to be independent. Otherwise, any changes you make in the window will also appear in the original.

4. Be sure you use Transfer Clear Window to clear a window, not Transfer Clear All. Note that **All** is always the default in the Transfer Clear command.

5. When using windows, always check which one is active before doing anything. Word shades the number of the active window at the top left corner.

6. Remember to save all documents you have changed before closing their windows or leaving Word. Word provides a reminder when you close the only window into a document.

7. Always close a window when you are finished with it. Extra windows clutter the screen and reduce the amount of text you can see. You can always split the screen again later.

8. Use windows when moving text a long distance. This reduces the likelihood of interruptions or errors along the way. It also ensures that you move all the text you need and allows you to make changes or adjustments at both positions.

9. Be careful when closing windows. Word fills the area and renumbers higher-numbered windows immediately. If you don't keep track of your windows, you may find it difficult to determine what is where after the rearrangement and renumbering.

KEY POINTS

Table 7.1 summarizes the keys and commands introduced in this chapter. Table 7.2 summarizes the new mouse operations.

Key or key combination	Function
F1	Make next window active
Ctrl-F1	"Zoom" the active window

Command	Function
Transfer Clear Window	Clear the active window
Transfer Allsave	Save the documents in every window
Window Close	Close (remove) a window
Window Split Footnote	Open the footnote window
Window Split Horizontal	Open a horizontal window
Window Split Vertical	Open a vertical window

Table 7.1   Keys and commands introduced in Chapter 7.

Operation	Mouse Pointer Location	Button(s)
Close window	Right border	Both
Open footnote window	Right border	Right
Open horizontal window	Right border	Left
Open vertical window	Top border	Left
Activate window	Inside window	Left

Table 7.2   Mouse operations introduced in Chapter 7.

1. Word can display up to eight documents (or parts of documents) at once in separate areas called **windows.**

2. To create (or open) a new window from the keyboard, issue a Window Split command. To open one using the mouse, position the pointer at the proper place on the right or top window border, and then press the left button.

3. Word operates only on the document in the "active" window. To activate a window, press F1 until Word shades that window's number, or position the mouse pointer inside the window you want to activate and press the left button.

4. To "zoom" a window so that it fills the screen, activate it and press Ctrl-F1. To restore its original size and position, press Ctrl-F1 again.

5. To save the documents in every window, issue a Transfer Allsave command.

6. To delete a window, issue the Window Close command or place the mouse pointer on the window's right border and press both buttons.

7. Word fills new windows with text from the current document. To put a different document in a window, you must either clear the window or load a disk document into it. To clear a window, issue the Transfer Clear Window command or position the mouse pointer on the window's right border and press both buttons.

8. The footnote window displays the footnotes that apply to the text on the screen. To open the footnote window, issue a Window Split Footnote command or position the mouse pointer on the footnote window's right border and press the right button. Any changes you make in the footnote window appear automatically in the original document.

[illegible] appear [illegible] significant for purposes [illegible] in [illegible]
[illegible] write arrays only, via this.

[illegible] seem like a [illegible] domain. We [illegible] use a Window's [illegible]
[illegible] to put [illegible] but we [illegible] use [illegible] pointer in arguments [illegible]
[illegible] to the [illegible] that [illegible] the [illegible] of column a [illegible]
[illegible] data [illegible] on the [illegible] column to [illegible] of the window [illegible]
[illegible] by Window's [illegible] the DNA Window's context pointer [illegible]
[illegible] until you [illegible]

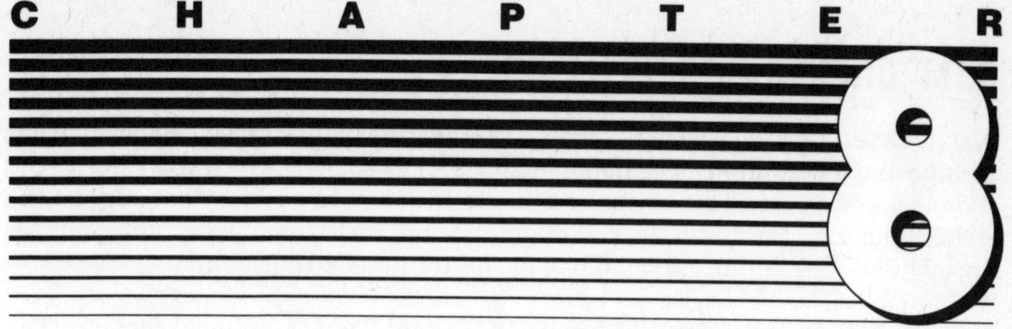

STYLE SHEETS

So far, you have set up Word for each new document by changing division and paragraph parameters such as margins, tabs, line spacing, and justification. In practice, you will probably use a few formats (e.g., single-spaced business letters or double-spaced reports) most of the time.

In this chapter, you will learn how Word lets you save style values in standard formats called **style sheets**, rather than making you set the same values repeatedly. All you must then do is "attach" a style sheet to a document. You can change a document's format (e.g., go from draft style to final form or from one journal's or company's standard to another's) simply by switching style sheets.

COMPONENTS OF A STYLE SHEET

A style sheet consists of a list of format combinations called **styles**. Each style has a name and a definition. The name includes a key code by which you refer to the style in a document. This key code consists of one or two letters that suggest the style's function. For example, you might use "np" for normal paragraph, "nd" for normal division, "il" for indented list, or "jp" for justified paragraph.

A style's definition consists of a "usage," a "variant," and an optional remark. The **usage** tells Word whether the style contains any of the following:

- character formats, such as bold and underline, or formats for page numbers, footnote numbers, and the like

- paragraph formats, such as indentation and line spacing

- division formats, such as margins and page length

The **variant** is used to give further information about styles with the same usage, to help keep them separate. Word provides commonly used variants for each of the three usages, and Table 8.1 summarizes those variants. Note that Table 8.1 also includes numbers to which you can assign variants of your own.

The **remark** lets you describe what the style means in more detail than the one- or two-letter code.

Usage	Variants
Character	Page number
	Line number
	Footnote ref
	Summary Info (document summary sheet)
	Line draw
	Annotation ref
	1-23 (numbers you can define)
Paragraph	Standard
	Footnote
	Running Head
	Heading levels 1-7
	Index levels 1-4
	Table levels 1-4
	Annotation
	1-55 (numbers you can define)
Division	Standard
	1-21 (numbers you can define)

Table 8.1   Word's predefined variants.

CREATING A STYLE SHEET

Now that you know what a style sheet contains, you will learn how to create one. You create style sheets in what Word calls the **Gallery**. To reach the Gallery, select the Gallery command. This makes Word clear the text area and display the Gallery menu:

```
GALLERY: Copy Delete Exit Format Help
         Insert Name Print Transfer Undo
```

Don't worry: any text you previously had on screen is still there even though you can't see it. By displaying **NORMAL.STY** at the bottom right corner of the border, Word reminds you that you aren't viewing text. This so-called "normal" style sheet is Word's default style sheet — the one it will use if you don't specify a different one.

To enter a style, you must name it by selecting **Insert** (not Name) in the Gallery menu. Word then asks you for the key code, usage, variant, and a remark.

To describe the style, select the Gallery menu's **Format** command. This lets you specify the character formats and printer font for this style.

After you define all the styles, you should save the style sheet on disk. This works just like saving a document. Use the Gallery menu's **Transfer Save** command and give the sheet a name that suggests its function. You might use FORMCORR for formal correspondence, MAGART for a magazine article format, or BUDGET for a budget format.

After saving the style sheet, you can return to the regular Edit menu by selecting **Exit**. Note that Exit in the Gallery menu does the same thing as pressing Esc in the Edit menu — it makes Word leave the menu and return to editing.

When you select Exit, Word displays your text instead of the style sheet. Both the text and the style sheet are available even though you can see only one at a time. You can, of course, always switch back and forth between text and style sheet with the Gallery and Exit commands.

Example

You will create a style sheet called "LETTER1" for letters that have the general format shown in Figure 8.1. The letter in Figure 8.1 has justified text and one-inch margins. It also has the return address, salutation, and writer's name and title at the center of the page. Finally, it has a list of items that are indented from the left margin.

```
                              2211 Washington Street
                              San Diego, CA 92121
                              May 16, 1989

Mr. Carl Johnson
1236 Summit Drive
San Diego, CA 92121

Dear Mr. Johnson:

In response to your recent request, we need the following
information to consider a credit application:

     1)  Name and address of your bank, along with your account
         number.
     2)  Three credit references.
     3)  A signed corporate resolution indicating responsibility
         for payment.

You may either use our enclosed form or submit a standard one of
your own. Please indicate any ratings you may have from credit
bureaus.

                              Sincerely yours,



                              Marie F. Gerard
                              Assistant Credit Manager

Enclosure
```

Figure 8.1   Sample letter.

To begin, type **g** to select **Gallery** in the Edit menu. This clears the text area and replaces the Edit menu with the Gallery menu.

Normal Division Style

To make Word start with one-inch side margins, you must create a normal division style. Proceed as follows:

1. Select **Insert** (not Name) from the Gallery menu. Word changes the bottom of the screen to show the following:

```
INSERT key code: {}        usage:(Character)Paragraph Division
         variant: 1        remark:
Enter one or two letter key code for style
```

2. Type the key code **nd** (for "normal division"), and then press Tab to reach the "usage" field.

3. Type **d** for Division and press Tab *twice* to reach the "remark" field.

4. Type **Normal, 1" side margins**.

   The remark is intended solely for documentation, to remind you what this style does. It can be up to 28 characters long.

5. Press Enter to save your entries.

   Word shows a highlighted summary of the active division settings (see Figure 8.2). Note that the "left" and "right" parameters are currently set to **1.25"**; you want to change both values to **1"**.

```
1   ND Division 1                          Normal, 1" side margins
       Page break. Page length 11"; width 8.5". Page # format Arabic. Top
       margin 1"; bottom 1"; left 1.25"; right 1.25". Top running head at
       0.5". Bottom running head at 0.5". Footnotes on same page.
```

Figure 8.2   Initial settings for normal division style.

6. To change the margin settings, first press Esc to reach the Gallery menu.

7. Type **f** for Format and **m** for Margins. Word displays a Format Division Margins form.

8. Press Tab twice to reach the "left" field, and type the number **1**.

9. Press Tab again to reach the "right" field, and type another **1** there.

10. Press Enter to record your new margin settings in the ND style (and put them in the on-screen summary).

Normal Paragraph Style

To make Word justify text, you must set up a normal paragraph style. Proceed as follows:

1. Select Insert from the Gallery menu.

2. Enter **np** (for normal paragraph) for the key code.

3. Press the Tab key to reach "usage" and type **p** for Paragraph.

4. Tab to "remark" and enter **Justified, single-spacing**. When you press Enter, Word will dispaly the normal paragraph style (Figure 8.3).

```
1   NP Paragraph 1                              Justified, single-spacing
        Courier (modern a) 12. Flush left.
```

Figure 8.3   Initial settings for normal paragraph style.

5. Select the Format command. Word displays the following menu:

```
FORMAT: Character Paragraph Tab Border pOsition
```

6. Type **p** for Paragraph. Word displays the paragraph parameter list.

7. Type **j** for Justified, and then press Enter. Now Word displays **Justified** at the end of its paragraph style summary.

You can also include a tab at the center in the normal paragraph style, as follows:

1. Select Format, and then type **t** for Tab and **s** for Set. Word displays the ruler and asks for the tab's position.

   Note that Word always starts a new Format with whatever settings you last used during Gallery operations; it does not change margins, tabs, or other parameters to reflect earlier style entries. This makes sense because the styles are not being currently implemented.

2. Because you are using 1" side margins on 8-1/2" paper, the text is 6-1/2" wide. Hence, to set a tab at the center, type **3.25**, and then press Enter. The center tab now appears in the style summary.

Indented List Style

To create the indented list style, proceed as follows:

1. Select Insert from the Gallery menu.

2. Type **il** for the key code.

3. Select Paragraph as the usage.

4. Enter **Indented list** as the remark. When you press Enter, Word adds the **IL** Paragraph style to its summary.

5. Select Format and type **p** for Paragraph.

6. Type **j** for Justified and change "left indent" to **.8** and "first line" to **-.3**, and then press Enter.

Word's style summary should now look like Figure 8.4. Check it to be sure you made all the changes correctly.

```
1  IL Paragraph 2                              Indented list
       Courier (modern a) 12. Justified. Left indent 0.8" (first line
       indent -0.3").
2  NP Paragraph 1                              Justified, single-spacing
       Courier (modern a) 12. Justified. Tabs at: 3.25" (left flush).
3  ND Division 1                               Normal, 1" side margins
       Page break. Page length 11"; width 8.5". Page # format Arabic. Top
       margin 1"; bottom 1"; left 1"; right 1". Top running head at 0.5".
       Bottom running head at 0.5". Footnotes on same page.
```

Figure 8.4   Final style summary.

If you were to later add another indented list format (say with "left indent" at 1.0 and "first line" at -.5), you would go through the same procedure with a different key code (e.g., "ID" for "Indented Deep"). You would also need to provide a different variant by entering it in the variant field. You can use any arrow key to obtain a list of the available variants.

Saving the Style Sheet

To save the style sheet, follow these steps:

1. Issue a Transfer Save command from the Gallery menu.

2. Enter **letter1** for the style sheet name and press Enter. Word supplies the extension **.STY** automatically because you're working in the Gallery.

3. To get a printed copy of the style sheet, turn your printer on and select Print from the Gallery menu. A printed copy will serve as a reference and help you remember the key codes. (Remember that you cannot see the style sheet and your text simultaneously.)

4. Select Exit to return to the regular Edit menu.

ATTACHING STYLE SHEETS

To apply a style sheet to a document, you must first "attach" it with a Format Stylesheet Attach command. Word will ask you for the style sheet's name. As usual, you can select it from a list by pressing F1. Of course, the list includes only .STY files.

Once you have attached the style sheet, Word automatically uses whatever you have selected as the normal division and normal paragraph styles (remember the assignments in Table 8.1). To use other styles (such as an indented list or an alternate paragraph format), you must hold the Alt key down and enter the style's key code. That style will then apply until you override it. If you don't remember the key codes, execute a Gallery command to display the current style sheet.

Applying Character Formats to a Styled Document

Having a style sheet attached to a document creates a minor change in the way you work. You must now press the X key to apply special character formats; that is, to obtain underlining, boldface, superscripts, or subscripts, you must hold the Alt key down, type **x** and then the format's key code. For example, underlining requires Alt-x-u rather than just Alt-u, and bolding requires Alt-x-b rather than just Alt-b.

If you forget the **x**, Word will display the message **Key code not defined**. You can still use Alt-Spacebar to remove formats and either Alt-h or Alt-x-h to obtain help (use x-h if you have key codes starting with h). Note that you must also now use Alt-x-c to center a title or table.

Example

Apply style sheet **LETTER1** to the letter in Figure 8.1. First, perform a Transfer Clear All command to clear the text area. Note that Word asks you to confirm loss of changes in both the text area and the style sheet. Next, perform a Format Stylesheet Attach command to attach style sheet LETTER1.

Because Word automatically applies the style sheet's normal division and normal paragraph (see Table 8.1), you need not specify those. Word obtains the margins, tabs, and other division and paragraph parameters from the normal division and paragraph without any action on your part. Note the margins and the tab in the center on the ruler. You can start the return address at the center by pressing Tab before entering each line.

Continue typing in the letter in Figure 8.1. When you reach the numbered list, follow these steps:

1. Hold the Alt key down and press **I** and then **L**. This makes Word switch to the style sheet's IL or "indented list" style.

2. Enter the three items in the list. Word will indent and align them just as if you had changed the paragraph parameters manually.

3. Press Enter twice to reach the line where the final paragraph belongs.

4. To return to normal paragraph style, hold the Alt key down and press **N** and then **P**.

Note that Word will continue a style until specifically told otherwise. When you finish the final paragraph of the letter, use the Tab key to enter the closing and the writer's name and title. After entering **Enclosure**, save the letter on disk under the name **credtltr**.

Be sure to type Alt-**x** to produce character formats. If, for example, you want to underline the words "any ratings" in the final paragraph, highlight those words and press Alt-x-u. To remove the underline from the space between the words, move the cursor to that space and press Alt-space-space (remember, the second space is necessary to remove formats from a single character).

Note that Alt-u-u, Alt-b-b, etc. no longer work on a single character; they produce **Key code not defined** messages. Nor do forms such as Alt-x-u-u work. With a style sheet, you must repeat the **x** as well as the key code. Hence Alt-x-u-x-u underlines a single character, Alt-x-b-x-b makes it bold, and so on.

NORMAL STYLE SHEET

If you issue a Gallery Insert command in a document that has no style sheet attached, Word assumes that you want to insert the style in its default or "normal" style sheet. This is (quite cleverly) called **NORMAL.STY**. Word attaches NOR-MAL.STY during startup or as part of a Transfer Clear All command.

Because new documents will start with NORMAL.STY, you should insert in NORMAL.STY the styles you use most often. (It initially has no actual styles, only the default tabs, margins, and other settings built into Word.) When you finish, save the style sheet and retain the name NORMAL.STY.

SUPPLIED STYLE SHEETS

Word's Utilities 2 disk (on your WORD5 directory, if you have a hard disk) includes a number of style sheets that you can attach to your own documents. To do this, issue a Format Spreadsheet Attach command, press F1 to obtain a list of STY files, and select the file you want.

The supplied style sheets include the following:

- **ACADEMIC.STY** can be used to produce a report. It has styles for formatting a title page, chapter and section titles, double-spaced text, quotes indented on both sides, bibliography entries, and so on.

- **SEMI.STY** and **FULL.STY** are style sheets for creating business letters. They have styles for a return address, date, the recipient's address, salutation, and so on.

- **OUTLINE.STY** contains styles for seven levels of headings, where each level is indented one-half inch to the right of the preceding level.

- **SIDEBY.STY** and **RESUME.STY** let you format text as side-by-side paragraphs.

- **SAMPLE.STY** contains styles for numbered lists, centered titles, bold and underlined subheads, side-by-side paragraphs, and three levels of headings.

REVISING STYLE SHEETS

You can edit a style sheet just as you can edit a document. Of course, you must have Word in the Gallery menu. First, issue a Transfer Load command to load the style sheet. Word summarizes the styles in it and highlights the first one. You can use the down arrow key to move the highlighting to the style you want to change.

Note the following:

1. To change the key code, usage, or remark, select "Name," which displays the same list as Insert, but fills in the fields with the current values.

2. To change the definition, select "Format." Word will then provide a submenu or parameter list.

3. To delete a style, press Del.

When you finish revising the style sheet, issue a Transfer Save command to save the new version on disk. If you use the same name as before, Word will save the old version with a .BAK extension.

To keep the old version available as a style sheet, either save the new version under a different name or use Transfer Load and Transfer Rename to load and rename the old version. You must load the old version with its .BAK extension; it does not appear in any directory except Transfer Delete.

SWITCHING STYLE SHEETS

You can switch style sheets at any time or apply a style sheet to a document that lacks one. Simply issue a Format Stylesheet Attach command to attach the new sheet. As soon as you select it (and, if necessary, confirm that you no longer want the old sheet), Word will reformat the current document; that is, Word will do the following:

- Change all automatic styles (remember Table 8.1) to their versions in the new sheet.

- Change all specified styles (usages and variants) to their versions in the new sheet.

- Revert to an automatic style if a specified style has no equivalent in the new sheet.

You can also use this approach to produce draft copies of a strictly formatted document. All you do is attach a simple style sheet and print. All the complex formats will revert to their defaults (see Table 8.1). In fact, if you press Del when Word asks for the new style sheet, Word will revert to its automatic style settings: 1.25" side margins, single-spacing, and so on.

Going from a simple style sheet to a more complex one or changing strict formats is more difficult. You will need to tell Word where to apply usages and variants that were not in the original style sheet. You may also need to reformat parts of the document if you have different purposes for a usage and variant in the different sheets. To avoid this, always employ usages and variants for the same purposes in all style sheets.

STYLE SHEETS AND WINDOWS

Each document can have its own style sheet. Thus, independent windows may have different style sheets. To see the style sheet that applies to a particular window, make that window active (by pressing F1 repeatedly or by using the mouse) and issue a Gallery command. Any style sheet you create or modify will apply to the active window only; you can return to that document window by selecting Exit from the Gallery menu. Transfer Clear Window clears a single text window and either loads NORMAL.STY (if it exists) into that window's gallery or clears the gallery (if NORMAL.STY is not on the data disk).

SWITCHING DOCUMENTS

If you load a new document, the current style sheet is not automatically applied to it. Word will load the new document with its own style sheet if it has one or will use the default settings if the new document doesn't have its own style sheet.

If you start a new document with Transfer Clear (either All or Window), Word attaches NORMAL.STY if it exists; otherwise, it applies the default settings. If you want to start a new document but retain the current style sheet, you must delete the old document. To do this, press Shift-F10 to select the entire document, and then press Del to delete the document but retain the style sheet.

QUESTIONS AND ANSWERS

I want to single-space a paragraph in a report, but my style sheet only provides double-spacing. How can I get Word to single-space?
Switch to single-spacing as usual, by changing the "line spacing" to 2 with a Format Paragraph command. The fact that you have a style sheet does not disable Word's regular formatting operations. Of course, if you do a lot of single-spacing, you might as well add it to your style sheet. It is much easier to type in a key code than to change the paragraph parameters. Remember to enter the Alt-key code combination when you are ready to go back to double-spacing.

I want to underline something, but when I type Alt-u, the computer says "Key code not defined." What's happening?
When you have a style sheet attached to your document, you must press **x** before you press the character code that selects a character format; that is, you must press Alt-x-u to underline, not just Alt-u.

I want to start a new document with Word's automatic format, but Word always attaches my normal style sheet when I issue a Transfer Clear. How can I get rid of the style sheet?
Issue a Format Stylesheet command. When Word asks for the name, press Del, and then press Enter. This detaches the normal style sheet and returns Word to its automatic format.

I want a style sheet that has special side margins but uses Word's automatic paragraph format. Do I still have to create a normal paragraph style?
No. If you omit a normal style (paragraph or division), Word will use its automatic settings.

I set up a new style sheet and used it to prepare a memorandum. It worked fine, but when I started Word the next day, the style sheet was gone. What happened to it?

You probably forgot to save it on your data disk. Always save a style sheet with a Gallery Transfer Save command before using it. Note that you can only save a style sheet from the Gallery menu.

How can I add a three-column table format to an existing style sheet?

Put Word in the Gallery mode and use Transfer Load to load the style sheet. Use Insert to specify the new style's key code (say, t3), usage, variant, and remark. Then use Format to define the style. Finally, save the revised style sheet, using Transfer Save. You may also want to use Transfer Delete to erase the old version.

I tried to insert a new style, but Word refused and said "Style already defined." Why?

Your style sheet already has a style with the same usage and variant: the one Word has highlighted.

I used my indented list style to enter a numbered list. That works fine, but now Word is arranging all my paragraphs as if they were list entries. What did I do wrong?

You forgot to return Word to the normal paragraph style. If that style has key code "np," press Alt-n-p. Remember that Word continues its current styles unless told otherwise.

I can't remember the key codes in my style sheet. How do I get a list of them?

Display the Gallery menu. It will show the current style sheet. You may want to issue a Print command and then press Enter to get a printed copy for future reference.

HINTS AND WARNINGS

1. Give each style in a style sheet a unique key code that is easy to remember. Take the time to put a comment in each "remark" field as well.

2. Don't try to cover every possibility in a style sheet. You aren't likely to remember key codes you hardly ever use anyway. Remember, you can always change formats from the keyboard to handle unusual situations.

3. Remember to use Exit to leave the Gallery menu. Note that this is different from pressing Esc to leave the Edit menu.

4. Be sure to use Insert (not Name) to add a style and use Name to change a name.

5. Always assign usages and variants to the same functions in different style sheets. Then you can switch style sheets with a minimum of reformatting.

6. Format a document initially with the most complex style sheet you are likely to use. Word will provide automatic defaults if you attach a simple style sheet. On the other hand, it clearly cannot guess where additional styles apply if you switch from a simple style sheet to a more complex one.

7. Remember that Transfer Clear attaches NORMAL.STY if it exists; otherwise, it leaves the document without a style sheet. You must directly attach another style sheet if you want it.

To start a new document while retaining the current style sheet, you must delete the entire current document by pressing Shift-F10 and then Del.

KEY POINTS

Table 8.2 lists the keys and commands introduced in this chapter.

Key Combination	Function
Alt-(key code)	Switch to the specified style

Command	Function
Format Stylesheet	Attach or detach a style sheet
Gallery	Move from text to Gallery
Exit	Return to Edit menu
Format	Format style
Format Tab Set	Set tabs in style
Insert	Define style attributes
Name	Change style attributes
Print	Print styles in a style sheet
Transfer Save	Save style sheet on disk

Table 8.2   Keys and commands introduced in Chapter 8.

1. A style sheet contains a list of formats or "styles" that you can apply to a document by entering their key codes. You must first create the style sheet and then attach it to the document.

2. To create a style sheet, issue a Gallery command to display the Gallery menu. You must have Word in the Gallery to create, edit, load, or save style sheets.

3. Each style has a name and a definition. The name consists of a one- or two-letter key code, a usage, and a variant (to allow alternatives for the same usage).

4. To add a style to a style sheet, use Insert to specify the name and use Format to define the meaning.

5. To apply (attach) a style sheet to a document, issue a Format Stylesheet Attach command.

6. To use a style in a document, hold the Alt key down and type the style's key code. Word automatically applies styles such as normal division and normal paragraph at the start.

7. Word has a default style sheet called NORMAL.STY that it attaches on startup or as part of any Transfer Clear command.

8. You can revise style sheets just like documents except that you must have Word in the Gallery menu. You must use the Name command to change a style's name.

9. You can change style sheets at any time. Word will automatically convert styles to equivalent usages and variants in the new sheet. It will use defaults for usages and variants that are not defined in the new sheet.

10. Each document can have its own style sheet. Thus, each independent window can have a different style sheet. To see or modify the sheet that applies to a particular window, you must make that window active and then issue a Gallery command.

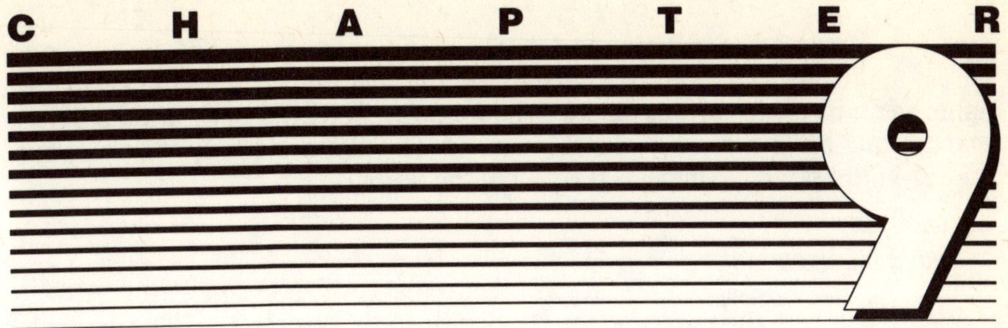

9

FORM LETTERS

Sometimes you must send the same letter (such as a request for payment, notice of credit terms, order acknowledgment, or report on account status) to an entire list of recipients. This chapter first presents a simple form letter in which Word replaces fields (items that will vary) in a generalized letter, or **main document**, with items from a **data document** on a one-for-one basis. Then Word's features for creating more elaborate form letters will be described. These features include inserting text conditionally, customizing groups of letters and individual letters from the keyboard, and using several data records in a single document.

Direct mail solicitors often use personalized letters that include the recipient's name and address in various places. The following is typical of the kind of letters that fill our mailboxes and wastebaskets (**note**: the underlined names would appear in the same typeface as the rest of the letter):

Dear <u>Mr. Brown</u>:

Would you like the name <u>James C. Brown</u> **to be associated with success? Yes,** <u>Mr. Brown</u>**, you can be a dynamic, successful person if you attend our seminar.**

With Word, creating this kind of personalized form letter takes three steps:

1. Prepare a model of the letter in which you name places or **fields** that will vary (e.g., the recipient's name, address, account number, outstanding balance, etc.).

2. Prepare a **data document** containing the items Word must insert into the multiple copies.

3. Use a Print Merge command to combine the model with the data and print the letters.

SIMPLE FORM LETTERS

As an example of a simple form letter, you will produce an invitation to a company's anniversary party. All you will do here is insert an individual address, a salutation, and a single reference to the recipient's affiliation. The procedures for creating a data document, entering the generalized letter, and printing the copies will be explained next.

Creating a Data Document

A data document is a Word document that contains a description of the **fields** (items) for each recipient and the recipient **records** (entries) themselves.

The description, or **header**, comes first. It contains the names of the fields in the order in which they appear in the records. Field names in the header may be up to 64 characters long and may be separated by commas or (for the sake of legibility) tabs.

The rest of the data document consists of the records. Each record must contain items in the number and order specified in the header, with commas or tabs separating them. Further, each record must end with an Enter. Note the following rules:

- You may not put blank lines between records or between the header and the first record.

- You must press Enter after typing in the final line in the data document.

Figure 9.1 shows the data document for the invitation. The header tells Word that each record consists of the following five fields: "name," "company," "street," "city," and "firstname." Below the header are the records for the two recipients.

```
name,company,street,city,firstname
Mr.  Phillip T.  Grange,Newton Plastics Corporation,1865 Industrial
Way,"Newton, FL 32786",Phil
Mrs.  Viola Wilson,"Wilson and Associates, Inc.",4399 Beach
St.,"Ocala, FL 32787",Vi
```

Figure 9.1   Data document for a simple form letter.

The quotation marks around the **city** fields and Mrs. Wilson's "company" field keep Word from mistaking the commas inside with the ones that separate fields. (Similarly, you must put quotation marks around data items that contain quotation marks. For example, if an item in your data document is **"prime" grade beef**, you must type it as **""prime" grade beef"**.)

Prepare the data document just as you would any document, and then save it under the name **address**.

Creating a Generalized Letter

Now you may enter the generalized letter as shown in Figure 9.2. As usual, use Format Division Margins to produce one-inch side margins and use Format Tab Set to set a tab at the center.

```
«DATA address.doc»
                             Gutenberg Printing, Inc.
                             1243 Flamingo Lane
                             Newton, FL 32786
                             January 22, 1989

«name»
«company»
«street»
«city»

Dear «firstname»:

This year is Gutenberg Printing's fifth anniversary in business.
To mark the occasion, we are hosting a cocktail party on Friday,
February 3, from 4:30 to 7:00 PM at the Newton Inn.  As one of
our most valued customers and friends at «company», we would be
honored by your presence.  I hope to see you there!


                             Best wishes,



                             James A.  Anderson
                             President
```

Figure 9.2   Simple form letter before merging

The material enclosed by chevrons (« and ») has a special meaning to Word. «DATA address.doc» tells Word what file contains the data; other fields in chevrons tell it the data field in which to insert when printing letters. The chevrons don't appear on the keyboard; you must press Ctrl-[to produce « and Ctrl-] to produce ».

When you finish entering the letter, save it under the name **invite**.

Printing Form Letters

To print personalized form letters, issue the Print Merge command. Word shows

```
PRINT MERGE: Printer Document Options
```

where the options have these meanings:

- **Printer** sends the copies to your printer.

- **Document** stores the copies as a document on disk. This lets you print later (with Print Printer) or modify certain copies, perhaps to add special messages to them.

- **Options** lets you choose specific data document records for printing, as opposed to printing a copy for every record.

When you select Print Merge Printer or Print Merge Document, Word displays the message **Merging record** *n* (where *n* is the record number) as it prints the copies or stores them on disk. Figure 9.3 shows the completed letter to Phillip Grange.

```
                                  Gutenberg Printing, Inc.
                                  1243 Flamingo Lane
                                  Newton, FL 32786
                                  January 22, 1989


Mr.  Phillip T.  Grange
Newton Plastics Corporation
1865 Industrial Way
Newton, FL 32786

Dear Phil:

This year is Gutenberg Printing's fifth anniversary in business.
To mark the occasion, we are hosting a cocktail party on Friday,
February 3, from 4:30 to 7:00 PM at the Newton Inn.  As one of
our most valued customers and friends at Newton Plastics
Corporation, we would be honored by your presence.  I hope to see
you there!


                                  Best wishes,




                                  James A.  Anderson
                                  President
```

Figure 9.3   Printed form letter after merging with data document.

Note that Word has replaced all the names with specific items from the data document. On the screen, however, you see only the generalized letter, not the individual copies with the data entered.

Separating Headers and Data Documents

Sometimes you may want to separate the header from the data document. This is particularly useful when the data document was produced by a database management program. Then you can use the database file directly; you need not modify it to insert header information.

Separating the header and data document also allows you to use the same header with many different data documents. This is convenient, for example, if you use several mailing lists that are all organized in the same way. You need not enter the header in each list.

To use separate header and data documents, you specify both documents in the DATA instruction at the beginning of the letter. If, for example, you are using the header contained in ADRHDR.DOC and the data document contained in ADDRESS.DOC, start the letter with the following DATA instruction:

«DATA ADRHDR.DOC, ADDRESS.DOC»

Note that you must put the header file first and a comma between it and the data document file. Be sure to type the comma. If you don't, Word will report **Not a valid filename** when you issue a Print Merge command.

VARIABLE FORM LETTERS

Word also lets you tailor letters to groups of recipients. For example, you can do the following:

- Print **Enclosures** on letters to people who are to receive additional material.

- Send both wholesale and retail price lists to regional managers but only retail prices to salespeople.

- Insert **The charges below include a $50.00 late-payment penalty.** on invoices to delinquent customers.

- Print either **Payment is due within 90 days** or **Payment is due within 30 days** on an invoice, depending on whether the addressee is an old or new customer.

- Include a local telephone number in letters to customers within your state and a toll-free number in all others.

- Print special messages such as **Remember to add 6% California sales tax.** for in-state customers or **Please remit in U.S. currency with checks drawn on a U.S. bank.** for international customers.

IF and ENDIF

The instructions IF and ENDIF let you include a specific block of text in selected letters, based on the contents of a field. The general form is as follows:

«IF *field* = *"string"***»***text***«ENDIF»**

This instruction line tells Word to print the enclosed text for every record in which *field* is set to *string*.

For example, suppose you are mailing a retail catalog and want to offer preferred customers a 15-percent discount. To do this, you could put a "preferred" field in each record and use the following paragraph in the cover letter:

As you can see, our prices are among the lowest in the business. «IF preferred = "yes"»And as a preferred customer, you are entitled to deduct an additional 15 percent!«ENDIF» Don't delay; order TODAY!

Word will then print all three sentences for preferred customers and the abridged version for everyone else. *Do not* type extra spaces between the conditional text and the chevrons because Word will include those spaces in the text if you do.

IF-ELSE-ENDIF

Word also provides an IF-ELSE-ENDIF variation that prints one block of text (*truetext*) if *field* matches *string* and a different block (*falsetext*) otherwise. IF-ELSE-ENDIF has the following general form:

«IF field = "*string*"»*truetext*«ELSE»*falsetext*«ENDIF»

For example, suppose you are offering a discount to customers who order before March 30. Preferred customers get 15 percent off; all others get 10 percent off. Your cover letter could include the following paragraph:

As you can see, our prices are among the lowest in the business. And «IF preferred = "yes"»because you are a preferred customer, «ENDIF»if we receive your order before March 30, you can deduct an additional «IF preferred = "yes"»15«ELSE»10«ENDIF» percent! Don't delay; order TODAY!

With this arrangement, letters to preferred customers will read as follows:

As you can see, our prices are among the lowest in the business. And because you are a preferred customer, if we receive your order before March 30, you can deduct an additional 15 percent! Don't delay; order TODAY!

Letters to other customers will read as follows:

As you can see, our prices are among the lowest in the business. And if we receive your order before March 30, you can deduct an additional 10 percent! Don't delay; order TODAY!

Remember that each record in the data document must contain a "preferred" field in the position indicated in the header. A typical record would be as follows:

Ms. Catherine Simpson,"1580 Cole St., Apt. 5","Clayton, MO 63105",yes

Numeric Comparisons

Earlier in this chapter, it was mentioned that you could put an equal sign (=) in an IF instruction, to make Word decide whether to insert a specified text string based on the text in a data field. You can also make Word omit or insert text based on the size of a numeric field by including a **comparison operator** in the IF component. Table 9.1 summarizes these operators.

Operator	Meaning
=	equal to
< >	not equal to
<	less than
< =	less than or equal to
>	greater than
> =	greater than or equal to

Table 9.1   Comparison operators.

For example, a bank might want to offer extra inducements to customers age 65 or over. The form letter could include the following paragraph:

With 85 years of service and over 100 branches statewide, you know you can depend on First National Bank. «IF age> = 65»And as a senior citizen, «name», we can offer you a free checking account and safe-deposit box! «ENDIF»When you think of banking, think of us--First National Bank.

Here, the condition **age> = 65** makes Word insert the "And as a senior citizen" sentence if the recipient's "age" field has a value of 65 or more. Note that you can put variable fields in the text of an IF-ENDIF or IF-ELSE-ENDIF statement; for example, in the above paragraph, *name* personalizes the extra sentence.

CUSTOMIZING FORM LETTERS FROM THE KEYBOARD

Word lets you add information to a form letter from the keyboard. You can use this feature to insert specific dates, times, places, subjects, event names, sponsors, numbers, or messages in a generalized letter. You can also customize individual letters with account status, achievement levels, or personal messages.

Word provides this capability through the SET and ASK instructions. These instructions make Word stop printing and wait for you to enter text for a field (type the text and then press Enter). If you use either instruction, always put it at the beginning of the generalized form letter, directly below the DATA line.

Customizing Groups of Letters

SET asks you to enter the text just once. You can use its field in every copy of the document. The general form is as follows:

«SET *field* = ? [*prompt*]**»**

In this example, *prompt* is a message that Word displays on the bottom line to tell the operator what it wants. The square brackets [and] indicate that the prompt is optional; *do not* type them. If you omit the prompt, Word will just display the uninstructive **Enter text** message.

SET lets you supply data items that apply to an entire group of letters. For example, Figure 9.4 shows a generalized meeting announcement that uses SETs to request the date and all the particulars of the specific meeting.

```
«DATA MEMBERS.DOC»
«SET date=?Date of letter»
«SET meettime=?Time of meeting»
«SET meetdate=?Day of week, date of meeting»
«SET place=?Place of meeting»
«SET speaker=?Speaker's name»
«SET affiliation=?Speaker's affiliation»
«SET topic=?Speaker's topic»
                              12568 Easy Street
                              Moolah, MI 67432
                              «date»

«title» «firstname» «lastname»
«street»
«city»

Dear «firstname»:

The regular monthly meeting of the Make-a-Million Investment Club
will be held at «meettime» on «meetdate» at «place».  Our
guest speaker will be «speaker» of «affiliation», whose topic
is «topic». Please plan to attend.

Best regards,



D.  Warbucks
Secretary
```

Figure 9.4   Generalized meeting notice using the SET instruction.

Customizing Individual Letters

ASK asks for text each time Word starts a new copy. You can use the ASK field only in that copy. Its general form is as follows:

«ASK *field* = ? [*prompt*]**»**

ASK lets you supply data items for individual letters. ASK is most useful when you have both a standard letter and a standard data document. You can then use it to customize each letter.

Suppose you want to notify all sales representatives of their last quarter's total and current quarter's goal for a particular item. Figure 9.5 shows a standard letter.

```
«DATA SALESREP.DOC»
«SET qrtno=?Last quarter designation»
«SET year=?Year»
«SET item=?Sales item»
«ASK sales=?Last quarter's sales»
«ASK goal=?This quarter's goal»

From: Richard Gordon, National Sales Manager

To: «name»
    «street»
    «city»

Subject: Sales of «item» for «qrtno» quarter «year».


According to our records, your sales of «item» for «qrtno»
quarter «year» were «sales». Your goal for the current
quarter for sales of «item» is «goal». If either of these
does not concur with your records, please notify me. These
numbers will be used in calculating commissions and in
determining progress toward overall sales goals. Please
acknowledge receipt of this notification and report any
discrepancies before the end of the current quarter.
```

Figure 9.5   Sales memorandum using the SET and ASK instructions.

Note that SET is used for the quarter number, year, and item name because these are the same for all recipients. ASK is used for last quarter's sales and this quarter's goal because these items are individualized. You can use this letter for notifications concerning many different items in different quarters without changing either the letter form or the address list. Following is a description of the actual production of a set of letters.

Suppose you are producing notifications concerning sales of tractors for the 3rd quarter of 1989. Your two representatives and their results and goals are as follows:

Name	Last Qtr's Sales	This Qtr's Goal
Joseph F. Murray	8	9
Gordon Johnson	12	14

You can proceed as follows, assuming the memorandum in Figure 9.5 is on the screen:

1. Issue a Print Merge command.

2. Respond to Word's overall questions as follows:
   - Last quarter's designation - 3rd
   - Year - 1989
   - Sales item - tractors

3. Respond to specific questions for Joseph F. Murray as follows:
   - Last quarter's sales - 8
   - This quarter's goal - 9

   Word will now print the memorandum to Murray.

4. Respond to Word's specific questions for Gordon Johnson as follows:
   - Last quarter's sales - 12
   - This quarter's sales - 14

   Word will now print the memorandum to Johnson.

Note the difference between the overall questions (the SET instructions) and the questions for each letter (the ASK instructions).

USING MULTIPLE RECORDS IN A LETTER

So far, you have seen examples in which Word uses only one data document record per letter. However, sometimes you may want to use more than one. Word's **NEXT** instruction lets you do this. It tells Word to advance to the next record in the data document.

For example, suppose you are sending prospective new members of an investment club the letter shown in Figure 9.6. Here, each copy contains two names and addresses for the prospective new member and the sponsor. Of course, you must organize records in the data document in the way the letter expects to find them: first a member, then a sponsor, and so on.

```
«DATA NEWMEMS.DOC»
                                    12568 Easy Street
                                    Moolah, MI 67432
                                    March 15, 1989


«title» «firstname» «lastname»
«street»
«city»

Dear «firstname»:

We are pleased to inform you that you have been selected for
membership in the Make-a-Million Investment Club.  This
honor is reserved for a selected few in the investment
community.  You will be inducted into the club at our annual
general meeting on April 1, 1989 at 8:00 P.M.  at the Bay
City Inn.  Your sponsoring member is:
«NEXT»
    «title» «firstname» «lastname»
    «street»
    «city»

We extend our congratulations to you on this achievement.

Sincerely yours,



D.  Warbucks
Secretary
```

Figure 9.6   New members' letter using the NEXT instruction.

Note that only new members receive the letter in Figure 9.6. Once you use NEXT, Word never returns to the previous record. However, you could use NEW-MEMS.DOC to send reminders and schedules to both members and sponsors.

You can also use NEXT to summarize short data documents. For example, the form in Figure 9.7 produces a current list of a company's five plant managers. Of course, this approach is sensible only if there are just a few managers, not if there are 30 or 40. Unfortunately, there is no way to tell Word to use NEXT a specific number of times or until it runs out of records.

```
«DATA PLTMGRS.DOC»
«SET qrtrno=?Last year's designation»
«SET year=?Year»
ROSTER OF PLANT MANAGERS - «qrtrno» QUARTER «year»

«plant»
«name»
«address»
«city»

«NEXT»
«plant»
«name»
«address»
«city»

«NEXT»
«plant»
«name»
«address»
«city»

«NEXT»
«plant»
«name»
«address»
«city»

«NEXT»
«plant»
«name»
«address»
«city»
```

Figure 9.7   *Plant managers' list using the NEXT instruction*

PRINTING SELECTED LETTERS

Sometimes you may want to send letters to a particular group of recipients within an address list. If you have a list of the recipients in the order they're posted in your data document, you can simply tell Word which records you want before proceeding with the merge. You can also have Word determine which records to merge, by including a SKIP instruction in your main document.

Selecting Records Manually

If you know the numbers of the records you want to merge, you can specify them ahead of time as follows:

1. Issue a **Print Merge Options** command. Word displays the following:

```
PRINT MERGE OPTIONS range: All Records        record number:
```

2. Type **r** for Records and press Tab to reach "record number."

3. Type the numbers of the records you want, separated by commas (for individual records) or hyphens (for a range of records).

   For example, if there are 100 records in your data document and you want to merge records 5, 13, and 30 through 37, type **5,13,30-37** for "record number."

4. Press Enter to return to the Print Merge menu.

5. Issue a Print Merge Printer or Print Merge Document command.

Print Merge Options is particularly handy for merging a few records you may have added after completing a previous merge operation. It is also convenient for resuming a merge you stopped (by pressing Esc) for some reason.

Selecting Records Automatically

Just as Word provides a NEXT instruction to work through a data document you are summarizing, it also has a **SKIP** instruction that skips a particular record (and its related form letter).

SKIP contains no inner terms; it has only one form: «SKIP». Hence, you would normally insert it just ahead of an «ENDIF» or an «ELSE» statement. For example, to send letters to clients who ordered at least $100,000 worth of goods from your company, you could put this statement at the beginning of your main document:

«IF orders < 100000»«SKIP»«ENDIF»

In working its way through your data document, Word would then skip any client whose "orders" field is less than 100000 and print letters to the rest.

You can even perform several tests to narrow down the selection further. For example, the following two statements make Word print letters to clients whose orders totaled between $100,000 and $300,000 (you may have special letters to send to the major buyers):

«IF orders < 100000»«SKIP»«ENDIF»
«IF orders > =300000»«SKIP»«ENDIF»

QUESTIONS AND ANSWERS

Word won't insert anything. It just prints field names as if they were regular text. What happened?
Either you used a Print Printer command instead of a Print Merge command or you entered the chevron symbols incorrectly. To insert «, press Ctrl-[; to insert », press Ctrl-].

Word printed the message "* Unknown field name ***" for one data item. Why?**
Word couldn't find that field name in the data document; you probably mistyped it or used a different name (e.g., "street" instead of "address" or vice versa). Make sure the names are exactly the same everywhere in the main document as they are in the data document's header.

When I tried using Print Merge, the computer beeped and displayed each of my field names, plus "Unknown field name" on the message line. What's going on?
You probably omitted the DATA line from the beginning of the letter. Word didn't know where to find the data to insert, so it gave you a series of audible "raspberries."

Instead of inserting an address, Word printed "address»" on my form letter. What did I do wrong?

You entered **address»** instead of **«address»**. Without the left chevron, Word didn't know that **address** was a merge item and printed it as regular text.

I made a typing error and the letters are all coming out wrong. Do I need to wait for Word to finish the entire data document?

No, press Esc to cancel the rest of the printing.

Whenever Word reaches an address with a suite number, it reports "Too many fields in data or header record" and then puts the suite number where the city and state should go. What am I doing wrong?

You're probably separating the suite number from the address with a comma. Word then thinks the suite number is the next data item. The solution is to put quotation marks around addresses with suite or apartment numbers. For example, enter 8400 Main St., Suite 2700 as **"8400 Main St., Suite 2700"**.

Every once in a while, Word prints a letter with blanks in all the fields. What's the problem?

You're putting extra blank lines between your data document records. Word thinks each blank line is a record by itself, so it prints a letter to no one. Remember, don't put extra blank lines anywhere in a data document!

Why is Word asking me for the same meeting date before it prints each form letter?

You used ASK instead of SET in the letter. ASK asks for text for each copy, while SET asks for the text once and then inserts it in all subsequent copies.

I want to send a letter to all my tenants notifying them of a rent increase. Do I have to put the old and new rents in my address list?

No, leave your address list alone. At the beginning of the letter, put

«ASK oldrent=?Old rent»
«ASK newrent=?New rent»

Use the names *oldrent* and *newrent* where you want the values to appear. ASK will make Word ask you for the new values before printing each letter.

Word is asking me for values for the next letter, but I'm not sure which letter it's doing. Is there a way for me to keep track of where Word is in the address list?

Yes, split the screen in two with a Window Split Horizontal command (enter 3 for the line value). Press F1 to select the small window at the top, and then use a Transfer Load command to put the address list in it. Move the cursor down (past the header) until you see the first record. Then use F1 to switch windows and start the Print Merge.

After Word prints a letter, press F1 to go to the top window, move the cursor down until the next record is visible, and press F1 to return to the letter window. This procedure will allow you to always see the current record in the top window.

Why do I get the message "Not a valid filename" when I issue a Print Merge command? I've used this file before for printing form letters.
You probably forgot to put a comma between the header file and the data file in a DATA instruction.

HINTS AND WARNINGS

1. Like the Print Printer command, Print Merge Printer and Print Merge Document use the Print Options settings to determine how many copies and which pages to print. The default values are one copy and the entire document printed.

    Print Merge Printer and Print Merge Document use Print Merge Options to determine which data document records to print. The default is all records.

2. Never put blank lines in a data document. Word will think they are records by themselves.

3. Be sure each record in a data document has its items in the same order as the names appear in the header. Because Word follows a simple item-by-item correspondence, ordering errors will result in incorrect alignments.

4. If data items contain extra commas, put quotation marks around them. Otherwise, Word will think the commas are separators between items. Typical problem examples are "White Drug Stores, Inc."; "Maltby and Co., Ltd."; "3583 Main St., Apt. 3-F"; "Mr. George Colby, Jr."; "Elaine W. McGregor, Vice-President"; "Pickwick, Bumble, and Cratchit, Attorneys at Law"; and "a prize of $1,000,000 (that's right, one million dollars!)."

5. When preparing a generalized letter, be sure to press Ctrl and [or] to get the special chevron symbols used to enclose variables. If [,], {, or } appears in your document, you probably forgot to press Ctrl or pressed Shift instead.

6. If Word displays error messages during a Print Merge operation, press Esc to stop printing and examine your data document. This usually means the

document has an extra blank line or a comma omitted, an extra comma not inside quotation marks, or a missing Enter after the last record.

7. When entering conditional text, remember the ENDIF at the end. Otherwise, Word will think the entire remaining text is conditional.

8. Put all SETs and ASKs at the beginning of your main document. Otherwise, Word will replace the variables with old values or blanks.

9. Remember the difference between SET and ASK. SET requests text just once and makes it available for all subsequent letters, whereas ASK requests text each time Word prints a new copy.

10. When using the NEXT instruction, note that the advancement in the data document is permanent. Word does not provide a way to go back to the previous record (i.e., there is no PREV instruction). Nor will Word ever use the current record again. That is, if it now proceeds to the next letter, it will also advance to the next record in the data document.

KEY POINTS

Table 9.2 summarizes the keys and commands introduced in this chapter.

Key Combination	Function
Ctrl-[	Left chevron («) for merge field name
Ctrl-]	Right chevron (») for merge field name
Command	**Function**
Print Merge Printer	Merge document to printer
Print Merge Document	Merge document to disk document
Print Merge Options	Select records for merging

Table 9.2   Keys and commands introduced in Chapter 9.

1. Word produces form letters by combining a generalized letter with records from a data document.

2. To tell Word which data document to use, begin the generalized letter with a command of the form «DATA *datadoc.*DOC». Enter a field name of the form *«name»* wherever you want Word to insert a data item. To produce the chevrons « or », type Ctrl-[or Ctrl-], respectively.

3. A data document starts with a **header** containing the field names in the order in which they will appear in the records. The records themselves follow. You must separate names or data items with commas and put quotation marks (") around items that include a comma or a quotation mark.

4. To print form letters, load the main document from disk with a Transfer Load command and then issue a Print Merge command. Select **Printer** to print the copies or **Document** to store them in a document file on disk.

5. Form letter documents may use the following instructions:

   - **IF-ENDIF** customizes groups of letters by inserting or omitting text, depending on the value of a selected field. For text fields, it inserts the text if the field has a specified string value.

     For numeric fields, IF-ENDIF inserts the text if the field has a value equal to (=), less than (<), less then or equal to (< =), greater than (>), or greater than or equal to (> =) a specified number.

   - **IF-ELSE-ENDIF** is similar to IF-ENDIF, but inserts one block of text if the field test succeeds and a different one if it fails.

   - **SET** and **ASK** let you enter field values from the keyboard. SET requests text only once, whereas ASK requests text for each copy. You can use SET to customize groups of letters and ASK to customize individual letters.

   - **NEXT** lets you use more than one data record in a single copy. It makes Word advance to the next record. This is useful for letters containing more than one address and for compiling short lists.

   - **SKIP** lets you omit letters from a merge. It makes Word advance to the next record, but (unlike NEXT) SKIP is generally used in IF-ENDIF or IF-ELSE-ENDIF statements, rather than alone.

Following are summaries of the form letter instructions introduced in this chapter:

IF *field* **="string"»text«ENDIF»**

Inserts text if *field* has the value *string*.

«IF *field* **<** *number***»text«ENDIF»**
«IF *field* **< =** *number***»text«ENDIF»**
«IF *field* **=** *number***»text«ENDIF»**
«IF *field* **= >** *number***»text«ENDIF»**
«IF *field* **>** *number***»text«ENDIF»**

Inserts text if *field* is less than, less than or equal to, equal to, greater than or equal to, or greater than *number*.

«IF field ="string"»truetext«ELSE»falsetext«ENDIF»

Inserts *truetext* if *field* has the value *string*; inserts *falsetext* otherwise.

«IF *field* **<** *number***»truetext«ELSE»falsetext«ENDIF»**
«IF field = *number***»truetext«ELSE»falsetext«ENDIF»**
«IF field > *number***»truetext«ELSE»falsetext«ENDIF**

Inserts *truetext* if *field* is less than, equal to, or greater than *number*; inserts *falsetext* otherwise.

SET *field* **=? [***prompt***]»**

Requests *field* value from the keyboard, with an optional *prompt* message. Uses typed response in every copy.

«ASK *field* **=? [***prompt***]»**

Same as SET, but uses response only in current copy.

«NEXT»

Makes Word advance to the next record in the data document but remain in the current form letter.

«SKIP»

Makes Word advance to the next record in the data document and start a new form letter.

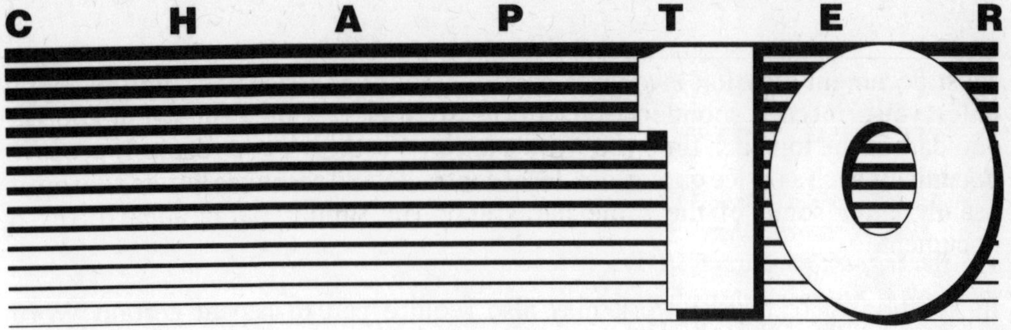

MACROS

This chapter discusses how you can use Word's macro recording and writing capabilities to save time and improve consistency when performing repetitive tasks.

Most document creation involves a certain amount of repetition. For example, unless you print correspondence on letterhead paper, you must enter your address and date at the top each time you write a letter. Further, if you regularly prepare documents such as price quotations, legal contracts, and response letters, you must usually enter some of the same paragraphs (or similar paragraphs) in each document.

In addition to text, your work may also require you to repeat certain Word commands. For example, if you often include single-spaced lists or tables in a double-spaced document, you must change the spacing (and perhaps the margins and tabs) before and after you enter the table.

With Word, you can avoid typing the same sequence of keystrokes every time by defining the keystrokes as a "macro." A **macro** is simply a sequence of keystrokes (text or commands, or both) that Word plays back when you tell it to.

In addition to saving typing time, macros also provide some other side benefits. For example, when using a macro to reproduce a block of text, you needn't worry about misspellings or typing mistakes. If you entered error-free text into the macro, Word will always replay it without errors. Moreover, because a computer is doing the work, the text will appear faster than anyone could type it in. Finally, using macros to replay key commands saves you from having to remember all of those key commands. Considering the many key combinations that Word furnishes for commands, you will probably appreciate that benefit.

Typical macro users include the following people:

- Attorneys who want to produce stock phrases or boilerplate paragraphs that refer to a specific person or company.

- Businesspeople who want to use a form letter to reply to someone who has requested the address of a local dealer or the price of a specific item.

- Engineers who want to prepare status reports that include variable items (e.g., dates, manpower estimates, and costs) within set tables or blocks of text.

- Anyone who wants to produce periodic meeting notices or bulletins that differ only in time, place, or purpose.

CREATING MACROS

Word lets you define a macro in two different ways:

- You can **record** your keystrokes as you type them.

- You can type, or **write**, the contents of the macro on the screen and then copy the contents to the glossary.

Recording a macro is generally easier than writing one because you simply type your text and commands in the exact order you want Word to replay them. By contrast, when you write a macro that contains commands, you must insert special codes to indicate the commands. For example, to make Word perform a backspace operation, you must type **<Backspace>** in your text.

On the other hand, if you write a macro, you can include the instructions described in Chapter 9 that make Word stop for text from the keyboard, display a message on the message line, and perform other useful jobs. If you are just beginning, try recording your macros. Then, when you get more experience and confidence, try writing a few macros.

Naming Macros

After you create a macro (by recording it or writing it), you must give it a name. The name can be up to 31 characters long. It cannot contain spaces, but you can insert underscore characters (_), hyphens (-), or periods (.) as separators. For example, if a macro both bolds and underlines a block of text, you could name it in any of the following ways:

- mac.Bold_Und

- Bold_Und.mac

- mac.Bold-and-Und

Note the "mac" here. It's not required, but it helps distinguish macros from other glossary entries when you ask for a list of available items.

Word also lets you assign a one- or two-keystroke command to the macro so you can replay the macro by pressing those keys. To assign a key command as well as a name, type the name, insert a caret (^) by pressing Shift-6, and then press the keys for the macro. Word translates your key command into a code. For example, you could assign Ctrl-B to the preceding bold-and-underline macro by giving it this name:

    mac.Bold_Und^<Ctrl B>

If there is already a macro assigned to the Ctrl-B combination, you can make the new macro require *two* key commands in succession. If you set up the bold-and-underline macro for Ctrl-B then U, its name would look like this:

    mac.Bold_Und^<Ctrl B>U

Note, however, that Word includes the key command characters in its 31-character limit for macros.

Recording a Macro

To record a macro, follow these steps:

1. Press Shift and F3 to issue a Record Macro command. The status line displays "RM."

2. Type the keystrokes you want Word to play back. In addition to text, you can include tab or margin commands, character formats (e.g., center, bold, underline, or subscript), or anything else you can use in a regular document.

3. When you finish, press Shift and F3 again.

4. At the "COPY to: { }" prompt, type the macro's name and, if you want, a caret (^) followed by one or two key commands you want to use to play back the macro.

5. Press Enter to store the macro in the glossary.

To cancel a macro you are recording, press Shift-F3 to stop recording and press Esc when the COPY prompt appears.

Writing a Macro

To write a macro, follow these steps:

1. Type everything you want in the macro, both text and key commands, but enclose each command with a "less than" (<) and "greater than" (>) character. Table 10.1 lists the keys and their names.

Key	Keyname
Alt and another key	<Alt *x*>
Ctrl and another key	<Ctrl *x*>
Shift and another key	<Shift *x*>
Asterisk on numeric keypad	<Keypad*>
Backspace	<Backspace>
Caps Lock	<CapsLock>
Del (Delete)	<Del>
Down arrow	<Down>
End	<End>
Enter	<Enter>
Esc (Escape)	<Esc>
Function keys	<F1> through <F10>
Home	<Home>
Ins (Insert)	<Ins>
Left arrow	<Left>
Minus on numeric keypad	<Keypad->
Num Lock	<NumLock>
Page Down	<PgDn>
Page Up	<PgUp>
Plus on numeric keypad	<Keypad+>
Right arrow	<Right>
Scroll Lock	<ScrollLock>
Spacebar	<Space>
Tab	<Tab>
Up arrow	<Up>

Table 10.1   Keys and keynames.

The <Enter> and <Space> codes tell Word to "press the Enter key" or "press the space bar." Word knows that the Enter at the end of a paragraph and a space between two words are regular text elements, so don't put the < and > symbols around them.

2. Highlight the entire macro.

3. Issue a Copy or Delete command to store the macro in the glossary. Copy leaves the text in place, and Delete removes it.

4. At the prompt, type the macro's name and, if you want, a caret (^) followed by one or two key commands.

5. Press Enter to store the macro in the glossary.

REPLAYING A MACRO

When you reach the document location in which you want to replay a macro, do one of three things:

- Type the macro's name and press F3 (for Expand Glossary).

- If you assigned the macro to a key combination, press those keys.

- To select from a list of available macro names, issue an Insert command, press F1 to get the list, and then highlight the name of the macro you want and press Enter.

EXAMPLE MACRO

Suppose your company's name is Ryan's Lawn Service, and you always underline it in your letters. Instead of typing it each time, you create a macro that will produce it when you press Ctrl-RL (that is, when you hold Ctrl down and type **rl**). To record the macro, do the following:

1. Press Shift-F3 to issue a Record Macro command.

2. When "RM" appears on the status line, press Alt-U (to turn underlining on); then type **Ryan's Lawn Service**, and press Alt-Spacebar (to turn underlining off).

3. Press Shift-F3 to stop recording the macro.

4. At the "COPY to: { }" prompt, type **mac.RyanLS^** and then press Ctrl-RL. For Ctrl-RL, Word displays **<ctrl r> <ctrl l>**.

5. Press Enter to store your new macro in the glossary.

You could also create the macro by typing this line on the screen

> **Ryan's Lawn Service <Ctrl R> <Ctrl L>**

and then highlighting it and copying or deleting it to the glossary.

When you reach a place in a document where you want the macro text, hold Ctrl down and type **rl**.

SAVING YOUR MACROS ON DISK

Word doesn't save changes to the glossary unless you tell it to. To update the glossary with its new macros on disk, issue a Transfer Glossary Save command.

MACROS THAT REPLACE ABBREVIATIONS

In Chapter 6, you used the Replace operation to expand abbreviations. However, using Replace forces you to enter the search and replace strings each time. Word doesn't remember them from one document to the next or, in the case of the replacement string, even from one Replace operation to the next. If you use an abbreviation often (say, "DoD" for "Department of Defense" or "pfp" for "party of the first part"), you should define a macro for it. The macro should perform a Replace command by entering your abbreviation for the "text" (i.e., search) string and entering the abbreviation's expanded text for the "with text" (i.e., replacement) string.

For example, suppose you want to set up a macro that replaces every occurrence of "aic" in your document with "Acme International Corporation." To define the macro, perform the following steps:

1. Press Shift-F3 to issue a Record Macro command.

2. Press Esc and type **r** to obtain the Replace form.

3. For the "text" option, type **aic** and press Tab.

4. For the "with text" option, type **Acme International Corporation** and press Tab again.

5. For the "confirm" option, type **n** (to perform global replacements) and press Tab twice.

6. For the "whole word" option, type **y** (to avoid replacing "aic" when it is merely part of a word and not intended as an abbreviation).

7. Press Enter to start replacing.

8. Press Shift-F3 to stop recording keystrokes.

9. For "COPY to: { }," type **mac.aic^** and press Ctrl-AI, and then press Enter.

After that series of instructions, you can replay the "aic" macro at any time, by holding Ctrl down and typing **ai**. Word expands the abbreviations throughout the document.

EDITING MACROS

Sometimes you may make a mistake in defining a macro, perhaps by leaving out a command or inserting some keystrokes you hadn't intended. Fortunately, it is easy to edit a Word macro. You simply Insert that macro's definition onto the screen, edit the definition, and then write the macro definition back to the glossary. Specifically, to edit a macro definition, follow these steps:

1. Issue an Insert command.

2. When "INSERT from: { }" appears, type the name of the macro you want to edit followed by a caret (^). The caret tells Word to insert the macro's definition, as opposed to replaying it.

3. Press Enter.

4. Edit the macro as necessary, using the keynames in Table 10.1 for commands.

5. When you finish, select the entire macro definition.

6. Issue a Copy or Delete command.

7. At the prompt, type the macro's name (or press F1 to select it from the glossary list) and press Enter.

8. When Word asks for confirmation, type **y**.

Changing a Macro's Key Command

When you save an edited macro back to the glossary (steps 6 and 7 above), you can also give it a different key command. Simply type a caret (^) after the macro's name and then press the keys you want. For example, if you Insert the definition for a macro called "mac.acme<ctrl y>" and you want it to respond to Ctrl-Z, type **mac.acme^** and press Ctrl-Z in response to the COPY or DELETE prompt.

NESTING MACROS

Word allows you run one macro from within another. The Word manual refers to this technique as "nesting" macros. The advantage of nesting is that it lets you combine a number of small macros to build bigger macros.

To nest an existing macro within a new one, define the new macro as usual, but when you reach the place where Word is to run the existing macro, enter a start command for it. Further, the macro that's called can call another macro within its definition, and that macro can call still another, and so on. Word allows up to 16 levels of nesting.

SUPPLIED MACROS

Word provides several glossaries that contain a variety of macros. Note that most of Word's supplied macros have key commands of the form <Ctrl *key1*>*key2*. This means that to run one of these macros, you hold the Ctrl key down and press the first key, and then release both keys and press the second key. Remember, to use a glossary other than NORMAL.GLY, you must load it, using a Transfer Glossary Load command or merge it with the current glossary, using a Transfer Glossary Merge command.

Following are summaries of the more useful macros contained in the default NORMAL.GLY glossary and in the MACRO.GLY glossary, including the keys (if any) you can press to run those macros. A third glossary, SAFEKEYB.GLY, contains macros that are useful in column operations.

Useful Macros Contained in **NORMAL.GLY**

Note: Macros marked with * are also contained in MACRO.GLY.

annot_collect.mac* <Ctrl-A>C
 Compiles a list of all annotations in a document.

annot_merge.mac* <Ctrl-A>M
 Merges review comments from several copies of a document into a single document.

annot_remove.mac* <Ctrl-A>R
 Removes all annotations from a document.

character_test.mac* <Ctrl-C>T
 Prints all of the characters in a selected font.

collect_guts.mac*
 Called by another macro. *Do not* call this macro by itself.

envelope.mac* <Ctrl-E>N
 Lets you print addresses on envelopes.

file_feeder.mac*
 Called by another macro. *Do not* call this macro by itself.

make_directory <Ctrl-M>D
 Creates a new hard disk directory from within Word, using the DOS **MD** (Make Directory) command.

make_table
 Called by another macro. *Do not* call this macro by itself.

mailing_label.mac* <Ctrl-M>L
 Lets you print mailing labels with one to three labels across the page. This macro performs a Print Merge operation, using a data document for which you supply the name of the address file.

merge_guts.mac*
 Called by another macro. *Do not* call this macro by itself.

move_file <Ctrl-M>F
  Moves a specified file, by copying it to its destination and then erasing the original.

print_letter.mac* <Ctrl-P>L
  Lets you print the first page of a document with different margins than the rest of the document.

remove_directory <Ctrl-R>D
  Erases a specified hard disk directory, using the DOS **RD** (Remove Directory) command.

rename_file <Ctrl-R>F
  Renames a specified disk file, using the DOS **REN** (Rename) command.

sidebyside.mac* <Ctrl-S>B
  Inserts styles in the attached style sheet that you can use to arrange text in side-by-side format.

stop_last_footer.mac* <Ctrl-S>L
  Prevents the footer on the last page of a document from being printed.

Useful Macros Contained in MACRO.GLY

Note: Macros marked with * are also contained in NORMAL.GLY.

3_delete.mac <Ctrl-D>D
  Deletes selected text and saves it to a temporary glossary entry. You can use **3_undelete.mac** to recover up to three of these deletions.

3_undelete.mac <Ctrl-U>U
  Recovers up to three of the most recent deletions made with the **3_delete.mac** macro.

annot_collect.mac* <Ctrl-A>C
  Compiles a list of all annotations in a document.

annot_merge.mac* <Ctrl-A>M
  Merges review comments from several copies of a document into a single document.

annot_remove.mac* <Ctrl-A>R
Removes all annotations from a document.

archive_author.mac <Ctrl-A>A
Copies all documents written by a specified author (based on document summary sheets) into a specified disk directory.

archive_keyword.mac <Ctrl-A>K
Similar to **archive_author** but copies documents based on summary sheet keywords.

archive_documents.mac*
Called by another macro. *Do not* call this macro by itself.

authority_entry.mac <Ctrl-A>E
Marks selected text for inclusion in a table of authorities.

authority_table.mac <Ctrl-A>T
Generates a table of authorities based on entries in the current document.

bulleted_list.mac <Ctrl-B>L
Lets you enter a list of indented paragraphs preceded by hyphens; keeps indenting until you press Esc.

chainprint.mac <Ctrl-C>P
Prints the documents whose names are contained in a specified disk file and numbers their pages consecutively.

character_test.mac* <Ctrl-C>T
Prints all of the characters in a selected font.

collect_guts.mac*
Called by another macro. *Do not* call this macro by itself.

copy_file.mac <Ctrl-C>F
Copies a file and any graphics associated with it.

copy_text.mac <Ctrl-C>T
Lets you select text, and then copies it to a specified destination.

dca_load.mac <Ctrl-D>L
Loads a specified DCA-RFT file. DCA stands for Document Content Architecture; RFT stands for Revisable-Format Text.

dca_save.mac <Ctrl-D>S
Saves the current document in DCA-RFT format and gives it the extension .RFT.

envelope.mac* <Ctrl-E>N
Lets you print addresses on envelopes.

file_feeder.mac*
Called by another macro. *Do not* call this macro by itself.

filename.mac <Ctrl-F>N
Inserts the name of the current document (or "Untitled") at the cursor position.

freeze_style.mac <Ctrl-F>S
Removes all formatting applied with styles from the current document.

index.mac <Ctrl-I>W
Indexes the current document, based on a file that contains the phrases to be indexed (one phrase per line).

index_entry.mac <Ctrl-I>E
Adds hidden index codes to the selected text.

mailing_label.mac* <Ctrl-M>L
Lets you print mailing labels with one to three labels across the page. This macro performs a Print Merge operation, using a data document for which you supply the name of the address file.

memo_header.mac <Ctrl-M>H
Inserts the beginning text for a memorandum at the cursor position. The text consists of the centered header MEMORANDUM, followed by fields labeled TO, FROM, SUBJECT, and CC, plus a DATE label with the current date marker **(dateprint),** and a horizontal line.

merge_guts.mac
Called by another macro. *Do not* call this macro by itself.

move_text.mac <Ctrl-M>T
Lets you select text, and then moves that text to a specified destination.

next_page.mac <Ctrl-J>N
Moves the cursor to the top of the next page.

prev_page.mac <Ctrl-J>P
Moves the cursor to the top of the previous page.

print_letter.mac* <Ctrl-P>L
Lets you print the first page of a document with different margins than the rest of the document.

repl_w_gloss.mac <Ctrl-R>G
Lets you search for a string and replace it with a specified glossary entry.

repl_w_scrap.mac <Ctrl-R>P
Lets you search for a string and replace it with the current contents of the scrap.

save_selection.mac <Ctrl-S>S
Saves the selected text to a specified file on disk.

sidebyside.mac* <Ctrl-S>B
Inserts styles in the attached style sheet that you can use to arrange text in side-by-side format.

stop_last_footer.mac* <Ctrl-S>L
Prevents the footer on the last page of a document from being printed.

strip_path
Called by another macro. *Do not* call this macro by itself.

table.mac <Ctrl-T>T
Sets tabs for a table.

tabs.mac <Ctrl-T>1
Sets tabs at specified positions and alignments; repeats until you enter **0**.

tabs2.mac <Ctrl-T>2
Lets you create a table by specifying the number of columns, the alignment of the table on the page, and the width of each column.

tabs3.mac <Ctrl-T>3
>Lets you create a table by specifying the number of columns, the alignment of the table on the page, and the width of each column.

toc_entry.mac <Ctrl-T>E
>Marks the selected text as a table of contents entry.

QUESTIONS AND ANSWERS

I always put my address and the date at the top of every letter. Can I make Word insert them for me?
>Yes. Store the information as a macro, using the Record Macro command (Shift-F3). To define the macro, type the address as you would normally. When you reach the place for the date, insert a (**dateprint**) command and then press Shift-F3 to end the macro.

>You might name this macro "addr" and assign the key command Ctrl-I-A (for Insert Address) to it. After that, if you press Ctrl-I-A, Word will insert your address and the date.

Sometimes I forget the names of my macros. How can I get a list of them?
>Issue an Insert command and press F1 at the prompt.

I defined a macro that inserts a standard paragraph in contracts that I prepare. However, when I ran it I noticed that a word was misspelled. How can I correct it?
>You can edit the macro. To do this, Insert its text on your screen (type the macro's name followed by ^), edit it, select all of its text, and then issue a Copy or Delete command; enter the name of the macro (including a key code, if desired) at the prompt.

HINTS AND WARNINGS

1. When recording a macro, remember to press Shift-F3 at the end of it as well as at the beginning. If you don't press Shift-F3 the second time, Word will continue building the macro indefinitely, and put everything you type into the macro.

2. Once you begin recording a macro, there is no way to cancel the operation. If you spot a mistake in an earlier part of the macro or want to stop for any other reason, press Shift-F3 to end the macro. When the COPY prompt appears, press Esc.

3. To stop a macro while it is running, press Esc.

4. Word doesn't save new macros or other changes to the glossary unless you tell it to by issuing a Transfer Glossary Save command.

5. A macro can contain as many keystrokes as you want to put in it. Its size is limited only by the amount of storage space on your disk.

6. If you write a macro, you can include IF, SET, ASK, and the other instructions described in Chapter 9.

KEY POINTS

Table 10.4 summarizes the keys introduced in this chapter.

Key or key Combination	Function
F3	Expand a macro name
Shift-F3	Start or stop recording a macro

Table 10.2   Keys introduced in Chapter 10.

1. A macro is a sequence of keystrokes (text or commands) that Word plays back when you tell it to.

2. To create a macro, you can either **record** it as you type or **write** it on the screen and then save it all at once.

3. To record a macro, press Shift-F3 to issue a Record Macro command. (Word displays "RM" on the status line.) Type the keystrokes you want the macro to replay, and then press Shift-F3 again to stop recording the macro.

    Finally, when the COPY prompt appears, type a name for the macro. If you want to activate the macro with a key command (e.g., Ctrl-X-Y)), type a caret (^) and then press the keys and press Enter.

4. To write a macro, type its text and command codes on the screen. (See Table 10.1 for the command codes). Then highlight the macro contents and Copy or Delete them to the glossary. Name the macro as described in Step 3.

5. When you reach the place in a document where you want to replay a macro, do one of three things:

    - Type the macro's name and press F3 (for Expand Glossary).

    - If you assigned the macro to a key combination, press those keys.

    - To select from a list of available macro names, issue an Insert command, press F1 to get the list, then highlight the name of the macro you want, and press Enter.

6. To edit an existing macro, first Insert its contents on the screen by typing its name and a caret (^). Edit it as usual; then select it and Copy or Delete it to the glossary with the same name or a different one.

7. Word lets you start one macro from within another, or **nest** them. To nest an existing macro in the one you're defining, issue a start command for the existing macro.

8. Word's normal glossary (NORMAL.GLY) contains a number of useful, predefined macros; Word's MACRO.GLY contains even more of them.

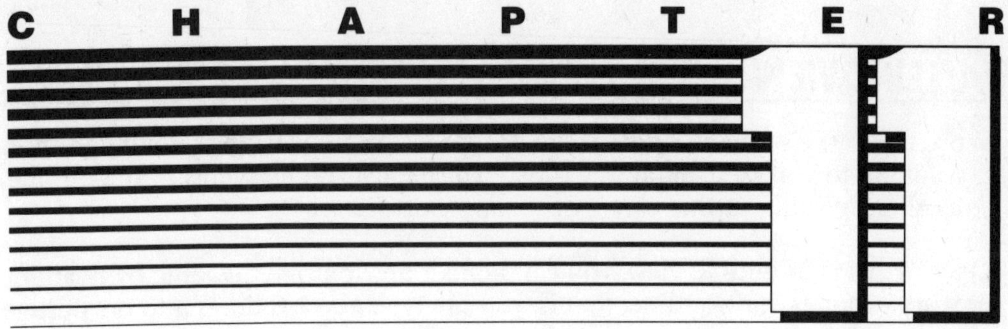

OUTLINING

Unless your document is simple and short, you will probably spend quite a bit of time preparing an outline for it. If you're like most people, you start by doing a simple outline that contains only first- and second-level headings. Then you examine this first attempt and decide what to change.

You may want to make the outline more detailed by inserting new subsection headings. You may also want to delete headings or change their priority (say, raise a second-level heading to first level). Or you may want to rearrange the outline, and move certain sections from one part of the outline to another.

You may also want to number the section headings in the outline. Section numbering is especially common for term papers, research reports, and technical specifications and manuals.

With some word processors, you must keep your outline in a separate document file or, worse, keep it at the beginning of the document. With Word's windows capabilities, either of those approaches would probably be tolerable, but Word's outline view is designed with a rather unique concept that makes it much easier to work with outlines. This chapter covers outlining with Word in detail.

OUTLINE VIEW

Word treats the outline as *part* of the document you're working on but can show the outline to you by itself at any time. To see just the headings in the outline, you call up Word's **outline view** by pressing Shift-F2.

Once Word is in outline view, you can build a new outline, heading by heading, or work on an existing outline; that is, you can type new headings into the outline or edit the headings that are already there. The Word manual refers to this as the **outline edit mode**. You can also switch to an **outline organize mode** in which you can move, copy, or delete headings.

Entering Headings

To enter outline headings on a typewriter, you must indent them manually by inserting spaces or using the Tab key. But with Word, the process is much simpler. First, Word always assumes that your next heading is at the same level as the current heading; thus, it positions the cursor at that indent value when you press Enter.

To enter a heading that has a different indent level from the previous heading, you must precede the heading with one of two key commands:

- Press Alt-0 to move the indentation to the right (to get a lower-level heading).

- Press Alt-9 to move the indentation to the left (to get a higher-level heading).

Figure 11.1 shows an outline that has three levels of headings. ("Fundamentals of Computers" is a first-level heading; "Loading DOS" is a second-level heading; and "Entering the Time and Date" is a third-level heading.) Further, it has the indentation that Word provides: four-tenths of an inch (0.4") between levels.

```
    Fundamentals of Computers
    Getting Started
        Loading DOS
            Entering the Time and Date
            Finding What's On the Disk
        Starting BASIC
            Running a BASIC Program
        Operating Your PC
            Setting Up the Computer
            Working with Disks
            Printer Care
            Keyboard and Display Care
            Computer Care
    BASIC
    Disk Operating System (DOS)
    Sound, Graphics, and Color
```

Figure 11.1   Sample outline.

Understandably, Word does not allow you to move the indentation more than one level up or down from the previous level. For example, if you have just entered a third-level heading, your next heading can only be at the second, third, or fourth level.

Editing Headings

In outline edit mode, you can edit headings just like regular text. That is, you can add, delete, or change characters or words. You can also raise or lower a heading's level by positioning the cursor anywhere in the heading and pressing Alt-9 or Alt-0, respectively.

As mentioned previously, Word will not let you make an illegal indentation change, however. For example, in the sample outline, Word would not let you move the second-level heading "Loading DOS" to the left because it has third-level headings below it.

Adding Text to an Outline

As mentioned earlier, Word treats an outline as part of a document. Thus, once you have finished your outline (or even while you're working on it), you can start filling in the text that follows each heading. In Word's terminology, you can start entering the **body text**. You can do this in either regular document view or in the outline view's outline edit mode.

To insert body text in outline edit mode, perform the following steps:

1. Move the cursor to the end of the outline heading that is to precede the text.
2. Press Enter to start a new paragraph.
3. Press Alt-P.

Word inserts a "T" in the left margin and shows "Text" at the bottom left corner of the screen to indicate that this is body text rather than an outline heading. From there, simply type whatever belongs in that section. Word always puts body text at the left margin. Figure 11.2 (see next page) shows the sample outline from before, but with some body text inserted.

```
     Fundamentals of Computers
     Getting Started
 T This chapter explains how to load the Disk Operating System
     (DOS), enter the date and time, determine what is on your disk,
     load BASIC, and run programs.  In short, you will learn
     everything needed to start working with your computer.
          Loading DOS
               Entering the Time and Date
               Finding What's On the Disk
 T The next step is to find out which programs your disk contains.
     To do this, type DIR (for Directory) and press Enter.
          Starting BASIC
               Running a BASIC Program
          Operating Your PC
               Setting Up the Computer
               Working with Disks
               Printer Care
               Keyboard and Display Care
               Computer Care
 BASIC
 Disk Operating System (DOS)
 Sound, Graphics, and Color
```

Figure 11.2   Outline with body text inserted.

ORGANIZING OUTLINES

As mentioned earlier, Word also has an **outline organize mode** in which you can move, copy, or delete headings. To switch from the outline edit mode to the outline organize mode, press Shift-F5. When you do this, Word displays "ORGANIZE" at the bottom left corner of the screen and highlights the current heading or text paragraph.

Once Word is in outline organize mode, you can move to the heading you want to operate on, select any additional material (if necessary), and then perform the operation. Word provides a variety of commands for selecting material, as summarized in Table 11.1. Remember that a "higher" level heading is one with less indentation, while a "lower" level heading is one with more indentation.

Material to be selected	Key
Preceding heading at the same level	Up arrow
Next heading at the same level	Down arrow
Preceding heading, regardless of level	Left arrow
Next heading, regardless of level	Right arrow
Nearest heading at the next higher level	Home
Last subheading at the next lower level	End
All subheadings and body text below the current heading	F6
The current heading, and later headings at the same level	F6, then Down arrow

Table 11.1   Selecting material in outline organize mode.

To **move** the material you have selected, issue a Delete command or press Del to delete it to the scrap. To **copy** selected material, issue a Copy command or press Alt-F3 to copy it to the scrap. Then move the highlight to the heading that should follow the moved or copied material and issue an Insert command or press Ins.

To delete material, select the material to be deleted, and then issue a Delete command or press Del.

COLLAPSING AND EXPANDING OUTLINES

Sometimes you may want to view just outline headings and hide the text and subheadings beneath them. In outline view, Word lets you hide body text and subheadings by **collapsing** them. (Note that collapsed material is only hidden from sight. It has not been deleted.) Later, you can **expand** the outline to display the hidden material. Table 11.2 summarizes Word's primary collapse and expand commands.

Operation	Key or key combination
Collapse subheadings and body text below a heading	Minus (-) on numeric keypad
Collapse body text below a heading	Shift-minus on numeric keypad
Expand the level below a heading	Plus (+) on numeric keypad
Expand all subheadings below a heading	Asterisk (*) on numeric keypad
Expand body text below a heading	Shift-plus on numeric keypad

Table 11.2   Outline collapse and expand commands.

You can also expand all headings and body text, that is, "uncollapse" everything, by following these steps:

1. Press Shift-F10 to select the entire document.
2. Press * (asterisk on the numeric keypad) to expand all the headings.
3. Press Shift-+ (+ on the numeric keypad) to expand all body text.

Word marks collapsed material in two ways:

- If you collapse a heading that has only body text below it, Word puts a **t** to the left of that heading.
- If you collapse a heading that has subheadings below it, Word puts a **+** to the left of that heading.

Figure 11.3 shows a sample outline with all body text and third-level headings collapsed. Only the first- and second-level headings remain displayed.

```
            Fundamentals of Computers
        t Getting Started
        +      Loading DOS
        +      Starting BASIC
        +      Operating Your PC
          BASIC
          Disk Operating System (DOS)
          Sound, Graphics, and Color
```

Figure 11.3   Collapsed outline.

OUTLINING AN EXISTING DOCUMENT

You can also outline a document that already exists by following these steps:

1. Press Shift-F2 to switch to outline view.

2. Select each heading and press Alt-9 to tell Word that the heading is a level 1 outline heading.

3. Go through the entire document and use Alt-0 to lower the appropriate subordinate headings.

4. Issue a Transfer Save to record your newly outlined document on disk.

NUMBERING DOCUMENTS

When you are in outline view, you can make Word number headings in a document automatically. You can use either of two predefined numbering formats for your documents:

Default	I. A. 1. a) (1) (a) i), etc.
Legal	1. 1.1 1.1.1 1.1.1.1, etc.

Numbering an Outline

To number an outline in Word's default format, follow these steps:

1. Press Shift-F2 to switch to outline view.

2. Issue a Library Number command.

3. When the Library Number form appears, select **Update** and set the "restart sequence" option to **Yes**.

4. Press Enter.

Figure 11.4 shows the sample outline (fully expanded again) after being numbered using the default format.

```
   I.  Fundamentals of Computers
   II.  Getting Started
 T This chapter explains how to load the Disk Operating System
   (DOS), enter the date and time, determine what is on your disk,
   load BASIC, and run programs.  In short, you will learn
   everything needed to start working with your computer.
      A.   Loading DOS
         1.  Entering the Time and Date
         2.  Finding What's On the Disk
 T The next step is to find out which programs your disk contains.
   To do this, type DIR (for Directory) and press Enter.
      B.   Starting BASIC
         1.  Running a BASIC Program
      C.   Operating Your PC
         1.  Setting Up the Computer
         2.  Working with Disks
         3.  Printer Care
         4.  Keyboard and Display Care
         5.  Computer Care
   III.  BASIC
   IV.  Disk Operating System (DOS)
   V.  Sound, Graphics, and Color
```

Figure 11.4   Outline numbered with default format.

To number an outline in the legal format, follow these steps:

1. Press Shift-F2 to switch to outline view.

2. Move the cursor to the beginning of the outline and type **1.** followed by a space or tab.

3. Issue a Library Number command.

4. When the Library Number form appears, select **Update** and set "restart sequence" to **Yes**.

5. Press Enter.

Renumbering

If you add new headings to your outline or reorganize the outline in outline organize mode, you can have Word renumber your document by following these steps:

1. Position the cursor on the first number in the outline.

2. Issue a Library Number command.

3. When the Library Number form appears, select **Update** and set "restart sequence" to **Yes**.

4. Press Enter.

Removing Numbering

You can also remove numbering entirely at any time. Simply position the cursor on the first number in the outline, issue a Library Number command, type **r** for **Remove**, and press Enter.

KEY POINTS

Table 11.3 summarizes the keys and commands introduced in this chapter.

Key Combination	Function
Shift-F2	Switch between document view and outline view
Shift-F5	Switch between outline edit and outline organize
Alt-0	Lower a heading level (move it right)
Alt-9	Raise a heading level (move it left)
Alt-P	Enter body text in an outline

Command	Function
Library Number Update	Number or renumber an outline
Library Number Remove	Remove numbering from an outline

Table 11.3   Keys and commands introduced in Chapter 11.

1. Word lets you create an outline, heading by heading, and add body text to it to build a document.

2. To work with an outline, switch to outline view by pressing Shift-F2.

3. When you enter outline view, Word puts you in an outline edit mode in which you can enter and revise headings and body text.

4. After you enter a heading, Word assumes that you want to enter another heading at the same level. To move the indentation to the right (to get a lower-level heading), press Alt-0. To move the indentation to the left (to get a higher-level heading), press Alt-9.

5. To add body text to an outline, press Enter and then Alt-P.

6. The outline organize mode lets you move, copy, and delete headings. To obtain it, press Shift-F5 from outline edit mode. ("ORGANIZE" appears at the bottom left corner of the screen.)

7. To move, copy, or delete a heading in outline organize mode, select it and issue a Delete or Copy command. To paste it in place, press Ins.

8. You can **collapse** headings and text to hide them and then **expand** the outline to reveal the hidden material. Word marks collapsed headings with a + and collapsed body text with a **t**.

9. To outline an existing document, switch to outline view and press Alt-9 on each heading. Then correct subordinate headings with Alt-0.

10. You can number or renumber outline headings by using the Library Number command and selecting **Update**. Similarly, you can remove numbering from an outline by using Library Number's **Remove** option.

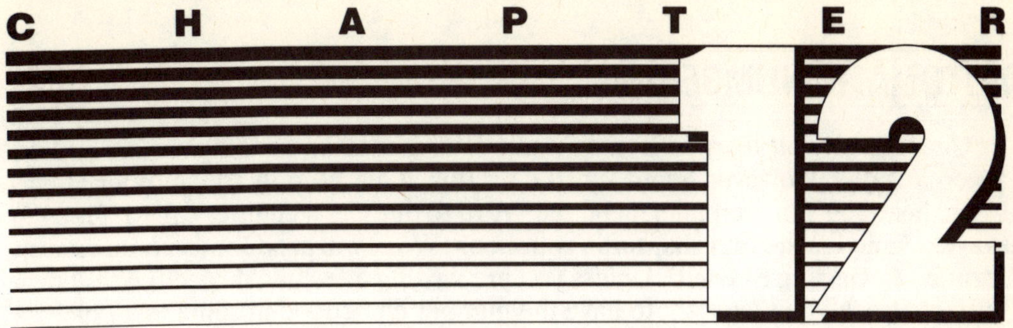

ADVANCED REPORT FEATURES

In addition to outlining, Word has a variety of other features that can speed up your work. With Word, you can perform the following tasks, all of which are covered in this chapter:

- Number headings and captions automatically.

- Generate a table of contents, index, and other lists and tables that are keyed to page numbers.

- Insert named **bookmarks** in your text, and jump to them from anywhere in the document.

- Create **cross-references** that let you produce citations such as "Figure 4 on page 12 lists quarterly sales for the Central Region."

- Perform mathematical calculations on rows and columns of numbers and on numbers embedded in text.

- Draw borders around paragraphs and shade them.

- Draw lines and boxes to create bar charts or organizational charts, or to simply dress up material.

- Insert comments, called **annotations**, that Word will number and print just like footnotes.

AUTOMATIC NUMBERING

In Chapter 11, you learned how to make Word number headings in an outline automatically. However, when Word does this, it always puts the number ahead of the heading. For example, if you tell Word to number a chapter called "Getting Started," and it's the first chapter in your book, Word will produce (with its default format) **I. Getting Started**. Unless you are writing a technical specification or a legal contract, you may want to have the number embedded in some text (such as "Chapter *n*" or "Table *n*"). You may also want to use Arabic numbering rather than Roman and produce **Chapter 1. Getting Started**.

Fortunately, Word has an automatic numbering feature that can number items in a series. The term "items," refers to figures, illustrations, examples, tables, chapters, sections, or parts. In fact, an item can be anything that is numbered consecutively. To make Word number items in a series, you assign a **series code** of your choice to the series and insert the code wherever the item's number is to be printed. (This is a minor drawback with automatic numbering. The outline displays its numbers on the screen; the numbers in a series only appear when you print the document.)

Numbering Items with a Series Code

To obtain automatic numbering for an item in a series, do the following:

1. Type any text that should precede the item's number. (For a table, you might type "Table" and a space; for a chapter heading, you might type "Chapter" and a space; and so on.)

2. Move the cursor to where you want Word to print the item number. Then type a series code name and a colon (:).

   A series code name can be up to 31 characters long. It can contain an underscore (_) character, period, or hyphen, but cannot begin or end with these characters. It cannot contain spaces. For example, you might type "table:" to number a series of tables or "chapter:" to number chapters.

3. Press F3 to designate the name as a series code. Word puts parentheses around the name, as in "(table:)."

4. Repeat these steps for each item in the series, that is, for each table, chapter, or whatever.

Specifying the Number for an Item

Word normally starts numbering items from **1**, but you can have Word start with a number you want. You can even have it restart the numbering at any time. You may want to restart numbering if, say, your report consists of several documents (one for each chapter) that you will Print Merge and you want figure numbers to start with **1** in each chapter.

To specify the number for an item, type its series code name, followed by two colons (::) and a number that is one less than the number you want to use. Then press F3. For example, to tell Word to assign the number 7 to the series code for a table, type **table::6** before pressing F3.

TABLES OF CONTENTS

Word can compile a table of contents if you tell it what to include, or **designate** the entries. The easiest way to designate entries for a table of contents is to define headings as outline entries, as described in Chapter 11. The Word command that compiles the table of contents can use the outline entries directly.

If you don't have an outline or don't want to use its headings, you can mark material (usually section headings) as table of contents entries and tell Word how much to indent each entry. Then you can compile the table of contents from those entries.

In either case, Word puts the table of contents in a new division at the end of your document so you can work on it (if necessary) without affecting anything else. You can make any changes to it there and then move it to the beginning.

Designating Table of Contents Entries

A table of contents entry consists of three things:

- a table code (.c.) formatted as hidden text
- the text for the entry
- a semicolon (;), which serves as the **endmark**, formatted as hidden text

The Word manual details the procedure for marking an entry with the hidden table code and endmark, but it's much easier to use a supplied macro for this purpose.

Designating Entries with a Supplied Macro

The macro that marks material for the table of contents is called **toc_entry.mac**, and is contained in MACRO.GLY. Thus, you must issue a Transfer Glossary Load command and specify MACRO.GLY before you start marking table of contents entries.

Once you have loaded MACRO.GLY, you can mark each table of contents entry as follows:

1. Highlight the text you want included in the table of contents. You can use F6 (Extend) for this purpose.
2. Press Ctrl-TE to run **toc_entry.mac**.

The **toc_entry.mac** macro puts a hidden **.c.** code ahead of your text and a hidden semicolon after it.

Designating Subentries

The hidden starting code and endmark define the enclosed text as a first-level contents entry that Word will print at the left margin. To designate a subentry, you must precede the subheading text with one hidden semicolon for each level you want it indented.

These semicolons belong between the starting **.c.** code and the first character in the entry. Thus, to designate a second-level entry, insert one hidden semicolon; to designate a third-level entry, insert two hidden semicolons; and so on, as in the following examples:

```
.c.Getting Started;              (First-level entry)
.c.;Loading DOS;                 (Second-level entry)
.c.;;Entering the Date and Time; (Third-level entry)
```

As you may recall, to produce hidden text, you must press Alt-E (or Alt-XE, with a style sheet), type the text, and then press Alt-Spacebar to turn off the hidden text feature.

Compiling a Table of Contents

You are now ready to generate, or **compile**, the table of contents—well, almost; you must first take care of a potential problem.

When Word generates the page numbers for the table of contents, it includes not only regular text, but any hidden text that is **visible** (i.e., if the "show hidden text" option is not turned off). Extra hidden text could produce incorrect page numbers. Hence, if your document contains hidden text (other than the table of contents markers), you should make hidden text invisible before you continue.

With that in mind, the procedure to compile a table of contents is as follows:

1. Issue an Options command, and set "show hidden text" to **No**.

2. Issue a Library Table command. Word displays the form shown in Figure 12.1.

```
LIBRARY TABLE from: Outline(Codes)      index code: C
         page numbers:(Yes)No           entry/page number separated by: ^t
         indent each level: 0.4"        use style sheet: Yes(No)
```

Figure 12.1   Library Table form.

3. What you do next depends on how you want to compile the table of contents. Note the following two options:

   - To compile the table of contents from an outline, select **Outline** in the "from" field.

   - To compile the table of contents from table codes, select **Codes** in the "from" field.

4.   Press Enter.

Word compiles the table of contents and moves the cursor to the beginning of the table. The table has right-aligned page numbers and its entries are indented according to the indentation of your outline entries or the number of semicolons in your table codes.

To mark the table of contents, Word encloses the table with two hidden paragraphs. It precedes the table with ".Begin Table C." and follows it with ".End Table C. " (See Figure 12.2.) Because you made hidden text invisible before compiling the table of contents, you will need to make it visible again (with the Option command) to see these paragraphs. When you move the table of contents to the beginning of your document, be sure to move these paragraphs too.

```
.Begin Table C.
Fundamentals of Computers                        1
Getting Started1                                 6
   Loading DOS1                                  7
         Entering the Time and Date1             7
         Finding What's On the Disk1             9
   Starting BASIC                               20
         Running a BASIC Program                22
   Operating Your PC                            25
         Setting Up the Computer                26
         Working with Disks                     28
         Printer Care                           31
         Keyboard and Display Care              33
         Computer Care                          35
      .            (Rest of table of contents)
      .
      .
.End Table C.
```

Figure 12.2   *Sample table of contents.*

Recompiling a Table of Contents

If you change the headings in a document or change text that affects the pagination, you will want to compile your table of contents again. To do this, make the hidden text invisible again and issue another Library Table command. Now, because you already have a table of contents, Word will let you replace it or append another table of contents to the end of the document (and leave the current table intact).

INDEXES

You can also make Word generate an index for your document based on words or phrases you specify. Generating an index involves the same procedures you use to generate a table of contents; that is, you designate the index entries by marking them, and then you compile the index.

Designating Index Entries

An index entry consists of three things:

- An index code (.i.) formatted as hidden text
- The text for the entry
- A semicolon (;), which serves as the **endmark**, formatted as hidden text

The Word manual details the procedure for marking an entry with the hidden index code and endmark, but it's much easier to use a supplied macro for this purpose.

Designating Entries with a Supplied Macro

The macro that marks material for the index is called **index_entry.mac**, and it is contained in MACRO.GLY. Thus, you must issue a Transfer Glossary Load command, and specify MACRO.GLY, before you start marking index entries.

Once you have loaded MACRO.GLY, you can mark each index entry as follows:

1. Highlight the text you want included in the index. You can use F6 (Extend) for this purpose.

2. Press Ctrl-IE to run **index_entry.mac.**

The **toc_entry.mac** macro puts a hidden **.i.** code ahead of your text and a hidden semicolon after it.

Designating Entries, Using a Separate Document

Sometimes you will want the index to contain *every* occurrence of a word or phrase. Word's MACRO.GLY glossary contains a macro called **index.mac** that will locate and mark all occurrences of specific words or phrases contained in a separate document whose name you specify. This document, often called a "concordance file," lists the entries that belong in an index, one entry per line. Once you have activated MACRO.GLY (with a Transfer Glossary Load command), you can run **index.mac** by pressing Ctrl-IW.

Designating Subentries

You can designate up to five levels of subentries below an index entry. To designate a subentry, you precede it with all higher-level subentries (and the main entry), and separate them with colons. Table 12.2 shows some examples.

To obtain this:	Type this in the text:
`Computer 16`	.i.Computer;
`Computer` `   starting 17`	.i.Computer:Starting;

`Computer`
`   starting`
`      With a hard disk 17`
`      With floppy disks 19`
	.i.Computer:Starting:With a hard disk;
	.i.Computer:Starting:With floppy disks;

Table 12.1   Sample index entries.

Naming Entries Yourself

Sometimes you may want your index to include phrases that don't appear in the text or don't appear in the form you want. You may also want to include an inverted entry, e.g., "Sales, foreign" instead of "Foreign sales." Finally, you may want to include "see" citations for cross-referencing, e.g., a "Foreign sales" entry with "*See* Sales, foreign" below it.

In each case, put the entry you want into your document, but format its text as hidden. For example, to obtain the following entry,

```
Foreign sales
    See Sales, foreign
```

type **.i.Foreign sales:See Sales, foreign;** as hidden text in your document.

As you may recall, to produce hidden text, press Alt-E (or Alt-XE, with a style sheet), type the text, and then press Alt-Spacebar to turn off the hidden text feature.

Compiling an Index

You are now ready to generate, or compile, the index. But, as with the table of contents, you must first take care of a potential problem.

When Word generates the page numbers for the index, it includes not only regular text, but any hidden text that is visible (i.e., "show hidden text" option is on). Extra hidden text could produce incorrect page numbers. Hence, you should make hidden text invisible before you continue.

With that in mind, the procedure to compile an index is as follows:

1. Issue an Options command, and set "show hidden text" to **No**.

2. Issue a Library Index command. Word displays the form shown in Figure 12.3.

```
LIBRARY INDEX entry/page # separated by:     cap main entries:(Yes)No
              indent each level: 0.2"        use style sheet: Yes(No)
```

Figure 12.3   Library Index form.

3. Press Enter.

Word compiles the index and puts it in a new division at the end of your document. To mark the index, Word encloses it with two hidden paragraphs. It precedes the index with **.Begin Index I.** and follows it with **.End Index I.** Because you made hidden text invisible before compiling the index, you would need to make it visible again (with the Option command) to see these paragraphs. If you move the index to anywhere else in your document, be sure to move these paragraphs too.

Recompiling an Index

If you add, delete, or change index entries or make text changes that affect the pagination, you will want to compile your index again. To do this, make the hidden text invisible (if it isn't already) and issue another Library Index command. Now, because you already have an index, Word will let you replace it or cancel the Library Index operation.

OTHER LISTS AND TABLES

You can also use Word's Library Table feature to produce other lists and tables that contain page numbers. This is handy for generating lists of figures or examples, or producing a table of contents for a chapter.

Designating Entries

Recall that each table of contents entry has a hidden table code (.c.) at the beginning and a hidden semicolon at the end. You can easily designate an entry for some other kind of list by preceding it with a hidden starting code that contains some other letter. In addition to **c**, Word uses the letters **d**, **g**, **i**, and **l** for its own purposes, so you can't use those letters. But you can use any other letter.

You might use **f**, for example, to designate entries for a list of figures. Or you might use **e** to designate entries for a list of examples. For example, the following,

```
.f.Figure 1.   Earning projections;
```

(with **.f.** and the semicolon marked as hidden text) designates this title as an entry in a list of figures.

Compiling a List or Table

To compile your list or table, do the following:

1. Issue an Options command, and set "show hidden text" to **No**.

2. Issue a Library Table command.

3. When the form appears, tab to the "index code" field and type the letter you used in the starting code for your list or table.

4. Press Enter.

Word compiles the list at the end of your document and moves the cursor to the beginning of it. To mark the list, Word encloses it with two hidden paragraphs. It precedes the table with **.Begin Table** x**.** and follows it with **.End Table** x**.**, where x is your code letter.

Because you made hidden text invisible before compiling the list, you will need to make it visible again (with the Option command) to see these paragraphs. If you move the list somewhere else in your document, be sure to move these paragraphs too.

BOOKMARKS

Just as you can mark your place in a book by putting a bookmark there, Word lets you insert computerized bookmarks in your documents. In fact, Word's bookmarks are even better than regular bookmarks because they mark a specific block of text instead of an entire page. Moreover, you can use as many bookmarks as you want; each has a name that you can use to reach it from anywhere in a document.

Word's bookmarks have a variety of uses. You can use one to mark the following:

- The place where you quit working on a document you are revising.

- A place in a report that needs a statistic or name that you don't yet have.

- A table or list that you want to view while you are writing about it. This would be handy if you had different parts of the same document in two Word windows. You could use the bookmark to locate the table you want to display in the second window.

- A page or footnote number you want to refer to within a report. Word has a cross-referencing feature that inserts bookmarked page and footnote numbers in a citation. This feature is discussed later in this chapter under "Cross-Referencing."

Designating a Bookmark

Each bookmark consists of the text you want to refer to and a name. A **bookmark name** can be up to 31 characters long. It can contain an underscore (_) character, period, or hyphen, but cannot begin or end with these characters. It cannot contain colons (:) or spaces.

To designate text as a bookmark, do the following:

1. Select the text you want to use.
2. Issue a Format bookmarK command.
3. Type a name for the bookmark.
4. Press Enter.

You can designate a specific block of text with as many bookmark names as you want, as long as the names are different from one another.

Jumping to a Bookmark

To jump to a bookmark, issue a Jump bookmarK command and enter the bookmark's name when Word asks for it. Word highlights the bookmark text.

Unmarking a Bookmark

When you no longer need to refer to a block of bookmarked text, you may want to unmark it. To do this, use Jump bookmarK to reach the text and issue a Format bookmarK command. When Word asks for the name, press Enter. Then type **y** to confirm that you want to remove the bookmark designation.

CROSS-REFERENCING

Reports, manuals, proposals, and other large documents often include references to pages, sections, chapters, figures, tables, or notes. For example, your document may include a reference such as the following: "As the Sales By Division graph on page 12 shows. . . ."

With many word processing programs, you must keep track of such references yourself and change the reference number yourself if the associated "target" (figure, page, table, etc.) is renumbered. However, Word provides a **cross-reference** feature that maintains these cross-references for you.

Creating Cross-References

Word lets you create a reference to a page number, footnote number, or the number of an item in a series (see "Automatic Numbering" at the beginning of this chapter). In all three cases, you must designate the target text as a bookmark, so read the preceding "Bookmarks" section, if you haven't already.

To mark a location on a page for cross-referencing, highlight the text you want to serve as the target of the cross-reference and use Format bookmarK to designate the text as a bookmark. To make an in-text reference to that page, type **page:** and the bookmark name, and then press F3. Word encloses "page:" and the bookmark name in parentheses.

For example, suppose your report contains a discussion of sales projections, and you designated the beginning of it as a bookmark named "sales_projs." You could then refer to it with a sentence such as the following:

See the discussion of sales projections on page (page:sales_projs).

To mark a footnote number for cross-referencing, highlight some text immediately following the footnote reference mark (the cross-reference target) and use Format bookmarK to designate the text as a bookmark. To make an in-text reference to the preceding footnote number, type **footnote:** and the bookmark name, and then press F3. Word encloses "footnote:" and the bookmark name in parentheses.

To mark an item in a series for cross-referencing, highlight a block of text that immediately precedes the series code name (e.g., "chapter:") and use Format bookmarK to designate the text as a bookmark. When you name the bookmark, use a name that is appropriate to that particular item (rather than the entire series). For example, suppose your report contains tables of sales for 1986, 1987, 1988, and 1989. You could use the name "sales88" for the 1988 sales table.

To make an in-text reference to the number of the item, type the series code name followed by the bookmark name (e.g., type **table:sales88**), and then press F3. Word encloses the names in parentheses.

Multiple References

In some cases you may want to refer to something in more than one way, as in the following example:

Figure 3 on page 12 lists the major accounts in the Southeast region.

Here, you would mark "Figure 3" with two bookmarks (one for its page number, the other for its item number) and make one cross-reference after "Figure" and another after "page."

MATHEMATICAL OPERATIONS

Word has a built-in calculator that lets you add, subtract, multiply, divide, and produce percentages. The calculator can perform these operations on numeric tables or even on numbers in text. It can also produce the answer to an equation, or **expression**, such as **23.5+16.74-32.1**.

Using the Calculator

Word provides five operators that you can use to tell it what to do:

<table>
<tr><td></td><td>To do this</td><td>Use this operator</td></tr>
<tr><td></td><td>Add</td><td>+ (or no operator)</td></tr>
<tr><td></td><td>Subtract</td><td>- (or parentheses around a number)</td></tr>
<tr><td></td><td>Multiply</td><td>*</td></tr>
<tr><td></td><td>Divide</td><td>/</td></tr>
<tr><td></td><td>Get percentage</td><td>%</td></tr>
</table>

Table 12.2   Word's arithmetic operators.

To use the calculator, simply highlight the material on which you want to operate and press the F2 (**Calculate**) key. Word puts the result in the scrap; you can insert it anywhere by pressing Ins.

For example, if you highlight the expression **112+243** and press F2, Word puts **355** in the scrap. This even works in text. If you highlight the phrase **112 cars and 243 trucks** and then press F2, Word's calculator ignores the text and puts **355** in the scrap. Note here that because the text does not include an operator, Word performs an addition. Similarly, if you highlight a row in a table or a column (using Shift-F6) and press F2, Word will add the numbers and put the total in the scrap.

You can also build an expression, using the operators. For example, if you highlight the following,

(112.4+36.765)/34.892

and press F2, Word will add the numbers in parentheses, then divide the sum by 34.892, and put 4.275 in the scrap. Word's calculator is quite precise; it can produce results up to 14 digits long.

DRAWING LINES, BOXES, AND BORDERS

Word has a **Format Border** command that can draw a border around a paragraph or draw a line to the left, right, above, or below a paragraph. Format Border can also add shading to a paragraph.

Word also has a related command, **Line Draw**, that lets you draw lines of any length or boxes of any size by simply moving the cursor. This feature is handy for creating bar charts, organizational charts, and decorative borders.

Format Border vs. Line Draw

The Format Border command and the Line Draw command have their own unique advantages and drawbacks, but together they make up a handy pair of line-drawing tools.

Format Border is convenient in that it always "knows" the size of a paragraph, and draws its borders accordingly. It will even change the length of the border lines if you change the size of the paragraph. Moreover, if you tell Format Border to draw a box around a paragraph (rather than draw selected lines), Word will always protect that paragraph against being divided between two pages. If any part of a boxed paragraph flows onto the next page, Word moves the entire paragraph to the next page.

On the other hand, Format Border can only draw with solid lines (although they can be bold, thick, or double lines), and it always operates on individual paragraphs. If you select several consecutive paragraphs and then issue a Format Border command, Word will draw border lines around each paragraph.

Line Draw is more versatile than Format Border but is more difficult to use. With Line Draw, you draw lines by moving the cursor; in effect, you attach a "pen" to the cursor. What's more, you can draw with a variety of characters, or even draw horizontal lines different from vertical lines.

But, unlike Format Border, Line Draw doesn't protect boxed text from being split between pages. Nor can you use it to draw a box around an existing paragraph. If you try to draw a vertical line down the left or right edge of a paragraph, Line Draw will *overwrite* any characters along those edges.

Of course, because Format Border and Line Draw are separate commands, you can use them individually to do what you want. As mentioned earlier, these commands together comprise a powerful pair of drawing tools.

Adding Paragraph Borders and Shading

When you position the cursor inside a paragraph and issue a Format Border command, Word displays the form shown in Figure 12.4. Here, you would type **b** to draw a box or type **l** to draw individual lines.

```
FORMAT BORDER type:(None)Box Lines    line style: Normal    color: Black
   left: Yes(No)         right: Yes(no)   above: Yes(no)       below: Yes(No)
   background shading: 0                  shading color: Black
```

Figure 12.4   Format Border form.

Fill out the rest of the form as follows:

- The "line style" option assumes that you want **Normal** single lines, but you can press F1 and choose from **Bold, Double,** or **Thick.**

- If you have a color printer, press F1 in the "color" field and select a line color from the displayed choices.

- If you choose Lines for "type," you must then tell Word which lines you want by typing **y** (for **Yes**) in "left," "right," "above," or "below."

- If you want a shaded paragraph, move to "background shading" and type a number between 1 (very light) to 100 (solid). Or you can press F1 and select from Word's choices. You can also specify the "shading color" if you have a color printer.

You can remove border lines or shading at any time with another Format Border command. To remove all border lines, type **n** (for **None**) in the "type" field. To remove a selected line, set that line's field to **No.** To remove shading, type **0** in the "background shading" field.

Using Line Draw

To draw a line or box, move the cursor to where it should start and press Ctrl-F5 to issue a Line Draw command. That turns the cursor into a "pen" that will draw a line wherever you move.

As usual, you can move one character position or one line at a time by pressing the arrow keys. Or you can press **End** or **Home** to draw a line to the paragraph's left or right margin. To turn off Line Draw, press Ctrl-F5 again.

Changing the Line Draw Character

Line Draw normally uses a regular single line to draw. But you can make it draw with something else by issuing an Options command and moving to the "linedraw character" field at the bottom right corner of General Options. (To reach this field quickly, press End followed by left arrow.) To draw with an *, $, or some other character, type that character in the "linedraw character" field. Or you can press F1 in this field to obtain a screen with 12 drawing options:

- **Single Set** (the default) and **Double Set** make Word draw with a single or double line. Both options draw a neat corner when you switch directions.

- **Hyphen/Bar Set** draws lines using regular characters, which is the best you can do if your printer cannot produce graphic lines. As its name implies, this set uses hyphens to draw horizontal lines and broken vertical bars to draw vertical lines. It uses a plus (+) character to draw corners when you switch directions.

- The remaining options let you use boxes and other graphics characters for drawing.

ANNOTATIONS

In Chapter 5, you learned how to insert footnotes in your documents. Word also provides special footnotes called **annotations** that you can use to insert comments in documents.

You could use annotations to insert reminders to yourself about jobs you still need to do. You could also use them to mark places that need information you don't yet have, such as a name, date, address, or number.

But annotations are especially useful for allowing reviewers to put in their comments. Like footnotes, annotations are numbered. But an annotation also includes a **mark** that allows a reviewer up to 28 characters for typing his or her name or initials. This mark can also include the date and time at which the annotation was created.

Entering Annotations

To enter an annotation in a document, move the cursor to where its reference mark belongs and do the following:

1. Issue a **Format Annotation** command.
2. When the form appears, type the text for the annotation "mark" (your name, initials, type of comments, etc.).
3. If you want Word to insert today's date, type **y** in the "insert date" field.
4. If you want Word to insert the current time, type **y** in the "insert time" field.
5. Press Enter.

Word moves to the end of your document, where it shows a number (**1**, if this is the first annotation) and your annotation mark, followed by the date and time, if you asked for them.

6. Type the annotation text.
7. To reach the annotation mark in the text, issue a **Jump Annotation** command.

You can also revise an annotation by highlighting the annotation mark in the document and issuing a Jump Annotation command.

Deleting Annotations

Deleting an annotation is similar to deleting a footnote: highlight the annotation mark in the document and press Del. Word also provides a macro in the MACRO.GLY file that removes all annotations from a document. To run this macro, called **annot_remove.mac**, press Ctrl-AR.

Printing Annotations

Word treats each annotation like a regular footnote and prints it on the same page as its in-text reference. However, you can easily make Word print annotations and footnotes at the end of the division or document. To do this, issue a Format Division Layout command and set "footnotes" to **End**.

QUESTIONS AND ANSWERS

I made Word number the tables in my document, but it numbered two consecutive tables "3." That threw the rest of the numbering off. What went wrong?

You probably mistyped the series code name for the second table. If you inserted "table:" for table numbers, you may have typed **tabel:** for your Table 4. Correct the table code name and reprint from there to the end.

The people who reviewed my report inserted their comments, using Word's annotation feature. I made all the changes and want to get rid of the annotations. Do I have to delete them individually?

No. The MACRO.GLY glossary includes a macro called **annot_remove.mac** that will remove all annotations at once. Press Ctrl-AR to run it.

HINTS AND WARNINGS

1. If you regularly use the same series code names to make Word number your chapters, sections, and tables, put those names in a macro. That way you needn't type them each time.

2. If your document contains any hidden text, remember to set "show hidden text" to **No** (using the Options command) before compiling a table of contents or index.

3. If you accidentally mark the wrong text for inclusion in a table of contents, list, or index, find the code at the beginning of the text and delete it. Entries for the table of contents or index begin with a code of **.c.** or **.i.,** respectively.

4. You can make Word put all occurrences of specific words and phrases into an index by listing those items in a separate document. To make Word use that document to designate index entries, load MACRO.GLY and press Ctrl-IW to run the **index.mac** macro.

KEY POINTS

Table 12.3 summarizes the keys and commands introduced in this chapter.

Key/ key combination	Function
F2	Calculate result of a math expression
F3	Mark an item for automatic numbering
Ctrl-F5	Draw a line by moving the cursor

Command	**Function**
Format Annotation	Insert a comment (annotation) in a document
Format bookmarK	Designate selected text as a bookmark, or unmark a bookmark (by pressing Enter)
Format Border	Draw border lines around a paragraph, or shade a paragraph
Jump Annotation	Move the cursor to an annotation
Jump bookmarK	Move the cursor to a bookmark
Library Index	Compile the index
Library Table	Compile the table of contents

Table 12.3   Keys and commands introduced in Chapter 12.

1. Word can number chapters, tables, sections, lists, or anything else that is numbered consecutively. To number an item in a series, type a series code name of your choice (e.g., type "chapter" where a chapter number belongs), followed by a colon (:). Then press F3 to mark the name. Word puts parentheses around the name. It will insert the numbers when you print the document.

2. Word can produce a table of contents from outline entries (as described in Chapter 11) or from entries you have marked manually.

3. Word's **toc_entry.mac** macro in MACRO.GLY marks selected text for the table of contents. Press Ctrl-TE to run it.

4. To designate a subentry for the table of contents, precede its table code (.c.) with a semicolon for each level past the first.

5. To compile the table of contents for a document, use Options to set "show hidden text" to **No**, then issue a Library Table command. Word always puts the table of contents at the end of your document.

6. You can also make Library Table compile other kinds of tables, such as lists of figures or examples. Simply precede each entry with a code of the form **.x.** (where x is any letter except c, d, g, i, or l) and follow it with a semicolon.

7. Word can generate an index from words or phrases you have marked.

8. Word's **index_entry.mac** macro in MACRO.GLY marks selected text for the index. Press Ctrl-IE to run it.

9. You can also make Word mark occurrences of words and phrases based on entries stored in another document (a "concordance file"). To do this, run the **index.mac** macro in MACRO.GLY by pressing Ctrl-IW.

10. You can designate up to five levels of subentries below an index entry. To designate a subentry, precede it with all higher-level subentries (and the main entry), and separate them with colons.

11. To compile the index for a document, use Options to set "show hidden text" to **No**, and then issue a Library Index command. As with the table of contents, Word always puts the index at the end of your document.

12. To mark text as a **bookmark**, highlight it and issue a Format bookmarK command. Enter a name for the bookmark when Word asks for it.

13. To jump to a bookmark, issue a Jump bookmarK command and enter the bookmark's name when Word asks for it. You can also unmark a bookmark by finding its text, issuing a Format bookmarK command, and then pressing Enter.

14. Word has a **cross-reference** feature that keys in-text references (e.g., "Figure 3 on page 12 summarizes our sales for 1988") to the figures, tables, footnotes, or page numbers they refer to.

15. To mark a location on a page for cross-referencing, highlight the text you want to serve as the target of the cross-reference and use Format bookmarK to designate the text as a bookmark. To make an in-text reference to that page, type **page:** and the bookmark name, and then press F3. Word encloses **page:** and the bookmark name in parentheses.

16. To mark a footnote number for cross-referencing, highlight some text immediately following the footnote reference mark (the cross-reference target) and use Format bookmarK to designate the text as a bookmark. To make an in-text reference to the preceding footnote number, type **footnote:** and the bookmark name, and then press F3. Word encloses "footnote:" and the bookmark name in parentheses.

17. To mark an item in a series for cross-referencing, highlight a block of text that immediately precedes the series code name (e.g., "chapter:") and use Format bookmarK to designate the text as a bookmark.

18. Word has a built-in calculator that lets you add, subtract, multiply, divide, and produce percentages. The calculator can perform these operations on numeric tables or on numbers embedded in text. It can also produce the answer to an equation, or **expression**, such as 23.5+16.74-32.1.

19. Word's calculator provides five **operators**: + (add), - (subtract), * (multiply), / (divide), and % (percent).

20. To use the calculator, simply highlight the material on which you want to operate and press the F2 (**Calculate**) key. Word puts the result in the scrap; you can insert it anywhere by pressing Ins.

21. Word has a **Format Border** command that can draw a border around a paragraph or draw a line to the left, right, above, or below a paragraph. Format Border can also add shading to a paragraph.

22. Word also has a **Line Draw** command that lets you draw lines of any length or boxes of any size by simply moving the cursor. To start or stop drawing lines, press Ctrl-F5. The character used to draw lines is controlled by the "linedraw character" in the Options form.

23. The Format Annotation command lets you insert footnote-like comments, called **annotations**, in your documents. An annotation also includes a **mark** (usually someone's name or initials) and the text of the comment. Word will also insert the date and time at which the annotation was created, if you tell it to.

COMMON DOS OPERATIONS

Y̲ou may occasionally want to perform some general "housekeeping" work on disks that contain Word documents. For example, you may want to copy an entire disk or a single document, or give a document a new name that's easier to remember. You can perform some of these operations from within Word, but it's often quicker and easier to perform them from the computer's Disk Operating System, **DOS**.

This appendix describes DOS operations you will probably use most often. For other operations or for more details, refer to the DOS manual that came with your computer.

STARTING DOS

To start DOS, do the following:

- With a dual floppy disk system, insert the DOS disk in the left drive (A) and switch the power on.

- With a hard disk system, simply switch the power on.

Press Enter when the computer asks for the date and time. The A (floppy disk) or C (hard disk) prompt on the screen tells you that the computer is waiting for a DOS command.

If you have two floppy disks and want to do something that involves one disk (e.g., delete a file or format a disk), put that disk in the right (or bottom) drive (B). If you want to do something that involves two disks (e.g., copy a disk), once DOS is loaded, replace the DOS disk with the source disk and put the second (destination) disk in drive B.

Using DOS from within Word

You can also enter DOS temporarily from within Word by issuing a **Library Run** command. When Word displays the following prompt,

```
LIBRARY RUN: COMMAND
```

type your DOS command and press Enter. The computer performs the DOS command and then displays the following message:

```
Press a key to resume Word
```

Press any key to leave DOS and return to your Word document.

FILENAMES

Every disk file has a name of up to eight characters. Optionally, it can have an "extension" — a period followed by one to three characters that describe what kind of information the file contains. For example, you may give letters the extension **.LET**, reports the extension **.RPT**, and so on.

When using DOS to operate on a disk file, you must enter both its name and extension. For example, to operate on a file named SALES.RPT, you would enter **SALES.RPT**. Furthermore, if the file you want is not on the active drive or hard disk directory, you must tell DOS where to find it. To do this with floppy disks, you must precede the filename with either **A:** or **B:**. Hence, you would enter **B:SALES.RPT** if A is the active drive and SALES.RPT is on the disk in drive B.

Paths and Filespecs

If you are working from a hard disk and the file you want is not in the active directory, you must precede the filename with a directory description, or "path." For example, if SALES.RPT is in the REPORTS directory of drive C, you would enter **C:\REPORTS\SALES.RPT**. The combination of drive name, path, filename, and extension is called a file specification or "filespec."

Operating on Groups of Files

DOS lets you operate on entire groups of similarly named files. You can, for example, copy or display a directory of a group of files with a single command. To do this, you use **wild card** characters that act as shorthand for "any character" or "any group of characters." You can compare them with the Joker in popular card games, a free number in Bingo, or a blank tile in Scrabble.

The character **?** means "any single character." You can put **?** anywhere in a filename — even several times. For example, the command **dir rptq28?.rpt** displays a list (directory) of report files for all second-quarter sales reports for the 1980s. Similarly, the command **dir rptq?8?.rpt** displays a list of *all* quarterly sales reports for the 1980s.

The * (asterisk) is an even more all-encompassing wild card. It tells DOS that any character can occupy that position and all remaining positions in the filename or extension. For example, the command **dir rptq*.rpt** displays all **RPTQ** report files, regardless of their quarter or year. Similarly, the command **dir rptq*.*** displays all files whose names begin with **RPTQ**, regardless of their extension.

COMMON DOS COMMANDS

The following list summarizes the DOS commands you will probably use most often. Note that here items shown in brackets are optional.

CD *\path*
    Makes the named directory active.

CHKDSK [*d:*]
    Displays a disk and memory status report.

COPY *old-filespec* [*new-filespec*]
    Copies files.

DIR [*filespec*]
    Displays name, size, date, and time of creation for file(s) on disk. If you omit the *filespec*, DIR summarizes all the files on the current floppy disk or hard disk directory.

DISKCOPY *source-drive target-drive*
    Copies an entire disk. DISKCOPY formats the target disk, if necessary.

ERASE *filespec*
    Deletes files.

FORMAT A: or **FORMAT B:**
    Prepares a disk to accept DOS files. **Note:** FORMAT *deletes* any files that are currently on the disk.

MD *\path*
    "Makes" (creates) the specified directory.

RD *\path*
    "Removes" (deletes) the specified directory. The directory must be empty.

RENAME *old-filespec new-filespec*
  Changes a file's name.

CD (Change Directory)

The CD, or "Change Directory," command puts DOS in the specified hard disk directory. The general form of the CD command is


```
CD \path
```


where *path* gives the location of the directory in respect to the higher-level directories above it.

Once you change to a directory, DOS assumes that every command you issue applies to that directory. For example, if you issue the command **ERASE REPORT.DOC**, DOS expects to find the REPORT.DOC file in the current directory.

Entering **CD **, the simplest form of the Change Directory command, puts DOS in the main or **root** directory, the one DOS starts in when you turn the power on. Similarly, **CD \WORD5** puts DOS in the Word 5.0 directory, whereas **CD \WORD5\DOCS** puts DOS in a DOCS (documents) subdirectory within the WORD5 directory.

If you specify a directory that doesn't exist, DOS ignores your CD command and displays **Invalid directory**.

CHKDSK (Check Disk)

CHKDSK tells how many files a disk contains and how many bytes (characters) are unused. It also reports on memory use. CHKDSK reports on the active disk unless you follow it with a drive name.

A typical CHKDSK report looks like this:

```
362496 bytes total disk space
350000 bytes in 12 user files
 12496 bytes available on disk

655360 bytes total memory
386672 bytes free
```

The top lines tell the disk's status. This particular disk is nearly full because only 12,496 bytes of its 362,496-byte capacity are still available.

If you try to copy a file to a disk that doesn't have room for it, DOS ignores your COPY command and displays a **Disk full** message. As a rule of thumb, when a data disk has less than 20,000 bytes available, you should change disks. Disks are inexpensive, and you do not want to lose some work because a disk is full.

COPY

As you might expect, COPY copies files. If you copy files onto another disk, you can give them the same names as the originals. If you copy them onto the floppy disk or into the hard disk directory where they are now, you must rename them. Either way, COPY does not affect the original files.

Of course, COPY requires two filespecs — a source and a destination — where the source's filespec comes first. You may omit the destination's name if it is the same as the source's. The following command copies SALES.RPT from drive A to drive B:

```
COPY SALES.RPT B:
```

You might also want to copy all document files to a new disk to make a backup. If you named the files with a .DOC extension, copy them with

```
COPY *.DOC B:
```

Finally, you might want to copy a document to use as a starting point for preparing a new document. For example, the following command makes a copy of 1989's sales report as a starting point for preparing 1990's:

```
COPY SALES89.RPT SALES90.RPT
```

DIR (Directory)

DIR displays the following information about files on a disk: filename and extension, size in characters, and the date and time it was most recently saved. A typical entry looks like this:

```
REPORT89 DOC 1920 5-29-89 9:45p
```

This tells you that the file REPORT89 has the extension DOC and is 1920 characters long. Further, 5-29-89 (May 29, 1989) is the date on which you last saved REPORT89.DOC and 9:45 p.m. is the time you saved it. Of course, these are correct only if you entered the time and date when DOS asked for them.

You can follow DIR with a filespec to limit the display to files in a particular group. Following are typical examples:

DIR   (Display all files on the active drive or hard disk directory.)
DIR B: (Display all files on drive B.)
DIR B:*.DOC   (Display all DOC files on drive B.)
DIR B:NEW*.DOC (Display only DOC files on drive B whose filenames start with NEW.)

Note that DIR differs slightly depending on whether you are using a DOS version numbered above or below the following:

- For DOS 3.0 or later, the command **DIR *.** lists only files that have no extension; to see all files regardless of extension, you must enter a **DIR *.*** command.

- For DOS versions earlier than 3.0 (e.g., DOS 2.10), the equivalent commands **DIR *** and **DIR *.*** list every file, while **DIR *.** lists files without extensions.

If your disk has many files, the directory entries may move or "scroll" by so quickly that you can't read them. To stop the scrolling temporarily, press Ctrl and Num Lock simultaneously; to stop the scrolling altogether, press Ctrl and Break (Ctrl-C).

DISKCOPY

DISKCOPY copies an entire disk's contents to another disk. The general form is as follows:

DISKCOPY *source-drive target-drive*

Note that the source drive comes first. You do **not** need to format the target disk; if necessary, DOS will format it automatically before copying to it.

ERASE

ERASE deletes files. It can delete a single file or a group of files. Typical examples are as follows:

ERASE REPORT88.DOC   (Delete only REPORT88.DOC.)
ERASE REPORT.*   (Delete every REPORT file.)
ERASE B:NEW*.DOC   (Delete DOC files that begin with NEW.)

Be careful if you use ? and * to erase a group of files, because a single misplaced character may result in the deletion of files you want to keep. To avoid disaster, issue DIR with the filespec you plan to use with ERASE. This will provide a list of all files that ERASE will delete.

If you tell DOS to delete all the files on a disk (by entering, say, **ERASE A:*.***), it gives you a chance to change your mind by displaying an **Are you sure (Y/N)?** prompt. To proceed with the deletion, type **n** and press Enter; to retain the files, type **y** and press Enter.

FORMAT

FORMAT prepares a disk to accept DOS files, including Word files. You can compare formatting a disk with drawing lines on a baseball or football field, or marking the origins and axes on a piece of graph paper. That is, formatting prepares the disk for use but doesn't actually do anything with it.

The drive name after FORMAT specifies the disk to be formatted, as in

```
FORMAT B:
```

This is the form you would normally use to prepare a new Word document disk.

Warning: If your computer has a hard disk drive (C, D, or whatever), do *not* enter **FORMAT C:**. Depending upon which version you have, DOS may wipe your hard disk clean, causing you to lose everything.

MD (Make Directory)

This command creates a new directory on a hard disk. The general form of the MD command is as follows,

MD *path*

where *path* gives the location of the new directory in respect to the higher-level directories above it. For example, the command **MD \LETTERS** creates a directory called LETTERS that is one level below the root directory.

The similar command **MD \WORD5\LETTERS** also creates a LETTERS directory, but the term \WORD5\ makes LETTERS a subdirectory *within* the WORD5 directory. Such a subdirectory is handy for storing files produced by the program contained in the directory above it. In this case, LETTERS could be used to hold letters that you create with Word.

The MD command simply creates a directory. To make the computer use that directory, you must issue a CD (Change Directory) command. For example, the command **CD \WORD5\LETTERS** puts DOS in the LETTERS subdirectory that is contained in the WORD5 directory.

RD (Remove Directory)

This command removes (deletes) the specified directory from a hard disk. The general form of the RD command is as follows:

RD *\path*

where *path* gives the location of the directory with respect to the higher-level directories above it. Note the following examples:

- The command **RD \LETTERS** deletes a directory called LETTERS that is one level below the root directory.

- The similar command **RD \WORD5\LETTERS** erases a LETTERS subdirectory that is contained in the WORD5 directory.

DOS will only remove a directory that is empty. (If you try to remove a directory that still contains files, DOS ignores your RD command and displays an **Invalid path, not directory, or directory not empty** message.) To remove all the files from a directory, issue a command of the form

ERASE *\path****.***

where *.* stands for "all files and any extension." For example, the command

ERASE \WORD5\LETTERS*.*

clears the LETTERS subdirectory that is contained in the WORD5 directory.

RENAME

RENAME changes a file's name. This command obviously requires two filespecs; the old one comes first. For example, the command

```
RENAME B:SALESRPT.DOC SALESRPT.OLD
```

changes the name of SALESRPT.DOC on drive B to SALESRPT.OLD (to keep the old version for reference while you work on the new one).

RENAME can also preserve files while you are deleting an entire group of files. For example, suppose you have documents named SALES86, SALES87, SALES88, and SALES89. To delete all except SALES89, you could use the following sequence

```
RENAME SALES89 TEMP
ERASE SALES8*
RENAME TEMP SALES89
```

Here, the TEMP file serves as a temporary "hideout" for SALES89, keeping it from being ERASEd.

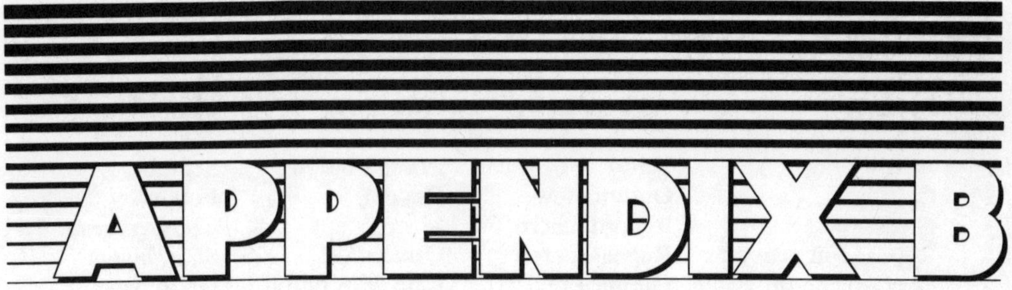

KEY COMMANDS

This appendix summarizes the key Word commands discussed in this book. It breaks key commands down into the following categories:

- Function key assignments
- Cursor-moving operations
- Text operations
- Text-selecting operations
- Applying built-in character and paragraph formats
- Command related operations
- Outline operations

FUNCTION KEY ASSIGNMENTS

Key	By itself	With Shift	With Ctrl	With Alt
F1	Next window	Undo	Zoom window	Set tab
F2	Calculate	Outline view	Header	Footer
F3	Glossary	Record macro	Macro step	Copy to scrap
F4	Repeat edit action	Repeat search	Case on/off	Show layout
F5	Overtype on/off	Outline org.	Line draw on/off	Go to page
F6	Extend selection	Select column	Thesaurus	Spell
F7	Previous word	Previous sentence	Load	Show line breaks
F8	Next word	Next sentence	Print	Font name
F9	Previous paragraph	Current line	Print preview	Text/graphics
F10	Next paragraph	Select document	Save	Record style

CURSOR-MOVING OPERATIONS

To move to:	Press:
Preceding character	Left arrow
Next character	Right arrow
Preceding word	Ctrl-Left arrow
Next word	Ctrl-Right arrow
Preceding line	Up arrow
Next line	Down arrow
Beginning of line	Home
End of line	End
Preceding paragraph	Ctrl-Up arrow
Next paragraph	Ctrl-Down arrow
Preceding screen	PgUp
Next screen	PgDn
Top of window	Ctrl-Home
Bottom of window	Ctrl-End
Next window	F1
Preceding column	Ctrl-5, left arrow
Next column	Ctrl-5, right arrow

To move to:	Press:
Beginning of document	Ctrl-PgUp
End of document	Ctrl-PgDn

TEXT OPERATIONS

Operation:	Press:
Delete preceding character	Backspace
Delete to scrap	Del
Delete permanently	Shift-Del
Insert from scrap	Ins
Replace selected text with scrap	Shift-Ins
Copy to scrap	Ctrl-F3
Start new paragraph	Enter
Start new division	Ctrl-Enter
Start new page	Ctrl-Shift-Enter
Start new column	Alt-Ctrl-Enter
Start new line in same paragraph	Shift-Enter
Turn overtype on/off	F5
Turn line draw on/off	Ctrl-F5
Type optional hyphen	Ctrl-hyphen (on top row)
Type nonbreaking hyphen	Ctrl-Shift-hyphen
Type nonbreaking space	Ctrl-space
Type left chevron for merge field name	Ctrl-[
Type right chevron for merge field name	Ctrl-]
Type ASCII character	Alt-*number* (on keypad)
Expand glossary entry	F3
Define selected text as header	Ctrl-F2
Define selected text as footer	Alt-F2
Zoom/unzoom window	Ctrl-F1

TEXT-SELECTING (HIGHLIGHTING) OPERATIONS

To select: **Press:**

Word left   F7
Word right   F8
Current or preceding sentence   Shift-F7
Current or next sentence   Shift-F8
Preceding paragraph   F9
Next paragraph   F10
Current line   Shift-F9
Entire document   Shift-F10

Turn extend mode on or off   F6 or Shift-Direction key
Turn column select mode on or off   Shift-F6

APPLYING BUILT-IN FORMATS

Character Formats

To apply this format: **Press:**

Bold   Alt-B
Italic   Alt-I
Underline   Alt-U
Double underline   Alt-D
Small caps   Alt-K
Strikethrough   Alt-S
Hidden text   Alt-E
Superscript   Alt-plus
Subscript   Alt-hyphen

Remove last character format   Alt-Z
Remove all character formats   Alt-space

Paragraph Formats

Format:	**Press:**
Center	Alt-C
Left-align (even with left margin)	Alt-L
Right-align (even with right margin)	Alt-R
Justify	Alt-J
Indent first line one tab stop	Alt-F
Reduce left indent one tab stop	Alt-M
Increase left indent one tab stop	Alt-N
Indent from left and right margins	Alt-Q
Create hanging indent	Alt-T
Open spacing between paragraphs	Alt-O
Remove all paragraph formatting	Alt-P

COMMAND-RELATED OPERATIONS

Operation:	**Press**
Move between menu commands	Direction keys
Reach next option in command field	Space
Reach next field	Tab
Reach preceding field	Shift-Tab
Perform command	Enter
Undo last action	Shift-F1
Repeat last action	F4
Repeat Search command	Shift-F4
Spell	Alt-F6
Thesaurus	Ctrl-F6
Redraw screen	Ctrl-Shift-\
Move between Edit menu and text	Esc
Cancel command, stay in Edit menu	Ctrl-Esc
Leave Edit menu, return to text	Ctrl-Shift-Esc
Get help	Alt-H

Macro Commands

Command	Press
Start or stop recording a macro	Shift-F3
Step through macro	Ctrl-F3

OUTLINE OPERATIONS

Operation:	Press
Switch between document view and outline view	Shift-F2
Switch between outline edit and outline organize	Shift-F5
Lower a heading level (move it right)	Alt-0
Raise a heading level (move it left)	Alt-9
Enter body text in an outline	Alt-H

APPENDIX C

MENU COMMANDS

This appendix summarizes Word's numerous menu commands. In the following table, the key combinations in parentheses are keyboard "shortcuts" that produce the associated menu command.

Command	Action
Command	**Action**
Copy	Copy text to scrap or glossary entry (**Alt-F3**)
Delete	Delete text to scrap or glossary entry (**Del**)
Format Annotation	Create an annotation
Format bookmarK	Create a bookmark
Format Border	Create paragraph borders and shading
Format Character	Change character formats (**Alt-F8**)
Format Division	Change division formats (Margins: **Alt-F4**)
Format Footnote	Create a footnote
Format Paragraph	Change paragraph formats
Format pOsition	Move graphic
Format repLace	Replace formats and styles
Format revision-Marks	Work with revision marks
Format Running-head	Create a header (**Ctrl-F2**) or footer (**Alt-F2**)
Format sEarch	Search for formats and styles
Format Stylesheet	Attach or detach a style sheet (Record: **Alt-F10**)
Format Tab	Set (**Alt-F1**) or clear tab stops
Gallery	Move to Gallery, to work on style sheets
Gallery Copy	Copy selected style to the scrap
Gallery Delete	Delete selected style from the style sheet
Gallery Exit	Return to Edit menu
Gallery Format	Define a style
Gallery Help	Get help for Gallery
Gallery Insert	Insert a new style
Gallery Name	Change a style's key code, variant, or remark
Gallery Print	Print styles in a style sheet
Gallery Transfer	Work with style sheet files
Gallery Undo	Reverse the last revision
Help	Get help (**Alt-H**)
Help Exit	Leave help
Help Next	Show next help screen
Help Previous	Show preceding help screen
Help Basics	Show help about help screens
Help Index	Show index to help screens
Help Tutorial	Run Learning Word
Help Keyboard	Show keyboard help
Help Mouse	Show mouse help

Command	Action
Command	**Action**
Insert	Insert scrap contents (**Ins**) or a glossary entry
Jump Page	Move cursor to a page (**Alt-F5**)
Jump Footnote	Move cursor between a footnote reference mark and its associated text
Jump Annotation	Move cursor between an annotation mark and its associated text
Jump bookmarK	Move cursor to a bookmark
Library Autosort	Sort paragraphs, columns, lists, or outlines
Library Document-retrieval	Work with documents that satisfy a specific search criteria
Library Hyphenate	Let Word hyphenate a document
Library Index	Compile the index
Library Link	Import graphics, spreadsheet data, or text from another document
Library Number	Number outline headings or paragraphs
Library Run	Run DOS commands
Library Spell	Spell-check (**Alt-F6**)
Library Table	Compile the table of contents
Library thEsaurus	Look up the selected word in the Thesaurus (**Ctrl-F6**)
Options	Change window options or general options (e.g., autosave, date and time format)
Print Printer	Print to the printer (**Ctrl-F8**)
Print Direct	Send keystrokes directly to the printer
Print File	Store a printer version of the document in a disk file for printing later
Print Glossary	Print the contents of the glossary
Print Merge	Print multiple versions of a document by merging a main document with other files
Print Options	Change print options, such as the number of copies
Print Queue	Queue documents for printing
Print Repaginate	Repaginate a document without printing it
Print preView	Preview a document's page layout before printing (**Ctrl-F9**)

Command	Action
Command	**Action**
Quit	Leave Word
Replace	Search for and replace specified text
Search	Search for specified text (Repeat last search: **Shift-F4**)
Transfer Load	Load a disk document into Word (**Ctrl-F7**)
Transfer Save	Save a document on disk (**Ctrl-F10**)
Transfer Clear	Clear the current window or all windows
Transfer Delete	Delete a disk file
Transfer Merge	Insert another document into this one
Transfer Options	Change the document directory
Transfer Rename	Rename the current document
Transfer Glossary	Load, save, or clear a glossary, or merge another glossary with the current glossary
Transfer Allsave	Save all open documents
Undo	Reverse the last command, by undoing its effects
Window Split	Open a new window
Window Close	Close a window
Window Move	Change the size of a window by moving its borders

replacing, 152
searching for, 149
table of, 108
Character_test.mac macro, 222, 224
Characters
changing, 20
deleting, 20, 21
in font, macro to print, 222, 224
inserting, 21
overtyping, 21
selecting with mouse, 116
CHKDSK (DOS Check Disk
command), 271
CL (Caps Lock) indicator, 9
Clearing the screen, 27
Clearing tabs, 52
CMP (dictionary) extension, 87
Collapsing outlines, 236
Columns
copying, 138
deleting, 137
moving, 137
text, 114
Combining paragraphs, 31
Comments
See Annotations
Comparison operators, 199
Compiling
index, 251
table of contents, 246
your own lists or tables, 253
Computers for use with Word, 6
Consecutive words, deleting, 23
Control keys, 7
COPY (DOS command), 272
Copy text, macro to, 224
Copy command, 62
Copy_file.mac macro, 224
Copying text, 136
Correcting errors, 19
Creating macros, 215
Creating style sheets, 175

Cross-referencing, 255
Cursor
described, 16
moving the, 19, 23
Customizing form letters, 200

D

Dark (control) keys, 7
Data document for form letter
creating, 192
described, 191
fields in, 192
header in, 192
DATA instruction, 209
Date
entering at startup, 16
inserting, 52, 64
Date glossary entry, 64
Dateprint glossary entry, 64
DCA files, macros for, 225
Decimal numbers, aligning, 112
Decimal tabs, 112
Del (Delete) key, 20
Delete command, 62
Deleted text, restoring, 32
Deleting
annotations, 262
character formats, 109
characters, 20, 21
columns, 137
documents, 37
footnotes, 112
groups of words, 23
lines, 29
paragraphs, 30
running heads, 101
sentences, 30
text (macro for), 223
to the left, 21
words, 23
Diamond (end mark), 17

Multicolumn material, 114
Multipage letters, 55
Multiple character formats, 109

N

Naming macros, 215
Nesting macros, 221
New features of Word 5.0, 5
New page, starting a, 56
Newline character, searching for, 148
Newspaper-style columns, 114
NEXT instruction, 204
Next_page.mac macro, 226
Nextpage glossary entry, 64
NL (Num Lock) indicator, 11
Nonbreaking space, searching for, 148
Normal
  division style, 177
  paragraph style, 179
  style sheet (NORMAL.STY), 183
NORMAL.GLY glossary, macros in, 222
Not a valid filename message, 196
Num Lock key, 11
Numbering
  automatic, 244
  headings, 238
  items in a series, 244
  pages, 66
Numeric keypad, 9

O

Opening a window, 164
Operators, comparison, 199
Optional hyphen, searching for, 148
Options form, 119
Organizing outlines, 235
Orphan line at top of page. 60
OT (Overtype) indicator, 21
Outline

adding text to, 234
an existing document, 238
body text in an, 234
collapsing an, 236
edit mode, 232
expanding an, 236
headings, editing, 233
headings, entering, 232
levels, 232
numbering, 238
organize mode, 232, 235
organizing, 235
removing numbering, 240
style sheet for, 184
view, 232
Overtyping, 21

P

Page
breaks, jumping to, 61
breaks, searching for, 148
glossary entry, 64
number, inserting, 64
numbering, 107
numbers, lists and tables with, 252
starting a new, 56
Pages
moving between, 60
numbering, 66
printing selected, 106
working with, 60
Pageview files, 123
Paragraph
format parameters, 53
formats, replacing, 151
formats, searching for, 150
mark, searching for, 148
style, normal, 179
that marks a graphic, 125
Paragraphs
adding borders to, 259

Timeprint glossary entry, 64
Toc_entry.mac macro, 227

U

Undeleting text, 32, 223
Underlining
  character format, 108
  creating, 61
  removing, 61
Undo command, 33
UPDAT-AM.CMP dictionary, 87
Usage, style sheet, 174
User dictionary, 87

V

Variable form letters, 196
Variants for style sheets, 175
Viewing
  graphics, 125
  ruler, 50

W

White space, searching for, 148
Widow line at bottom of page, 60
Wild card
  DOS, 269
  searches, 146
Windows
  active, 164
  and style sheets, 185
  footnote, 168
  independent, 165
  moving text between, 166
  on-screen, 161
  opening, 164
  options form for, 119
  saving documents in, 167
  thesaurus, 88
  zooming, 167

Word 5.0, new features of, 5
Word Finder Thesaurus window, 88
Words
  changing, 22
  deleting, 23
  duplicated, 82
  how Word defines, 38
  moving between, 23
  selecting with mouse, 116
Writing macros, 217

X

X key for styled character formats,
  181

Z

Zooming windows, 167